Dennis Kelly Purchased
7/12/86
San Juan Island
Griffin Bay Book
Store
$13.00

The Pig War

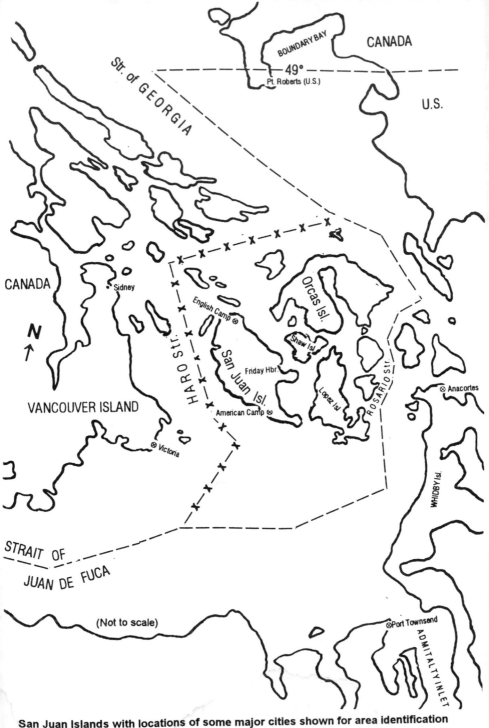

San Juan Islands with locations of some major cities shown for area identification

The Pig War

And Other Experiences of William Peck
—Soldier 1858-1862—
U. S. Army Corps of Engineers

∧

The Journal of William A. Peck, Jr.

Senior Editor: C. Brewster Coulter
Special Editor: Bert Webber

WEBB RESEARCH GROUP
Books About the OregonCountry

Please address all inquiries to the publisher:
WEBB RESEARCH GROUP
P. O. Box 314
Medford, Oregon 97501
U.S.A.

Illustration Credits:
The cover was designed by Bert Webber, Central Point, and executed in oils on china by Beverly Jungwirth, Gervais, Oregon. Contemporary photographs of scenes on San Juan Island were made by Susan Eyerly, Friday Harbor.

Library of Congress Cataloging in Publication Data:

Peck, William A., fl. 1858-1862.
    The Pig War and other experiences of William Peck : soldier 1858-1862, U.S. Army Corps of Engineers, San Juan Islands, Washington Territory : the journal of William A. Peck, Jr. / senior editor, C. Brewster Coulter : special editor, Bert Webber.
       p.   cm.
    Includes bibliographical references and index.
    ISBN 0-936738-17-0
    1. San Juan Islands (Wash.)—History. 2. Washington State) History—To 1889. 3. Frontier and pioneer life—Washington (State)—San Juan Islands. 4. Peck, William, fl. 1858-1862—Diaries. 5. Soldiers—Washington (State)—Diaries. I. Coulter, C. Brewster. 1915- . II. Webber, Bert [1921]. III. Title.
F897.S2P43   93-26331
979.7'7403'092—dc-20   CIP

Preface

In 1941, the Washington State Legislature passed an act requiring a one-year course in the history of the United States and a one-semester course in the history and government of the State of Washington as a prerequisite to graduation from high school. These courses were usually taught in the 9th grade and in the spring for 12th graders who had not taken the course earlier, mainly those who had moved into the state while in high school.

At the college level, these courses were required of every student who wanted to obtain a license to teach in public schools. In the fall of 1945 I became a professor at the College of Puget Sound teaching American history. At the end of my first academic year, I was told that in the fall I would have to teach a course on the History of Washington. I started from scratch and learned all I could as I went along. In that first year I concentrated on the Westward Movement and started researching sources to locate where I could find anecdotal material to provide life to the course.

By divine benevolence I was given access to the *Journal of William A. Peck.* He had been a soldier in the U.S. Army Corps of Engineers and was doing his duty in Oregon and Washington Territory in the years from 1858 to 1861. He died in 1897 when he was 63 years old.

His daughter, Sarah Emma Peck, then moved to Redlands, California, where she was a school teacher. In the early 1920's she retired from teaching and went to live with the White family, where she was a governess, i.e., took care of the family's daughter when the girl was very young.

(The White family, which lived in Redlands, had considerable wealth as the father had invented the White truck, the White sewing machine and the White steam automobile which competed with the Stanley Steamer.)

As a governess, she was called "Pecky." She was adopted by the Whites and lived with them for almost 50 years. The child grew up, married, and had a daughter, Debra Hall. Debra went to college at the University of Puget Sound where she met Robert V. Sepetoski, of Tacoma, who was also a student. They married. Robert was a member of the Sigma Chi Fraternity of which I was also a member as well as faculty advisor so I had contacts with him. This was in the early 1960's when I had over 300 students each semester.

The President of UPS told me that I had more students than any other professor except Alcorn (Biology) and Battin (economics). Because of rivalries in the History Department, students who specialized in European history were not allowed to take classes in American history. Both of the Sepetoskis said they attended my classes but neither was registered. Somehow, out of brotherhood and interest in history, results came.

In 1970, when "Pecky" was 96 years old and still living with the White family, the question came up as to what should be done with the Peck *Journal*. Robert Sepetoski contacted me and asked if I would like to read it. Of course I would so he sent it to me.

Deciphering the faded ink on the pages proved to be time-consuming so it was obvious that a short-term loan would be ineffective. I asked if Sarah Emma Peck would present the *Journal* to the University of Puget Sound, where it could be kept in archives along with the letters of Marcus Whitman, a pioneer missionary. She agreed therefore the *Journal* became an official gift to the university.

Working with the Peck Journal involved turning my focus back many years to the Wallen Expedition across south-central Oregon in 1858, and to the Pig War on San Juan Island in 1859. I determined that Peck remarked about a number of the major events of the day as well as recording his accounts of the ordeals experienced by the common soldier. What a fascinating *Journal*!

C. Brewster Coulter
Tacoma, Washington

Contents

To readers:

When reading this work and a numbered footnote occurs, it is suggested that one refer at that time to the Notes starting on page 217 for additional or explanatory information.

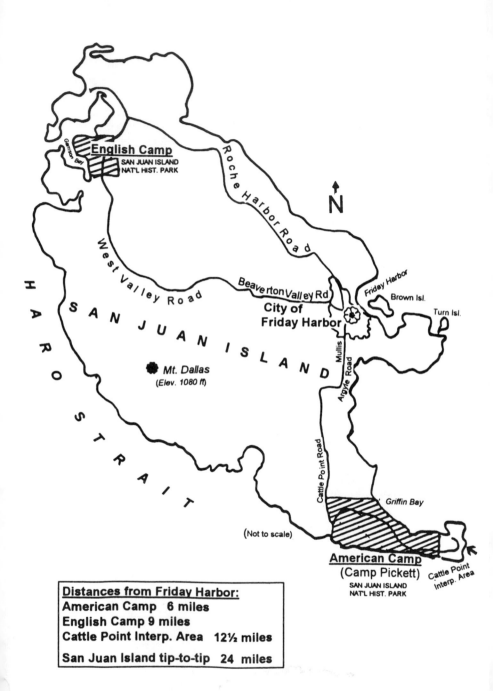

Distances from Friday Harbor:
American Camp   6 miles
English Camp 9 miles
Cattle Point Interp. Area   12½ miles

San Juan Island tip-to-tip   24 miles

Publisher's Introduction

The challenges confronting the publisher about how best to present the *Journal of William A. Peck* occupied space on agendas for meetings for nearly two years. The major discussions hinged around format. As the Pig War seemed the most enticing, it was suggested we publish a short work only on those events. Then there was thought of using all the *Journal* but as Pig War section was deemed high interest, to place that section in front, then "flash back" for the rest of the story. There was consideration about breaking up the *Journal* and bringing out three separate books as the *Journal* includes episodes that are not over-lapping. Then from a military history standpoint, there was strong feeling that the *Journal* should be done chronologically in its entirety. From the experience gained with the success of our other books of military history, the latter course was taken. These books are *Silent Siege* published in 1983; *Silent Siege II,* 1988; *Silent Siege III, Japanese Attacks on North America in World War II, Ships Sunk, Air Raids, Bombs Dropped, Civilians Killed,* 1992, *Aleutian Headache, Deadly World War II Battles on American Soil,* 1993.

Peck's *Journal* contains personal experiences written mostly on the days on which they happened to him and to the handful of soldiers he lived and slaved with and a little of what was doing in his immediate neighborhood. True, as readers will see, Peck had the ability to include conjectures and some observations from a larger horizon. But from one-man's view, a complete story does not emerge. Dr. C. Brewster Coulter, retired Professor of History at University of Puget Sound, Tacoma, has provided numbered Notes to the *Journal* to clarify and expand Peck's diary. These are in a Notes section at the back of the volume. Readers, who want to grasp a complete picture of the "scene," will turn to the Notes for Professor Coulter's additions whenever one of the numbers, as (15), occur in the text. These Notes have been held to a minimum so as not to unduly interrupt reading.

The publisher has brought out a number of diaries and it has always been policy to keep diaries as pure as possible by not changing words. Bert Webber, Research Photojournalist and Special Editor for the *Journal,* offers a few corrections and expansions on some of Peck's comments. These are [bracketed inserts] or show as footnotes in this size type at the bottom of the pages where they occur.

The Peck *Journal* is a rare piece of literature and the publisher hopes this explanation will assist reader enjoyment of it.

The Publishers

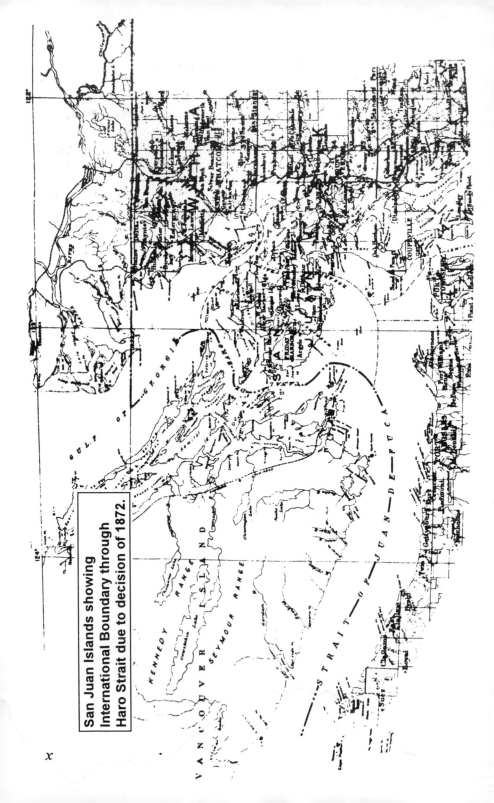

San Juan Islands showing
International Boundary through
Haro Strait due to decision of 1872.

x

Introduction
Historical Overview

When the colonies became independent at the end of the Revolutionary War, the young United States extended to the west only as far as the Mississippi River. The river, and the areas farther west was foreign territory for it was held first by Spain and then by France.

In 1803, when Thomas Jefferson was President, he negotiated the purchase of what became known as the Louisiana Territory from France. In what was probably the first "cost overrun" of the U.S. Government, the $2 million set aside for this transaction exploded into $12 million. The new territory extended the boundary west to the Rocky Mountains.

The President arranged to have Lewis and Clark go into the area on an exploratory expedition and report just what it was that had been bought. These explorers didn't stop at the top of the mountains but proceeded all the way to the Pacific Ocean. On their heals came fur traders. Among these, the Wilson Price Hunt party of 1810-12 is particularly notable. It was as a result of the Hunt Expedition, which had been sponsored by furrier John Jacob Astor, that all of the links of what became the Oregon Trail came together in 1812.

Missionaries started arriving in the Oregon Country in 1834. The federal government needed more information so dispatched Captain John C. Fremont on major exploring trips in 1842-1844. It would be Fremont's official report, at least that part of it concerning what became the Oregon Trail, that emerged as a guide book for emigrants.

There had been crop failures in the middle-west which contributed to an economic depression that lasted from 1839 through 1843, therefore thousands of farmers became disillusioned with their lot and thought they saw a bright future if they could resettle in Oregon.

Dribbles of pioneers had taken what was first called the Old Emigrant Trail to Oregon and returnees and letters revealed details of the great opportunities there. (In the early days of the migration there was little trouble with Indians who, in fact, had often been helpful.)

The "Great Migration" of 1843 followed. But the urge to move to Oregon was so strong that for more than 25 additional years, covered wagons loaded with a family's belongings, alongside of which the family walked the 2,000 miles, left the mid-west every spring.

11

In 1848, as a result of the Mexican War, the United States acquired Texas and much of the area that became New Mexico, Arizona and California. Gold was discovered that year thus the tremendous rush to California in 1949 by men who planned to strike it rich. A few did. During the period the United States Army entered the scene. The army built a number of forts along the Oregon and California trails to protect the emigrants from Indians who were becoming discontented with the onrush of whites.

Troops were also stationed at Fort Vancouver and Fort Steilacoom to protect American settlers from the British Hudson's Bay Company. The only international boundary still unsettled was in the northwester most corner of the United States where controversy centered. This was in the San Juan islands. In the meantime, towns sprang up near forts because soldiers provided a lot of the local business.

There was serious difficulty with Indians in the 1850's which led to numerous Indian wars. To better connect military posts, towns and seaports, roads were urgently needed therefore special troops, The United States Army Corps of Engineers, entered the picture.

*   *   *

Peck's *Journal* recalls the experiences of a soldier, but a special soldier because he was one of the earliest trained engineers. His training was at West Point, New York. Here was a foot soldier, a "grunt" with a grammar school education but with a keen sense of duty. He felt he had an obligation to record his own "errand into the wilderness." He had a self-effacing manner which makes his personality elusive and largely a matter of inference. He has no sense of destiny or of being involved in any great cause. This very fact is what makes his account valuable.

This is a history of a humble man with no pretentions of being involved in some sort of grand movement – "the opening of the west." He simply had the urge to do his job in the best manner he could.

His foes were the elements. His account reveals what "the opening of the west" was really like. He faced the challenge of the land as a builder of roads, bridges and fortifications in a nearly impassable wilderness. He was not concerned with a vague grand design or caught up in any manifest destiny. What could be the grandeur to one who is cold, muddy, wet, frequently bored and yet somehow swept up enough in his duty to make a career of it without the slightest glamour and with the risk of losing his life – not to a bullet or an Indian arrow but to a refractory mule!

Peck, a taciturn Yankee, experienced real discomfort and physical ills during his duty in the Oregon and in Washington Territory in the late 1850's. He almost had to rely on his sense of humor to get through and record the hardships of the poor soldiers out there in the cold and snow and wet forests. They did not have fresh supplies, not even enough food coming to them. They never knew when a ship would arrive.

The snow blew through the cracks in the log cabin where they slept. They didn't have waterproof clothing. Each man had only a single blanket. The army at this time in American history did not supply a lot of things we now take for granted. These soldiers, who were ordered to strenuous duty beyond imagination, were usually over-tired and often sick from lack of energy because they seldom had enough to eat.

Peck was writing his diary for his family. When he writes of the soldierly carousing with Indian women, there is little expression of moral outrage which he would hardly need to suggest. More likely, he refrained because of the expense and peril to his health of speaking out (the practical Yankee). His overt displeasure is reserved for the superior who made life difficult for him and was obnoxious in a personal way and who eventually received his just desserts.

From an historical stance, Peck's *Journal* provides day-to-day details that historians crave to learn for the experiences revealed are generally not found in other books or literature.

The publisher has worked from apparently the only typed transcript ever made from the original. In so doing, nothing has been changed. In a few instances where a statement by Peck where he guesses at elevations of mountains, footnotes have been added showing the true elevations.

The Peck *Journal* is expected to be of great value to writers, librarians, scholars and to a public that has demonstrated a great interest in books of this kind where the facts, in clear language, speak for themselves.

C. Brewster Coulter, Ph.D.
Bert Webber, MLS

We William

by the Grace of God, German Emperor, King of Prussia

After examination of the treaty concluded at Washington on the sixth of May, 1871, between the Governments of Her Brittanic Majesty and of the United States of America, according to which the said Governments have submitted to our arbitrament the question at issue between them, whether the boundary line which, according to the Treaty of Washington of June 15, 1846, after being carried Westward along the forth-ninth parallel of northern latitude to the middle of the channel which separates the continent from Vancouver's Island is thence be drawn southerly through the middle of the channel and of the Fuca Straits to the Pacific Ocean should be drawn through the Rosario Channel as the Government of Her Brittanic Majesty claims, or through the Haro Channel as the Government of the United States claims; to the end that it may finally and without appeal decide which of these claims is most in accordance with the true interpretation of the Treaty of June 15, 1846.

After hearing the report made by us by the experts and jurists summoned by us upon the contents of the interchanged memorials and their appendices

Have decreed the following award:

Most in accordance with the true interpretations of the treaty concluded on the 15th of June, 1846, between the Governments of Her Brittanic Majesty and of the United States of America, is the claim of the Government of the United States of America that the boundary-line between the territories of Her Britannic Majesty and the United States should be drawn through the Haro Channel. Authenticated by our autographic signature and the impression of the imperial great seal. Given at Berlin, October 21, 1872.

William

October 1858

West Point, New York October 5th

In accordance with a General Order recently issued by the Commander in Chief of the Army, the Detachment of Engineers at this Post commanded by Second Lieutenant David C. Houston and Brevet Second Lieutenant H.M. Robert of Engineers Corps, after a number of days preparations fitting out an Engineer train, and other necessaries likely to be of use on an expedition among the Mountains, embarked on the Steamer *Thomas Powell* en route for Fort Vancouver, Washington Territory via New York. (1)

We left the quarters at eight o'clock A.M. and marched directly to the wharf. While crossing the plains the entire Cadet Corps formed in line and gave us three times three in a hearty style. Upon arriving at the wharf we found a vast number of people amounting to about the entire population [of] Buttermilk Falls assembled to bid us a final good-bye. There are a number of men among us who have family connections, wives and children and as a consequence a display of feeling ensues which does nothing towards raising the spirits of those who are un-blessed from such sources. But to balance this unpleasant scene Mother Hall's good natured countenance is prominent. A suspiciously large basket from which the necks of several bottles protrude, assures us that there will be some cheer for the inner man accompanying her final adieu.

At last at nine o'clock the good steamer comes in sight and a final and vigorous attack of hand shaking, kissing and good-byes accompanied by a copious flow of tears and promises to write and not forget, ushers us aboard and away we drive down the ever glorious Hudson. Now commences our real soldiering.

The passage down is of course new, for we are traveling as troops and in the character of soldiers for the first time most of us. The afore mentioned basket has been opened and found to contain a goodly supply of cakes, pies, cigars, brandy, etc., all of which was partook of most freely.

Arrived at N.Y at 12 M. marched directly to [ship] *Moses Taylor's* wharf. I find Mother, George, Caroline and Sherman awaiting me, a most pleasant and unexpected surprise. But among the noise and confusion around and on the wharf of a departing California steamer, one cannot think of what one wishes and express what one thinks. Suffice to say that I am overjoyed at seeing those, that I imagined, I should not again see for a long time and grateful for such an evidence of affection as well as the articles for my future amusement and safely presented by them to me, and I must aboard ship with a good-bye to friends and shore for some months or years.

Upon the steamer making her first revolution towards start-ing, a breakdown occurred in her engine (so reported) causing a delay of one or more days. We are transferred to a tug boat, thence to Governors Island, and finally, amid the gaping crowd of recruits, to Castle William second tier of casemates among the guns, half of the men allowed to go to New York on pass, the balance to go upon their return in the morning. If the prospects tonight are indicative of our future, then indeed ours is a most un-pleasant campaign, for our accommodations are next to no accommodations at all. We are to sleep among the guns in the second tier of casemates, which have not been swept for years, the dust and filth of years accumulating around us. The floors of granite for our bed form a most striking contrast to our comfortable quarters at West Point.

Governors Island, October 6th.

This morning finds us in a considerable quandary how we are to get a decent breakfast. We were taken to the general mess hall where a table had been spread with the view of making us break our fast, each individual being supplied with a plate, knife, fork and bowl of villainous stuff called coffee. A huge slice of half cooked pork and some of the sourest kind of bread constitutes our morning meal. The poor recruits looked on immensely pleased that we should treat the vile stuff with contempt.

I succeeded in obtaining a decent meal of ham and eggs, coffee, etc. from a family here, and about noon went to the city on pass, wishing to make some purchases. I have been busy during the afternoon and evening, returning about nine o'clock, and took lodging again in the shadows of a forty-two pounder gun.

Governors Island is a general rendezvous for recruits for the department of the East. And here within a half hour's pull of the largest market in the country are the future heroes of our country, brought and robbed of even the food the law allows them by a few unprincipled non-commissioned Officers permanently fixing a thorough distaste for the service in their minds, causing them to desert upon the first possible chance thereby robbing [the] government of the services of many good men, and at the same time causing them, the men, to become outlaws in their own land. Those who remain are oftentimes so thoroughly imbued with a sentiment of injustice sustained at the hands of the officers ap-pointed by government, that they merely drag through an aimless five years and leave the service in utter disgust.

On Board Steamer *St. Louis,* October 7th.

This morning opened rainy and miserable for an embarkation. None of the men went to the mess hall for breakfast considering it merely a waste of time. At eleven and one half o'clock A.M. we bid adieu to Castle William and proceeded to wharf, where we find a tug boat to take us aboard this steamer. During the short passage Corporal Supplee who has, in view of the perils about to be encountered by both sea and land, been indulging largely in spiritual subjects and thereby becoming to a certain extent oblivious to earthly things, most carelessly and foolishly broke his arm while on the tug.

We transferred our baggage to the *St. Louis* at one o'clock P.M. and took up quarters in a portion of the ship previously assigned to us but whose berths had been again given to other passengers, whom we very unceremoniously routed amid curses, loud and deep, both on our poor heads and those of the officers of the ship. However as soldiers are not of a temperament to be shocked by a simple damn, uttered by an unoffending citizen, I think none slept less sound for them nor for the fact that in spending precious time cursing us simple beings, some lost all chance of a bed at all, and must sleep on the deck during the run to Aspinwall.

We left our mooring at two o'clock and pass down the bay. The rain [came] down so furiously as to drive every one to cover and depriving me of a fine view of New York Bay, a circumstance quite annoying, inasmuch as I have never had the pleasure of visiting any of the interesting resorts in the harbor.

Seasickness begins to be thought of as early as dark 'ere we are fairly outside and many are now paying to the demands of Neptune all of the good things with which they have gorged themselves during their stay in the city. We have about eight hundred passengers and many presume that the breakdown of the *Moses Taylor* was merely a

17

pretext, she being a smaller ship.

Steamer *St. Louis,* October 8th.

Observations at 12 M. place us in Latt. 37° 10" North 74° 10" West and 202 miles from New York. A strong north wind is blowing but the weather is cool and pleasant. About half of the men are suffering from seasickness, and the rest anticipating an attack of that nauseating feeling which causes one to make a flank movement by the double quick for the leeside of the vessel. of course, we who are well thus far, do all in our power to help the unfortunate ones, but our services are not at all times appreciatingly accepted.

One large Hoosier took my endeavors to assist him by greasing his throat with some fat pork, most cruelly unkind, and I felt sure by the expression of his countenance and working of his arms, that, had not the proprietor of said arms had business at the ships rail, he would have fed an innocent shark with my precious person.

However we have a pleasant day and running over a smooth sea is enjoyed by us who are capable of enjoying anything. In the evening some of our boys who can sing a good song and crack a joke are enjoying our first pleasant night at sea much. Sergeant Wheeler is scarcely recognizable such a woebegone looking specimen of humanity has 22 hours seasickness made him.

Houston says he will be damned if ever he puts himself on water if he once more treads soil. And a number of others protest against sea.

Steamer *St. Louis.* October 9th.

Observations today, 35° 51" North Latt. 73° 43" West Long., distance run 218 miles since noon of yesterday. Weather continues cool and clear. The sea is smooth and most of the men have recovered their spirits and appetites and enjoying themselves wonderfully. Flying fish are seen for the first time by many of us and cause some delight watching their antics above water.

Steamer *St. Louis,* October 10th

Observations, 29°44" North 74° 0" West, distance 247 miles.
The weather is warm and spring like. We are fast approaching perpetual summer and the sudden change from October to May is another novelty for us who have never before visited southern

18

latitudes. Nothing of especial interest transpired.

Steamer *St. Louis,* October 11th

Observations today 25° 33" North Lat. 73° 33" West Long. distance run 252 miles. We have a fine breeze from westward, but the weather continues to grow warm. One begins to look for a shade and complain of heat. The passengers are about all re-covered from their sickness and many of the gold seekers are grumbling lustily at their fare and accommodations, which are not bad, but not equal to home privileges in the country. All of this causes a great many of these country boys, who never left their mothers before, to grow heart sick and wish they had stayed at home and continued to milk the cows, never dreaming of the Land of Gold.

Steamer *St. Louis,* October 12th

Today's observations 21° 19" North Lat. 73° 42" West Long., distance run 155 miles. The weather continues pleasant and warm, the men in most excellent spirits. We made the island of Inaqua [*sic*] at 12 M., being the first land made everybody take a look and now we are at last in that oft dreamed place the Caribbean Sea, where but a few years since those bold Buccaneers held sway, and collected tribute of the wealthy Spanish Don, and any other who might come their way. We made the Island of Cuba at about 5 o'clock P.M., passing by its eastern end and affording us but a glimpse of that beautiful isle, never once giving us a glimpse of the old Moro Castle, and in fact not going on that side of the Island even. Tonight has been a jovial one on deck and such a one as a miscellaneous crowd can make.(2)

Steamer *St. Louis,* October 13th.

Observations 17° 40" North Lat. 75° 34" West Long., distance 244 miles. We rose the Island of Haiti early this morning, far over our port bow, and far off as it was, it caused a considerable interest. The weather is very warm. Jamaica hove in sight in the morning, also keeping up a round of excitement for us green ones and as a matter of course, amusing the old salts by our remarks, queries, etc.

Steamer *St. Louis,* October 14th.

Observations 15° 35" North Lat. 77° 42" West Long., distance 275 miles. The weather very warm. Considerable excitement caused by a fire in the ship, extinguished without great damage. Aspinwall tomorrow.

Steamer *St. Louis,* October 15th.

Today's reckoning 9° 40" North Lat. 79° 50" West Long., distance run 268 miles, and now 18 miles from Aspinwall. We are getting frequent showers during the day and the weather very warm. We run into the wharf at 3 o'clock and, unlike the balance of the passengers, must or may remain aboard all night as the train leaves for Panama in the morning.

On board Steamer *Senora,* October 16th.

We quartered on board the *St. Louis* last night, but a greater portion of our men were ashore among the hotels and fandangos about town. These places of amusement are decidedly novel, and somewhat primitive, the code of morals being not the most stringent. Native women are on the street selling fruit and at every step you are accosted with, "three for a dime sweety," in tones intended to loosen the purse strings of the most parsimonious wretch ever met with on the passage to California.

Aspinwall is a place of importance so far as its connection with the transit route is concerned only. There are a number of white persons here, but only to prosecute what business there is attached to, and consequent upon, the line of travel. These look as though they had been through a course of smoking and drying to shrink their flesh away to nothing leaving a little yellow shriveled up person in the place of man.

We left Aspinwall at seven A.M. The morning beautiful, a good fresh air after yesterdays rain. The men in the best possible spirits, and (all of it natural) few of them having ever been in tropical climates before. Consequently every shrub and tree is new and strange.

We occupied one whole car [on the railroad] and being provided with some prime cigars, gave ourselves up to the enjoyment of the scene, having been previously advised to abstain from eating fruit during the after portion of the day. Myself, and I presume others, had hardly tasted the tempting oranges and bananas, so freely offered in the streets of Aspinwall. But now upon arriving at the native villages we may indulge to almost any extent; of course having due consideration for the length of ones purse, which in most instances were short. At these native villages one could see nature unadorned in earnest, for most of their young children's limbs were unfettered by clothes and their only covering was the accumulated dirt upon their persons.

Their huts or dwellings are mostly constructed with bamboo and roofed with palm leaves, giving room for no complaint for want of ventilation, they having no sides. After passing a number of villages we are conscious of approaching higher country And although our train has been about three and one half hours in traversing forty-seven miles, one has been so interested as to consider it a remarkable short ride for the distance.

Arriving at Panama we were landed on the wharf and almost immediately transferred to lighters, thence to the steamer laying about five miles in the offing, in the Bay of Panama, thereby causing no little degree of disappointment to myself, for to visit the old cathedrals and battlements of its ancient walls was an object of some importance. But since the riot here between passengers and natives, the Company gives as little time as is possible at the end of the route.

Steamer *Senora*, October 17th.

We remained in the Bay of Panama until this morning. We find poor accommodations on this craft, so much so as to cause one to feel inclined to evil forebodings. And if supper and toadies fare are a sample of the ships stores, we will be anything but gouty upon our arrival at San Francisco. There are about fifteen hundred passengers aboard, with accommodations for about eight hundred, leaving every inch of deck room occupied in the night.

During last evening a shower sprang suddenly up and many a one comfortably snoozing were rudely enough disturbed in their golden dreams, and some choice blessings heaped on the heads of the company officers of this particular line of transit, one quarter of which being realized will render an expenditure of fuel, quite superfluous in a future world on the part of some officers. We occupy a portion of the ship designed in particular for suffocating purposes, and admirably adapted to the purpose.

Cockroaches are more plenty than bedbugs, bedbugs more plenty than rats, and rats as plenty as house flies in a hotel kitchen. One can amuse oneself looking at them, so confoundedly familiar are these long tailed devils that any fruit carelessly laid away for future use is soon confiscated for the benefit of the rat family. Weather continues rainy and sultry during the day, causing a deathlike feeling to penetrate ones system, and those unfortunately weak stomached individuals are once more holding party with old Neptune endeavoring to square accounts.

Supplee is drunk and particularly obnoxious today, he being the most unmitigated fool extant when drunk.

Steamer *Senora*, October 18th.

Today's reckoning finds us at 7° 20" North Lat. 82° 28" West Long., having run 250 miles since leaving our anchorage. There is a strong breeze and rough sea, tending considerably to the dis-comfort of not a few. Our boys are finding all manner of fault with our accommodations, and especially living. Lieutenant [Henry Martyn] Robert [1837-1923] has been inspecting our fare and it is hoped some good may come of it.

Steamer *Senora*, October 19th.

Midday finds us in 9° 10" North Lat. 85° 28" West Long., distance run 230 miles. Men all in the worst possible humor, myself anything but well. Our craft is uncomfortable in its present trim. The living anything but good. A strong North West and heavy sea running. The Sergeant is unwell and ugly and in fact everything to make this our most uncomfortable day at sea.

Steamer *Senora*, October 20th.

Observation 11° 25 North Lat. 88° 43" West Long., distance 231 miles, a good run considering the state of the sea and wind. The weather continued heavy until evening when all hands were on deck for a general airing. I remained on deck most of the night, glad to be rid of my too sociable companions below, who have a better claim on the space than myself, for they must be old residents of these parts, having bred generation after generation in those old cracks and holes. Lieutenant Houston has finally secured some privileges for us on this abominable craft which renders us somewhat more comfortable.

Steamship *Senora*, October 21st.

We are in 12° 43" North Lat. 91° 41" West Long., distance run 230 miles. Weather fine and everyone more disposed to try and live through our trip. Amusements are resumed and anything to create excitement is hailed with delight. Whales have been seen two or three times during the day, and a source of fun found therewith. The hurricane decks are flush with the guards of the ship and continually crowded. Upon the cry of whale on this side, there is a general rush to get a sight of the monster, putting the ship sadly out of trim, which is sure to bring the Second Officer on deck. He being a broad shouldered, good natured Scotsman, finds considerable difficulty in inducing the anxious sightseers to leave the side in question, which is finally accomplished with many assurances in the broadest Scotch accents that we will never get to Frisco.

Duff was served for dinner today, and the way the compound was devoured is a caution to Sees [sic] in New England, no sooner would a dish of the coveted dough strike the table than it would be transferred to the plates of the greedy passengers. Perhaps to be again transferred to another who was so unfortunate as to fail in getting his plate filled from the original package. Knives and forks were often times ignored, and the sticky and hot stuff would find its way under the nails of the anxious prober, causing some of the tallest kind of antics, and altogether were the several scenes of today's dinner table portrayed in *Frank Leslie's Illustrated Newspaper* it would secure the work a circulation incomparable in news and *Illustrated* paper circulation. Day passed most agreeably by us.

Steamer *Senora*, October 22nd.

Observations today 14° 49" North Lat. 95° 23" West Long., distance run 240 miles. Weather fine, and the boys amusing themselves in every possible manner. Judging from the present state of affairs, shipboard is not exactly the place to imbibe a moral sentiment.

Steamer *Senora*, October 23rd.

Today's reckoning finds us in 16° 32" North Lat. 99° 9" West Long., distance run 237 miles. We are running in sight of land all day, and [one] spends hours watching the mountain peaks as they come in view, some of them towering far above the clouds. The dark green of the verdure is a welcome sight to us who have been only so few days at sea. What must it be to the mariner who has been from land for months.

We entered the bay of Acapulco at four o'clock P.M. where the steamer gets coal, water and fresh provisions, there being a depot here for the accommodations of this line. This is an entirely land locked harbor, easy of access, and perfectly safe from any storm. High hills or mountains completely surround it.

Coal was taken aboard by naked natives, or greasers as the Mexican Indians are termed, water in large tanks towed alongside and pumped aboard. Wild Spanish beef was taken in alive and in a novel manner. Their heads were securely tied to the sides of a large canoe, or dugout, four on a side and towed alongside our steamer. A strap or rope made secure around the horns, and a tack hooked to it. All being ready, they are hoisted inboard, a distance of twenty or thirty feet up the ships sides entirely by the head. Once aboard they refuse all feed and water, having never been accustomed to it in such a manner, and are killed as often as required for use. This beef when taken is free [from] tallow, so much so that a Hindoo would not have to stretch his conscience in partaking of it. But after the animal has fasted two or three weeks, one fails to find a semblance of beef in it. For myself, I eat none of it at all.

Soon after coming into the bay our vessel was surrounded by men and boys anxious to dive for a dime. The water is very clear and they so expert swimmers, that it is almost impossible to throw a dime so [far] from one of the heathen that he will not overtake it and return to the surface with his, to him easily earned, dime.

The ship was also soon surrounded by bunges laden with all kinds of tropical fruits, of which the passengers bought most freely, and many a laughable scene occurred. Poor Umbra being duped in several instances with the new nickel cents, causing a flow of oaths of the direct nature; but as the Mexicans are not allowed aboard under any pretext, there is no redress for him.

Acapulco is an old Mexican town composed of low, one story houses and one or two cathedrals, strongly as well as rudely built of stone. As I was not ashore I could see nothing of the better class of society and know little concerning its resources or wealth. It is surrounded by mountains and cannot be supported by agriculture unless the country beyond the hills is more favorable. It is defended by one fort commanding the entrance to the harbor, mounting one tier of guns in barbette. They appear of small caliber and I should suppose be of little importance against the heavy guns carried by some of our craft. I believe this place was left unmolested during the war between us and them, being considered of no importance I presume.

We left this snug little harbor about nine o'clock P.M., the evening being one of the pleasantest I ever saw, the moon shining almost as bright as day. All hands on deck till midnight.

Steamer *Senora*, October 24th.

In Lat. 17° 24" North 101° 58" West Long., distance 178 miles. The weather continues fine and beautiful. Services were held on deck in the afternoon. Nothing of particular interest occurred during the day.

Steamer *Senora*, October 25th.

In 19°30" North Lat. 104° 59" West Long., distance run 203 miles. Entered the port of Manzanilla at eight o'clock A.M. to leave mails and one passenger. This seems a small hamlet, whose only importance is derived from it being accessible from the silver mines about forty miles inland, whose products are brought here for shipment. After an hour's delay we left for our final port of [*sic*] San Francisco.

Steamer *Senora*, October 26th.

In 21° 21" North Lat. 108° 2" West Long., run 220 miles. The weather gradually grows cooler and indicates that the moisting [*sic*] being continued, we will eventually find some cold weather. A case of small pox is reported among the passengers. The joke of whale on this side continues to be perpetuated to the annoyance of the officers.

Steamer *Senora*, October 27th

In 23°59" North Lat. 111° 27" West Long., distance 241 miles. Weather continues to grow cold. Met the Steamer *Oregon* at nine A.M. this morning. Off the island of Margartia at M. and don't feel inclined to stop, also saw a whaleman about 2 P.M.

Steamer *Senora*, October 28th.

In 27° North Latt. 114° 32" West Long., made 249 miles. The weather continues to grow cold. The men spent the majority of the day between decks, cards and singing the principal amusement.

Steamer *Senora*, October 29th.

In 30° 35" North Lat. 117° 25" West Long., distance 260 miles. We are now nearing our destination and getting sight of land often. Weather is about like early April at home.

Steamer *Senora*, October 30th.

In 33° 30" North Latt. 120° 4" West Long., distance 245 miles. A strong wind from northwest makes it extremely un-pleasant on deck.

We expect to arrive in San Francisco tomorrow. Every body is cleaning rifles, are undergoing a thorough over-hauling and some will be sorry as we bid final adieu to this craft.

Steamer *Senora*, October 31st.

In 37° 18" North Latt. 122° 28" West Long., distance **255** miles, and only 30 remaining before we reach the promised land. In sight of land all of the day, the decks constantly crowded. Passed in by the Golden Gate at 3 P.M. and made fast at wharf at four thirty. Crowds of people are on the wharf. It being Sunday, some are looking for friends, others for mere pastime. We are to remain on the ship tonight. Some disgraceful conduct occurred during the evening. Were it not for those ominous looking holes in the wharf, I should hardly remain aboard.

November, 1858

Presidio Barracks, November 1st.

We left the ship at about one o'clock P.M. today and came directly to the post to remain until the Oregon steamer sails. This was formerly an old Spanish mission built up by the priest, the materials used in its construction being adobe or sun burnt bricks. It is situated about three miles west of San Francisco and used as barracks and garrisoned by Government. There are about 35 prisoners, chiefly deserters with ball and chain, a detachment of Infantry guarding them.

The City of San Francisco is built on the west shore of the bay by the same name, is of course a new place built up since the gold discovery, many of the buildings having been put up and brought from the States. Some new handsome stores have been built but the city as a general thing bears evidence of its rapid growth. I have seen little of the place unless in passing through it. A dance is gotten up this evening for amusement.

Presidio Barracks, November 2nd.

This morning finds the men in a general state of grumbling, most of them having slept little for the fleas. For myself I am about half devoured by the little devils. It is my first experience among the vermin of this species. Went to the City in company with a number of our men.

26

Proceeded at once to find Aunt Dudley, which object I accomplished quite easily. Failed to surprise her inasmuch as she had received an intimation of my being enroute by the steamer. Found her and Florilla quite well and was kindly met by them. Spent the remainder of the day with them but returned to quarters in the evening.

On board Steamer *Columbia*, November 3rd.

We left the Presidio at seven o'clock this morning and march-ed immediately through the City to the wharf of the Oregon line, where we embarked for Fort Vancouver on board this steamer. Corporal Supplee was absent, drunk as usual, but made his appearance just in time to get aboard. We find better accommodations here than on either of the ships before occupied by us.

Quite a number of our fellow passengers out, are still in our company bound up the coast. This being a way-steamer we will call into all of the ports of any size on the coast but will be longer on the route than on other boats.

During my stay here I have been considerably surprised to see trees, plants and vegetables growing as finely as in May at home. The markets contain as good variety of fresh vegetables in January as in July. Flowers are in blossom, the climate is such as to grow crops the entire year. one will see a potato lot with the vegetables in all stages of maturity from planting to digging. The city is built on made land the sand hills, having been carted into the bay, making building room both ways. The bay itself is one of the finest, and most commodious in the world, being some seventy or eighty miles long by about eight wide.*

We left the wharf at about 12 M, a drizzling rain having set in, the wind blowing from the northwest, being quite chilly, passing Fort Alcatraz on our right and Fort Point on the left. Alcatraz is on an island of the same name and said to be quite formidable when completed [as a prison in 1868]. Fort Point is a high work, mounting three tiers of guns immediately at the Golden Gate and presenting serious impediment to a hostile fleet.

Steamer *Columbia,* November 4th

Weatner grows cool. There was more sea during the night than agreeable. Some of the men are paying dearly for their two nights ashore, [now] being constantly over the lee rail. We will be in Eureka during the night, as we are only about 50 miles away at 6 P.M. I must

---

*San Francisco Bay is approximately 30 miles long extending from Alcatraz Island, east of the Golden Gate, to a line between Mountain View and Irvington. –bw

mention the great number of Chinese abounding in San Francisco. One cannot pass through an alley without encountering many of these Oriental beauties, whose morals are some-what dilapidated. In the streets one constantly meets these long tailed Celestials, who do every menial service for small pay, washing and ironing seems their favorite employment. They are grown rich, in some instances, and one sees in letters of not the most symmetrical proportions. The Sing Sing sells peas and Wung. Chung deals in sausages, meats of all kinds, and for myself could not but make the mental inquiry used (no doubt my old schoolboy recollections) I wonder if there are any rats and puppies sold also.

Steamer *Columbia* November 5th.

We lay off and on at the mouth of the Humboldt River during the greater portion of the night, but came over the bar about eleven A.M. The fog having lifted sufficiently to induce our Pilot to try to navigate the channel, which is one of the worst on the coast, being so different and crooked. Eureka is a new and smart town built up in a very few years, important chiefly for its lumber, being surrounded by fine timber. There are several sawmills already in operation here. Some of the passengers are going to locate here. Being on guard [duty] I have little liberty ashore, more especially as some of the boys are inclined to the spiritual, which keeps the guard somewhat busy and on the alert.

Steamer *Columbia,* November 6th.

We remained at Eureka during the night and cast off from the wharf about 8 o'clock A.M. There were some choice scenes enacted during the evening. Levee, true to his natural inclinations, took a souvenir from each hotel, from ours a good table cloth, another a decanter of whiskey, another tobacco and so on besides owing two or three dollars in each place. We made Trinidad, a small seacoast town about eleven A.M., discharged freight and at eight o'clock P.M. run into the harbor (if it may be called one) of Crescent City. Coming in the steamer touched a rock, enough to cause quite a jar all through the steamer.

Steamship *Columbia,* November 7th.

This morning the breakers are running so high it is impossible to land freight or passengers. The harbor is merely an open road-stead with not the least protection from the ocean. The morning is a beautiful one, and it being Sunday makes the occasion more still and attractive. We left at eleven o'clock A.M., arrived off Rogue River at 3 o'clock and expect to be off Umpqua River our next post this evening.

Steamship *Columbia,* November 8th.

Arrived off Umpqua bar at 2 o'clock A.M. [then] lay to until 8 A.M., and started in. When just inside the outer bay, the ship struck hard on the bar followed immediately by a breaker which carried away our wheel, after bulwarks, and stove the two after boats, twisting the davits like seeds and causing the ship to strike so hard as almost render a footing on deck impossible.

Then commenced a scene of excitement and confusion. These steamers have few sailor men aboard, the crew being composed chiefly of longshoremen and laborers, who know little of steamship [work]. Our boys turned to and assisted in working [the] ship and throwing over freight, which labor we accomplish-ed in short meter. During the first fifteen minutes, little excitement occurred but the ship commenced wearing around, side to the breakers and in such case we were sure to find more here than accords with my fancy.

Life preservers now appeared. One old fellow felt sad that he could not get on two, being of somewhat extended composity, was sure he needed a double allowance. I saw one individual throw overboard a mattress to lighten ship. Mrs. Dobbs, who has been a fellow passenger since we left New York, quietly seated herself with a bottle of brandy in hand, ready to administer to any unlucky wet ones, and on the whole displayed more courage than most of the men. Ned Gilbert made a raid on the cooks galley and took a sumptuous repast during the height of excitement.

For myself I must confess to have come to the conclusion that I should never vegetate in old Connecticut more at one time, but fortunately we were favored with a fair wind, and flood tide, and after about forty-five minutes pounding we gradually wore off, and got into the channel with no great amount of damage to our ship.

We steamed to Gardiner City, a distance of ten miles, and here discharged a considerable freight and repaired so much as was absolutely necessary. There are several rumors regarding the accident this morning. The Pilot avers the channel has shifted, others say it being Capt. Patterson's first trip, that it was a concerted plan to injure him.

Steamship *Columbia*, November 9th.

Gardiner City is a smart town consisting of one house and the company's storehouse. It is important only as a depot to land freight for Scottsburg and other towns, back in the interior, as the goods are transported to the upper town in small boats. We left the wharf at 12 M. and proceeded down the river to near the bar, but such a dense fog arising, we put back to opposite the Post and dropped anchor for the night. Indians in their canoes are paddling about and the scenery roman tic [*sic*] and delightful.

Steamer *Columbia*, November 10th

We are still lying opposite Fort Umpqua. The weather being too foggy to cross [the bar]. Captain Patterson says he will never try to get out until the pilot knows the channel perfectly. This bar is laid down by the coast survey as unnavigable from the first of November to the first of April hence if the steamer is lost there is no insurance to be got. Fort Umpqua is a mere station or garrison, situated on the point of land running down between the ocean and river. It is garrisoned by Company "L" 3rd Artillery some of whom have been aboard and carried some of the boys ashore where we were very well treated, myself being one of the party.

Steamship *Columbia*, November 11th.

We are still looking for the fog to lift but disappointed thus far. Provisions are growing scarce. Ashore during the day, we are anxious to move in some direction as this constant expecting is tiresome.

Steamship *Columbia*, November 12th.

Weather is somewhat stormy this morning [so] we remained at our anchorage. Went ashore in the afternoon and remained during the eve. Spent a pleasant night. The men are glad to see any person here [as] they are so secluded and shut out from the rest of the world.

Fort Umpqua, November 13th.

I returned aboard ship this morning after visiting the ranch of Indians here and saw more filth than I have ever seen before, I verily believe. Whale oil in skins and salmon smoked were the only objects of food in view. Ye Gods, where is Cooper? After dinner took the ship's boat, and went on an expedition for crabs, which abound here in

30

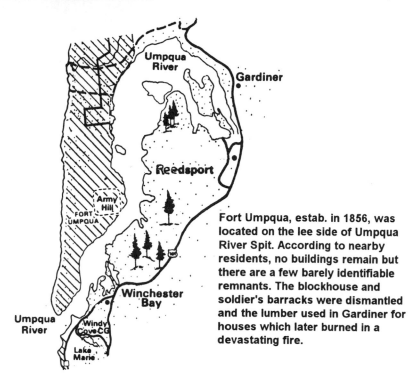

Fort Umpqua, estab. in 1856, was located on the lee side of Umpqua River Spit. According to nearby residents, no buildings remain but there are a few barely identifiable remnants. The blockhouse and soldier's barracks were dismantled and the lumber used in Gardiner for houses which later burned in a devastating fire.

great quantities and of a respectable size, some measuring eight to ten inches across the back.

Were recalled from the excursion and found the ships anchor being taken from the mud. We run up river to opposite the fort or garrison and came ashore to remain until the weather will permit us to go to sea. Took quarters in an unoccupied barrack room and were not the fleas so troublesome should be very comfortable indeed.

Fort Umpqua, November 14th.

Turned out for inspection in the morning, out on the river in the forenoon. Small steamer came down from Scottsburg at 3 P.M. We embarked at 7 o'clock, expecting to get to sea in the morning.

Fort Umpqua, November 15th.

Storming the worst sort this morning. We were ordered ashore at 11 A.M. and went in the rain; must be preparing business to send us off in the rain.

Fort Umpqua, November 16th.

I am on guard today and night. There seems little prospect of our leaving here unless by land. The distance is 200 miles by land to Fort Vancouver.

Fort Umpqua, November 17th.

I left the ship this morning and came ashore, have done little during the day, but this evening took a long walk down on the sand point where the breakers roar the loudest, and look the grandest, as they come rolling in from the sea. I have much more respect for these fellows than before. I felt and saw their strength the other morning. The moon is shining brightly. Shirts is my companion and he has done about all of the talking, having got on a string concerning his wife and like most of the others, believes there never was one like her.

Steamer *Columbia.* November 18th.

Fort Umpqua is most admirably situated for fishing and hunting. There are plenty of deer a few miles from the post. Shirts and myself were in the woods today, returning about six P.M., found the detachment under orders to embark, went off in the ship at once expecting to go to sea in the morning.

Fort Umpqua, November 19th.

Morning broke rainy and disagreeable, wind blowing a perfect hurricane. Went ashore at 3 P.M. and Lieutenant Houston swears he will not leave again until we can get away.

Fort Umpqua, November 20th.

Today is raining and I busy myself putting my arms in order, running pistol balls and general repairs. Had a most horrible dream last night concerning hoe [*sic*]. Confoundedly unpleasant night in consequence of the fleas.

Fort Umpqua, November 21st.

Cleaned up for inspection [but] were excused in consequence of the rain. The men are mostly unwell suffering from colds. I am decidedly so and feel hardly fit to go around. The men are growling and discontented and out of sorts.

Fort Umpqua, November 22nd.

I was out in the woods with Shirts again today. Game did not seem to fancy our style and excepting one good deer, we saw nothing and got nothing unless it be a good wetting.

Fort Umpqua, November 23rd.

Two parties are out after game today. Kendall, Woods, and Shirts are gone up the river after ducks. Carter, Walsh, and Wright to Ten Mile creek for salmon, who returned with four fine ones weighing about forty lbs. each. Lively and Shilling came in with one duck and one salmon, Kendall and party with nothing.

Fort Umpqua, November 24th.

The steamer came down from Gardiner City, where she has been but, although the day is fine and warm, I do not think we will get out of the river. The water is still so warm that we bathe in it.

Fort Umpqua, November 25th.

This being a day set apart for Thanksgiving and praise in the good state of Connecticut, it would be highly proper for one to do something great, outlandish, or patriotic, but as the only opining I can see is to get drunk on that miserable peus poor liquid, I have preferred to go out and pick a good quantity of whertleberrys (they being plenty, but of a different species than those back home) and have them put into a pudding for dinner.

Although there was a scarcity of turkey, chicken, and the usual routine for a Thanksgiving dinner at home, we dined very well from salmon and one simple pudding. The salmon are delicious, and being the first I ever ate, relished well. I presume home sees a gathering of all my brothers and sisters, and much as I would like mountains and prairie of Oregon, and my wishes seem so nearly being gratified. Of course we are now resting on one corner of it, but I wish to penetrate far into the interior.

Fort Umpqua, November 26th.

We seem destined to become old settlers here inasmuch as there seems not the least likelihood of getting out in any of the fine days we have had. The channel seems so rough, that a pilot cannot go out and take soundings, so we remain in this sand hill.

Steamship *Columbia,* November 27th.

Morning fine and were at once ordered aboard. Found the pilot gone, but returned at 10 A.M. hove up anchor at 1 P.M. crossed bar at 2 and one-half P.M. safe, the channel being perfectly smooth and calm.

Steamship *Columbia,* November 28th.

During the afternoon and evening of yesterday we had a beautiful time. Arrived off Columbia River bar at about 12 M. today, but as they had no pilot [who] came out, we must lay off and on till morning. There is a heavy sea running which causes the ship to toss around like a spirit in hell.

Steamer *Columbia,* November 29th.

The pilot came aboard of the ship at 8 A.M. and we at once steamed for the bar, crossed in safety, and at 12 P.M. were at Astoria, the place where the millionaire made a considerable part of his immense fortune. Perhaps if the poor Indians had been dealt with fairly, Mr. John Jacob Astor would have grown rich more slowly. Astoria is a town of about 200 inhabitants on the right [south] bank of the Columbia River, about 10 miles from its mouth, seems to be of little importance at present. Was built to some extent during a gold excitement nearby but does little business at present.

Fort Vancouver, November 30th.

We arrived at this place about midnight last night, and came ashore this forenoon, and quartered in one of the Hudson's Bay Company's buildings. We have been eight weeks accomplishing the trip from New York, a distance that usually occupies 4 to 5.

I found letters awaiting me from Jennie Frost, and George, and was more than pleased to do so. Vancouver is situated on the Columbia River about 45 miles from its mouth in Washington Territory. [It] was formerly the most important trading post belonging to the Hudson's Bay Company and is the head quarters of this military department. The Hudson's Bay Company still occupy their property here, but do very little trade. Their lease according to the treaty runs out on the first of June 1860.

Their post here is an enclosure about 500 yards long by 300 yards wide built of logs set in the earth forming a perfect stockade, inside of which are all of their buildings, stores, arms, and ammunition and a tower upon which is mounted a sentinel and cries the time of night and rings a large bell every half hour. We occupy one of their houses, some of the quarters at the garrison having been recently burned. The garrison is about 1/2 mile from the town and laid out in the form of a rectangle on a slight elevation. There is a garrison of five companies of Artillery and one of Infantry.

It seems that Colonel George Wright went into the mountains and pretty effectually whipped the Indians that so severely handled Colonel Steptoe in the first of the summer, so that the especial duty for which we came out is accomplished and hopes are entertained that we will be sent to West Point before long. (3) I spent the evening writing and reading letters.

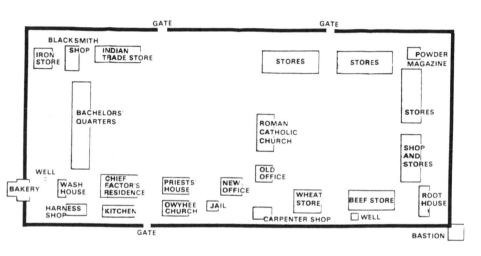

Fort Vancouver, W. T.
—National Park Service

December 1858

Fort Vancouver, December 1st.

I spent the day visiting the town and garrison, and in playing ball. The weather is mild and fine so far. The town is supported principally by the garrison. There is one or two sawmills here and some little farming done in the back country, but I think after the business furnished in consequence of the garrison is done, [that] the most of the business is done. Some few Indians are seen here, most of which are inferior specimens of humanity filthy and dirty to a disgusting degree. The women are a little or considerably loose in morals.

Fort Vancouver, December 2nd.

Mount Hood looms up in the east and south some 15 to 16,000 feet above the ocean,* it's ever snowcapped head far above the clouds, making a grand sight to the eye. There is little of interest today, some of the boys are trying the experiment of how much Vancouver whiskey will kill them, and judging from the present appearance, it will take very little time and no vast amount to complete the job.

Fort Vancouver, December 3rd.

The weather grows cooler and more winterish. I have been in quarters all of the day, writing to friends home. Commenced snowing this evening.

Fort Vancouver, December 4th.

Snow fell to the depth of about two inches during the night, the weather is not very cold. I have been in the town during the evening. The citizens here are to me a set of cut-throats and robbers who to loosen ones purse strings would not hesitate putting the muzzle of a revolver in ones face for an opera glass in order that one can more clearly see the necessity of coming to their terms.

---

* Elev. 11,235. –bw

Fort Vancouver, December 5th.

This being Sunday, we were out to inspection in the morning. The weather is considerably cool and keen. Some of the men have been in church. For myself, I have been reading most of the day. We are very uncomfortable here, sleeping on the floor so thick as to make rolling a job of considerable movement. The floor is very open and the cold gets in as much as is comfortable.

Fort Vancouver, December 6th.

I am on guard [duty] today, which duty here amounts to remaining in quarters during the entire tour. In the night one keeps up the fire and looks out for the lights. The rumor is going the rounds that we go up the river to the Cascades to spend the winter. It is said to be one of the most outlandish places in the world.

Fort Vancouver, December 7th.

I have spent the day doing little outside of going down town and around the quarters. A General Order promulgated today assigns us to duty at the Cascades, where we are to remain during the winter.

Fort Vancouver, December 8th.

We were out betimes [*sic*] this morning and preparing to leave the fort. Went to the wharf at nine o'clock A.M. and remained until ten. Found that we would be unable to go up the river in consequence of the ice and returned to the quarters. The mail arrived from the states and I'm the fortunate possessor of two letters and papers.

Fort Vancouver, December 9th.

The weather is cold, a drizzling storm of rain and snow falling. Carmichael is so unwell as to be compelled to go to hospital. Corporal Walsh's time expired today and we will see how he will proceed, for he was to come to this country looking for gold when he should be discharged, so he told me when I enlisted.

Fort Vancouver, December 10th.

Today has been like yesterday, rain and snow all day. I have been on duty most of the day, overhauling the pontoon train at the Quartermasters building. We amused ourselves dancing this evening.

Fort Vancouver, December 11th.

This morning broke warm and fine. The ice in the river is breaking up and we may look for a move soon. Corporal Walsh has re-enlisted for a second five [years] and his gold visions have gone. He will undoubtedly do well for of course he will be most likely to be discharged [when we get] home.

Fort Vancouver, December 12th.

This being Sunday we were out for inspection in the morning, and around quarters during the balance of the day.

Fort Vancouver, December 13th.

We packed up and got ready for the trip up river, but it proved a false alarm and we are still here, unsettled and growling.

Fort Vancouver, December 14th.

Weather continues moderate and some rain. Day spent as others. An order was promulgated this evening giving us the route tomorrow.

Fort Cascades, December 15th (4)

Left the quarters at nine A.M. embarked on the Steamer *Senontta* at ten and left the wharf at half [hour] after. Made one landing at a place called Sandy to take in wood. Arrived at this place at 3 o'clock P.M. but are not at our final destination [yet].

The scenery on the Columbia must equal that on the Hudson for beauty in summer. After leaving Vancouver for 20 miles or so the land bordering on the river is level and finely adapted to agricultural pursuits, unless the river overflows it at high water and, I am informed, that this never occurs unless it be some of the lower portions of it.

About midway we begin to come into the [Cascade] mountains, after which there is one continuous stretch of precipices and palisades with small streams or cascades running down their sides, bubbling and boiling, making oftentimes pleasing sights (and forming no mean subject for a sketch.) About 35 miles from Vancouver is Cape Horn, as it is called by the intrepid navigators of this great river. A high bold rock makes out, causing a bend in the river, and at times the wind draws down through the mountains with such force as to give the boat considerable trouble in getting around it. For the last ten miles or so the country begins to be more level and now and then is again seen the log house of some hardy settler peeking out from some piece of timber, with its piece of cleared ground around it, and finally upon arriving we find the fort situated on the edge of a prairie some three miles long and 3/4ths wide.

It comprises a block house and some other necessary build-ings, one or two families living here keeping a hotel, for here the boats stop, and travelers must spend the night here or five miles above at a place called Upper Cascades, where we are to stow ourselves for the winter in a most doleful place, as we are informed, and in fact one is hardly disposed to doubt it, for it has been raining here like the devil ever since our arrival. (5)

Fort at Upper Cascades, December 16th.

We have finally found our probable resting place for the winter. Took up our beds and traveled early this morning over five miles of the worst mud imaginable, amid rain in torrents, and camped in a very substantial block house built about two years since. It is two hundred and fifty feet above the river and com-mands everything. This is the upper terminus of the portage road built by Lieutenant Derby (alias Doesticks) for transporting freight around the rapids which give this place its name. These rapids are of such force as to prevent boats passing them at all indeed, were there no other obstructions. But as the river, which is about a half mile wide at this point, is full of large boulders, there is no possible chance for navigating it.

A boat plies regularly between here and Fort Dalles, a distance of 45 miles, carrying passengers and freight. There are some 6 houses here and one sawmill. One of the houses is occupied as a store by Messers Bradford, who owns largely in the boats and has also constructed a kind of railroad, two miles of the distance to the lower landing, which greatly facilitates the transporting of freight. This rail-road is simply made by grading and laying down wood string pieces of sawed stuff, and drawn by mules. Last year during the Fraser River Gold excitement, there was a great deal of travel over this route across the country by land.

The place was attacked two years since and a number of the inhabitants massacred by a combined force of Indians. There is a tribe of the red devils about midway between this and the lower landing, but mostly whipped to subjection, it is said. Some of the boys exhibit some timidity in view of this.(6)

Fort Cascades, December 17th. *

Raining, and if correctly informed, we may expect it all winter. (7) This is a fine place, is about like being in a well, one can see less than a mile in any direction unless it be right in the air, being surrounded by mountains rising 1 to 2000 feet. The citizens around here are a rough crowd most of whom carry a six gun battery on their sterns, with a rifle that for size may be termed a sabre [sic]. They are mostly men driven from California by the vigilance committee, and have murdered their man. They hang around here and if a traveler shows a twenty dollar piece they want and, if fair or foul means wail get it for them, they will not hesitate to use it. They boast of such names as White Salmon Bob, Up-the-Creek California Jim, Texas Bill and others with which I am not conversant.

Fort Cascades, December 18th.

We are still favored with copious showers of rain and mud. There is no end to or beginning to either, for everything is mud. We commenced operations today on the portage road, where it seems we are to expend our strength and patriotism for a few months to come. I could not but think with someone I know not who said, "when I think of what I am now and what I used to be, I think I've throwed myself away without sufficient cause." For when I stood there in mud nearly up to my knees, I had some curious reflections and asked old Wright if he would not as soon do a few tip tees as be there, but he said no, not by a damned sight. Corporal McEnaney was made a Lance Sergeant today.

Fort Cascades, December 19th.

This being Sunday, we are around quarters doing our wash-ing, mending, and general repairs. I took up an unfinished job, i.e., some shirts and drawers that I had expended all of the skin on my knuckles on upon a former occasion, but this time I improvised a washboard, which did the work admirably. I took a slab from a length of log, long

---

* Fort Cascades 1855-1861. The fort consisted of three separate locations all occupied at the same time called Main Fort, Middle Blockhouse and Upper Blockhouse. This installation was established to protect settlers and travelers along the Columbia River, who were detained there by the severe rapids in the river, from raids by Indians. The Main Fort was garrisoned by up to 79 enlisted men plus officers. There were as few as 11 men in the blockhouses, each of which had a 6-pounder cannon. The location of this post was in today's Skamania County, Washington near Bonneville Dam, about 40 miles upriver from Vancouver. See page 218 about Fort Rains which was the name given to a blockhouse. – bw

enough to reach across the tub and wide enough to make a good sized board. It is of what is termed Oregon Pine, not like any pine I have ever seen, has a coarse grain, which upon rubbing the clothes across, took out the dirt with amazing rapidity (some woolen too) but there is enough left. Some of the boys declare it a Yankee invention, but I notice others brought it into requisition after I had finished. Must remark that I had first rate luck, *ala* old women.

Fort Cascades, December 20th.

This is one of the most wonderful things in creation, that the people of Maine do not emigrate to this delightful country, for they are so confoundedly fond of water and it is so plenty here. In order to enjoy oneself he ought [to] be amphibious, for the atmosphere is full of water and it rains continually. Hereafter I shall only make note of the weather days that are more than usually stormy and that there are no storms (if these stay on).

Fort Cascades, December 21st.

Spent the day on the road and came in at evening more dead than alive. This is decidedly tough on the men, and Lieutenant seems to care little for it. Wheeler is sick of it enough.

Fort Cascades, December 22nd.

Immortal Gods; hear ye a day without storm, but even so we get three or four hours sun, it being so late when it gets over the mountains and goes down so early. I have today indulged in some of that invigorating beverage so much prized among Christians (i.e. beer) and find it much better than I imagined I should.

Fort Cascades, December 23rd.

Today finds me in quarters during the entire day and evening. Have written to my friend, Joe Day.

Fort Cascades, December 24th.

The great event of the day is the arrival of the States mail, by which I received letters from George & Mother, also papers, which are quite welcome. Worked and [it] rained.

Fort Cascades, December 25th.

Well, if this hasn't been a merry Christmas I would not say so. We were to go hunting, but it rained so intolerably that it would be pursuing pleasures under difficulties, so we shot at target out of one of the port holes. Had a dinner of bean soup and only for the newspapers received yesterday, I fear I should have passed a dull Christmas.

Fort Cascades, December 26th.

This being Sunday, there is nothing going on. I am on guard. Rain of course. Went out shooting with pistol awhile this after-noon, when we were honored by a visit from one of the red devils this afternoon for the first time. There is a numerous camp below here.

Fort Cascades, December 27th.

I am on guard pass today. Went out looking for specimens in the afternoon with Corporal Walsh, found very good ones. Some of the men were out hunting in the afternoon, but got wet was all. In the evening some person maliciously inclined throwed a large stone at Sergeant Wheeler's door, which causes some inquiries as to who did it. Most of the men blame Cecil, as he is on his beer and left quarters a very few moments before it occurred.

Fort Cascades, December 28th.

Today has been more pleasant than often occurs, and may be termed pleasant. Little of the so-called mountain mist has fallen. Men employed on [building] the road.

Fort Cascades, December 29th.

In consequence of the stone being thrown last evening, there is to be a full guard mounted hereafter. In this way all must be punished for the misdemeanors of one. We signed the pay rolls in the morning and went to our work as usual.

Fort Cascades, December 30th.

Raining so very hard this morning that we were not out on the road [work]. An order published to the detachment tonight shows a great amount of vindictiveness on some person's part. We are almost termed cowards enough for the act that no one hardly knows who is guilty.

Fort Cascades, December 31st.

We were out on the road, but passed off at noon and mustered again. For the last two months many of the men are on a spree and [it will be] strange if we do not have a noisy New Year's day.

January, 1859

Fort Cascades, January 1st, 1859.

Today we are excused from duty [as] the rain is pouring in torrents. Some of the men are on a drunk, for myself I am not inclined to put down more of this villainous whiskey than I can travel with. This is a decided change, since the first of last year. I am six thousand miles from home, quartered in a stout but not very tight block house, the logs so open that one can put his hand out through the spaces between the logs, sleeping on a floor of hewn timber which never made any pretensions to being tight, and oftentimes being compelled to shake the snow from my blanket on arising in the morning, and living on Uncle Samuel's rations razeed [*sic*] by the avarice of the Quarter Master Sergeant and I fear some others, and still I was never more healthy in my life. Am gaining flesh every day, not withstanding the continual drenching we are subjected to and hard duty compelled to perform. I took supper at the Exchange Hotel this evening with my bunkee, Wright.

Fort Cascades, January 2nd.

Rain prevails still and I presume will continue to do so until spring. It being Sunday, we had our usual inspection. I spent the day in quarters writing and reading.

Fort Cascades, January 3rd.

I mounted guard in the morning, took off my belts and went to work during the day, did my tour of guard during the night. The mail came from the States and I received letters from George and Caroline, also papers. I am the most favored of any of the party thus far receiving more mail than all [others].

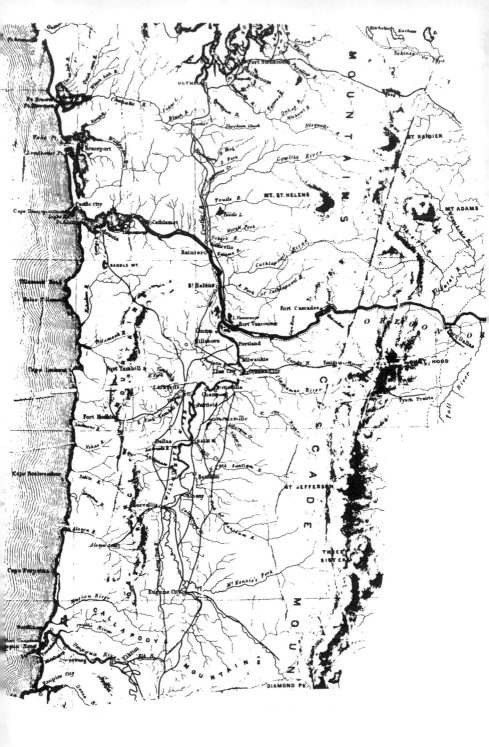

44

Find locations of a number of places Peck mentions in his
Journal. Note that San Juan Island is identified as "Bellevue I."

Fort Cascades, January 4th.

Today is tolerably pleasant. I was relieved from guard at eight A.M. and went to work in the forenoon. The Lieutenant finds considerable fault with the progress being made. We are beginning to get considerably acquainted with the Indians, their ways and customs. The beauties of these forest maidens is considerably less than portrayed by Cooper and others of his compeers. One is very much disappointed if he has formed his ideas from such works of the Indians, and when seen in their native filth and dirt, it looks amazing [that] so many live.

The women are especially degraded and have very little virtue left them if they arrive at the age of sixteen or seventeen. They are fast being destroyed by disease and whiskey, and [this is] I think the quickest and cheapest method to exterminate them. There is one of them hanging around here and one is somewhat surprised in seeing the idolatry and superstition existing among them. They hand the dead up to dry in trees for the first three or four months. At their final burial, all of their personal property is put in the grave with them. They have a number of slaves taken from other tribes here, and compel them to perform every menial service for them.

natural bridge over the Columbia, just over the islands above the rapids in the river, and by some great convulsion of nature it was thrown down, causing the river to be changed from its natural course to the one it now follows. And in fact, the mountains on either side look as if at some time they may have formed the abutments to such a formation, and the islands and rapids they claim to have been formed of the earth in the bridge, all of which does not appear altogether improbable.

Fort Cascades, January 5th.

Today is clear and cool. The wind is coming down the river enough to take one off [his] feet. Shirts and myself measured the road from the upper to lower landing today and found it just five miles, and that covered by mud on an average about one foot deep.

Fort Cascades, January 6th.

Weather continues cool and windy. I mounted guard in the morning, but owing to some strain received during the day was so lame at evening as to be unable to do my duty.

Fort Cascades, January 7th.

Continues to blow cold and disagreeable. Not feeling able to travel five miles this morning, I did not go to the lower landing to see the doctor. But upon the boat returning at noon, found myself booked for duty. But as I am considerably relieved, I do not suffer much. we are in a hell of a fix if we go to the doctor. He informs us that a man who can go five miles in the mud and return can do duty, hence books him for duty. And if one is so unwell as to be unable to travel to see him he is marked duty as he, the doctor, won't have any person on the sick list unless he knows he is sick. On guard tonight.

Fort Cascades, January 8th.

Weather much as during the last few days. The wind is perfectly furious in its passage.

Fort Cascades, January 9th.

This is Sunday. We were inspected in the morning. The weather continues the same as has been. The men could hardly stand on the parade at inspection.

Fort Cascades, January 10th.

Weather continues as the last few days, duty the same.

Fort Cascades, January 11th

Rain is now the order of the day, and cold with it. Livermore took in an extra cargo of poor whiskey and fell down stairs, being on guard was relieved and I am detailed in his place.

Fort Cascades, January 12th.

It continues to rain and freeze everything in a perfect glare of ice. I am on guard pass today, thank fortune, for the storm is quite severe. In fact when the men came in from work, they were completely encased in ice. Their overcoats would stand upright on the floor. Who would not sell a farm to be a soldier?

Fort Cascades, January 13th.

There is no change in the weather but some in us, as the Paymaster came today and squared up for the last muster.

Fort Cascades, January 14th.

There is no change in weather, doing nothing. The boys are gambling at a great rate. Faro [and] bluff are the amusement.

Fort Cascades, January 15th.

Detachment doing nothing in consequence of the rain. The Lieutenant must have been troubled in his dream to give so much respite in consequence of the weather.

Fort Cascades, January 16th.

I mounted guard in the morning. It being Sunday, we were inspected in the morning by Lieutenant Houston, Lieutenant Robert not being out.

Fort Cascades, January 17th.

Relieved from guard in the morning. Out through the back country trying to find a new and better route for a portage road from upper to lower landing. The country is of the roughest possible formation, most of the part passed through by us appears to have been the bed of a river at some time and suddenly became dry, it being in many places destitute of soil and vegetation. We scrambled over rocks until about three o'clock P.M., when we came out into the road and our inimitable chevalier Walsh acknowledged to have become tired out and that [in] some way he can't travel well today. I am somewhat fatigued myself, but would not say so to him, he being the recognized champion pedestrian of our party.

Fort Cascades, January 18th.

On the road as usual, we are really persecuted. Och [*sic*] why did [...] enlist in what our mugging says and further declares he's not himself at all, <u>Molly Dear.</u>

Fort Cascades, January 19th.

<u>Damn</u> the rain is the general exclamation uttered in tones that doth most strongly savor of discontent. Fraser River gold diggings are particularly the subject of discussion just now.

Fort Cascades, January 20th.

Today is here, quite pleasant all day. We are very much disappointed in not getting letters. The mail is three days overdue.

Fort Cascades, January 21st.

I mounted guard this morning, took off my belts and went out to work, as the grand custom now. After coming in from a hard days work one finds it immensely agreeable to put on his belts, shoulder his 12 lb. rifle, do a tour of guard, go out to work the next morning. But we are in for five years. All hands are taking to gaming, firstly as a means of driving off dull care and after for the love of gain. one is reminded of the far famed Eldorado of San Francisco notoriety upon looking in our quarters of an evening.

Fort Cascades, January 22nd.

There is little of interest occurring, now and then a visit to the Indian ranch constituting about our only excitement. But with the mud and rain the fun is dearly purchased. he timber in these parts is of a pine species and grows to an immense size. Often one sees trees five, and six sometimes feet in diameter. The sawmill here does a good business getting out lumber and sending [it] up country.

Fort Cascades, January 23rd-

Today is Sunday, inspection as usual by Lieutenant Houston. I was relieved from guard in the morning and spent the remainder of the day mending, washing, and other domestic duties. A chief whose name is said to be Bully Bully honored our place with his presence today. There seems a gloom cast over the entire party today, and for myself I feel as if my heart had a space of about ten thousand miles square to inhabit by itself, so lonely do I feel.

Fort Cascades, January 24th.

Today has been a remarkably fine one. Everybody has been on the grieve ever for letters during the day, for the mail is overdue. And when our expressman hove in sight down the trail there was a general shout for joy, for the red flag fluttered from his saddle pommel assuring us there was mail. Rifles were loaded and when he rode upon the parade [ground - ?] a salute or volley and three cheers with a tiger greeted him. After saluting with becoming dignity he presents myself

> I mounted guard this morning, took off my belts and went out to work.... After coming in from a hard days work one finds it immensely agreeable to put on his belts, shoulder his 12 lb. rifle, do a tour of guard, go out to work the next morning. But we are in for five years.
>
> —January 21, 1859

with one solitary letter, pronounces that's all, and rides off. I have never seen men's countenances drop so suddenly as did these same men's, and up to the present writing they are about as cross-grained lot as one would wish to meet, and many a damn has been uttered since. I am considered the luckiest of all in the mail line. The letter is from Jimmie Frost and exceedingly welcome.

Fort Cascades, January 25th.

Rain prevails. One must indeed be amphibious to thrive in this detested country. I am on guard again today.

Fort Cascades, January 26th.

Relieved from guard and on the road in forenoon, inside in the afternoon. Don't rain much I reckon, oh no!

Fort Cascades, January 27th.

......I can chronicle little of interest, only it rains.

Fort Cascades, January 28th.

Like yesterday we are favored with invigorating showers. We continue our labors on the road despite the storm.

Fort Cascades, January 29th.

We are really going to be intimate with roots once more, for no less than fifty bushels of potatoes have been landed in our block house for us today. Well we sadly wanted them, for our rations are quite poor. Our beef is good for nothing, or next to it, and it is with difficulty one has found sufficient food.

Fort Cascades, January 30th.

This being Sunday we were inspected as usual. Thank heaven there is one circumstance which keeps us from work on the road, I am on guard. Corporal Supplee, who has during the last few days shown signs of an approaching spiritual crisis, today culminated the affair by getting drunk while in charge of the guard, is under arrest and will undoubtedly be tried by a Court Martial, <u>Rum, Rum</u>!

Fort Cascades, January 31st.

I was relieved from guard this morning, on the road in the forenoon, in quarters in afternoon, spent my time writing home.

The mail arrived today and nearly everybody received letters, hence a great amount of good feeling tonight. Nothing so encourages one as letters from home, and surely we need encouragement.
—February 21, 1859

February, 1859

Fort Cascades, February 1st.

Today has indeed been fine. The men are in the best possible spirits and we have enjoyed ourselves more than we ever expected to in this hole of inequity. And we have great hopes of bright days in the future.

Fort Cascades, February 2nd.

Alas for our hopes for fine weather, for now in their very earliest bloom they are dashed to the ground. It rains like the devil. Everyone can see that this work on the road is all humbug and only labor thrown away.

Fort Cascades, February 3rd.

Weather continues unpleasant. We are excused from work for the rain.

Fort Cascades, February 4th.

Rain continues to predominate. I have been down to the lower landing with Gray. The ten mile tramp is no small job considering the mud is about leg deep. Sergeant W. Smith and Shirts are gone to Vancouver to attend the Court Martial that tries Corporal Supplee. I am on guard.

Fort Cascades, February 5th.

Relieved from guard this morning. Storm continues. I have been in the quarters all day.

Fort Cascades, February 6th.

We were inspected about ten o'clock by Lieutenants Robert and Houston. The day has been fine, a beautiful day for one to do one's washing. I visited the Indians this afternoon in their ranch. It is disgusting to witness their filth and degradation. Virtue or chastity is entirely ignored and to see them in their crude state eating lice makes me involuntarily [declare]: Lo: the poor Indian.

Fort Cascades, February 7th.

Weather continues fine. We have been on the road as usual. Artificer Cecil's time expires this morning and he is gone to Portland to wait for Wood, who will also [be] discharged soon.

Fort Cascades, February 8th.

Storm again, snow fell fast during the afternoon. Some of the men from below came up this evening and we had a dance in the evening, the old blockhouse was quite lively.

Fort Cascades, February 9th.

Snowing like the devil today. We were out at work in the morning, but came in for the storm. This afternoon has been spent in the general way for, when off duty, we continue to find some amusement. Mock Court Martials are much in vogue and woe to the man who is selected for a victim and tried for some imaginary fault and is sure to get from six to twenty with a bunk board. This mode of punishment is simple and easy to execute. The prisoner is laid on a table face downward, a board about three feet long by six inches wide is put into the hands of the executioner and he performs the functions of his office in a satisfactory manner generally.

Fort Cascades, February 10th.

Snowing still and we are doing nothing. Gambling among the men increases and this amusement is the most resorted to [in the] evenings.

Fort Cascades, February 11th

It is snowing and disagreeable. I have been out surveying with Corporal Walsh over the proposed new trail or road. It is indeed an almost endless task to attempt to go out through timber here. The country is so rough and broken that we cannot get over it readily. Add to this about eighteen inches of snow and one is fixed.

Fort Cascades, February 12th.

We are greeted with a change this morning, for in the place of snow we have severe cold. So much so that Lieutenant broke off the party from work, a thing of such rare occurrence as to cause a feeling of wonder to run through the crowd. And many a compliment has been paid to him (Lieutenant) for the consideration he shows for us.

Fort Cascades, February 13th.

Inspection by Lieutenant Houston at 10 o'clock A.M. The day being fine, there has been a general scattering from the quarters. For myself, I took a long ramble up the river in company with our Schilling, but found little of interest beyond large trees, rocks and mud. A number of our boys are down to one of the dens here gambling and so far quite lucky, nearly all having won. Poor seems to be the most lucky of any.

Fort Cascades, February 14th.

Today is raining as usual, but we were out at work. General Harney is at the lower landing. We expected a visit from him but he did not come. Inclined to make us more comfortable than in the past. They can do it and still our situation will be none too pleasant.

Fort Cascades, February 15th.

The General did not inspect us as was expected. Today Shirts and myself measured the distance from here to the lower landing. Found it just five miles and that five miles of as deep mud as could be possibly found anywhere.

Fort Cascades, February 16th.

At last the General passed by our place today, but did not call. Undoubtedly seeing at a glance that it is a most disagreeable hole and one that offers few attractions to any.

Fort Cascades, February 17th.

Snow is falling very fast all day, does not come in flakes but [in] handfuls. I am on sick report and feel quite unwell.

Fort Cascades, February 18th.

Today continues stormy. Wood is discharged and I, with some others, went to the lower landing with him. The men generally regret [his departure] for he was the life of the Detachment.

Fort Cascades, February 19th.

Unpleasant weather still prevails. We were doing nothing all day. Through Lieutenant Robert we hear of an expedition to go into the mountains in the spring, I suppose we will go.

Fort Cascades, February 20th.

Inspection at ten o'clock A.M. by Lieutenant Houston. There has been preaching at the Rail Road House today. I remained in quarters all day. Our men are gambling with a rush, men who never before indulged in the game are foremost.

Fort Cascades, February 21st.

The work, so long and arduously pursued on the road, is abandoned and today we commenced on another portion of it. The mail arrived today and nearly everybody received letters, hence a great amount of good feeling tonight. Nothing so encourages one as letters from home, and surely we need encouragement.

Fort Cascades, February 22nd.

This, the birthday (or anniversary of) the Father of our country, has been spent dreary enough. In the forenoon we were at work, but excused in the afternoon, but as it rained like the devil, one only could remain inside. The Artificers of the Detachment are required to give in a written statement of the manner in which our mess is conducted with a view to reform. it is needed sadly, for to come down to the fine thing we don't get half enough to eat.

Fort Cascades, February 23rd.

It continues stormy as usual. We were out on the road at work and when the storm increased the Quartermaster ordered his teams in, said it was too severe for his mules to be out in. I noticed no one took much interest in us.

Fort Cascades, February 24th.

We were out on the road as usual until 1 P.M. It is stormy of course. There is lots of fun now, and the late investigation regarding our mess is termed The Irish Conspiracy or The Blockhouse Plot. Shirts shot a cougar tonight, a large fellow, and would it prove an ugly customer in a fight.

Fort Cascades, February 25th.

Work and rain are the only events occurring now. A Detachment of men came in from Fort Vancouver to work on the road today. They are rough looking customers.

Fort Cascades, February 26th.

Out on the road today. The men from Vancouver are in the middle block house for quarters. Some of them are good and drunk tonight.

Fort Cascades, February 27th.

Inspection at 12 M. by Lieutenant Houston. I spent the day writing home.

Fort Cascades, February 28th.

We were mustered by Captain Wallen in the forenoon and as the day is extremely stormy did not go out to work on the road. Gambling is all the rage, and almost all of the men indulge in it.

March, 1859

Fort Cascades, March 1st.

I mounted guard in the morning, remained in quarters all day, continues to rain.

Fort Cascades, March 4th.

Weather has been stormy and the men employed as usual. Still there are indications of approaching spring. Frogs have been heard and everything indicates the approach of the season. We were payed off today and gambling received a fresh impetus thereby. We are much honored by a member of the Territorial Legislature who is in our quarters gambling tonight.

Fort Cascades, March 8th.

Weather continues stormy and very disagreeable. The men are employed on the road as usual. Today at noon one of the soldiers from the middle block house, who came up to the whiskey mills, was severely punished by one of the citizens here, and after[wards] fetched to our quarters by some of our men. During dinner Private Bradford came up to our place loaded with revolvers and knives, claimed that some of our boys had insulted his wife, and kicked up a terrible fuss about it. It seems this drunken soldier had been to his house for something, hence the mess, but he found a good number of men who were quite as belligerent in character as he and so left. He afterwards came and apologized for his conduct.

Fort Cascades, March 9th.

The weather is almost intolerable, rain with a wind that searches one through. Still, we were out at work as usual, the Quartermaster sent his teams in again. The mail came, I received papers but no letters, the first mail that has missed me.

Fort Cascades, March 12th.

We have received any amount of snow during the last few days, but today is fine and spring like. We continue our work, storm or no, which causes some fearful oaths to be piled on some poor officer, either Lieutenant Houston or General Harney.

Fort Cascades, March 18th.

No change has occurred in weather or our duties. It's rain, work and guard duty. The Hibernian portion of the Detachment were down to the lower landing celebrating St. Patrick's day and came home pretty drunk–nice times. The boys continue to amuse themselves with Faro, and some of them think very little of losing $100.00 per evening.

Fort Cascades, March 20th.

The weather continues of the most disagreeable nature and Lieutenant Houston more so. Rain and sour looks are our consolations. We were inspected by Lieutenant Robert at 10 o'clock A.M., after which the men dispersed. We had a good roast beef dinner and every one looked better pleased than is usual over the bean soup.

Fort Cascades, March 23rd.

There has been no change in the weather. I am on guard tonight. The mail came tonight. I received papers but no letters as yet. There is a grand ball at the R.R. House, the ball of the season. They advertise 20 ladies will be in attendance. Of course, I cannot go, being on guard. Shirts and myself often take a run through the woods but seldom see any game.

Fort Cascades, March 31st.

I have nothing to chronicle but bad weather up to today, which is very fine. The men continue the usual routine of duty, but the stream and river is rising fast in consequence of the snow melting on the mountains. Trout begin to be found in the streams and the men are after them. We look for some fine days in April. Our road business is progressing finely, and if we could have some fine weather we would soon wind it up.

April, 1859

Fort Cascades, April 1st.

Today is really fine. The sun shines brightly and not withstanding, a coolness in the atmosphere caused by so much snow still on the mountains all around us. It is fine. We were out at work as usual, but after it was done for the day, all hands were off for trout. I am detailed inside to assist the cook.*

Fort Cascades, April 6th.

We have been blessed with fine weather since the month came, until this morning when our old friend, the Mountain Mist, made its appearance in good earnest. It is an odd spectacle. one can stand in the door looking out, sees a heavy rain falling and looking a little further up the mountain side sees snow in good earnest. I believe one loses his identity to a certain extent, living in this out of the world, uncivilized place, and eventually becomes half savage. I dislike the country much and would not be compelled to remain in for a term of natural life, for the entire Territory. In the entire village, small to be sure, there is hardly a person whom I would trust.

Fort Cascades, April 8th.

The weather continues wet, the men engaged as usual. I am still [standing in] slush and dislike it much. Private Poor has gone to Portland today on pass, and in my opinion will fail to report when his pass has expired. Should he not do so, the officers will have the satisfaction of having driven a good man from the company and more will surely follow him unless some of this rigor is abated.

---

* "Assist the cook" undoubtedly referred to being on "K.P." - Kitchen Police, that is, peal potatoes, wash the dishes and pots, scrub the floor. The term apparently became popular during the First World War. The duty generally had little to do with actual assistance to the cook. Most soldiers considered being assigned to "K.P" to be a day or drudgery. —bw

58

Fort Cascades, April 11th.

Weather continues about the same. Poor's pass expired today, but no Poor came, and he of course has deserted. I am surely tempted to follow him for our treatment this winter has cooled all of the military ardor I possessed. However, we lose a good comrade by it.

Fort Cascades, April 12th.

There is no change in the weather, rain, rain, constantly. We received the mail today. I received [letters from] seven of my former friends and a number of papers. Brother George seems to have struck a streak of luck and finally became established in business. I am glad of it and would feel gratified to the fickle goddess would she smile on me once or so.

Fort Cascades, April 13th.

Storm continues. Sergeant Wheeler was sent to Portland today, probably in search of Poor. He was sent quite suddenly and some fear he will give Poor trouble in Portland, but my opinion is that it is understood between the parties. In a letter from Jennie I receive some most excellent advice and I would I could follow it, but poor weak nature forbids.

Fort Cascades, April 17th

The weather for the past four days has been extremely fine. The men are disposed to enjoy it to the fullest. I remain in the kitchen still. The men are on the fish exclusively. Trout are becoming quite plenty. Inspection at eleven o'clock A.M. and after[wards] a general raid on the finny tribe.

Fort Cascades, April 22nd.

Weather continues much more endurable and the men show the effect of a little sunshine perceptibly. For, instead of constantly sitting around the fire growling, they take themselves off on numerous excursions. Fishing continues the principle recreation. Trout weighing from 2 to 4 pounds are often brought in. There are any number of rumors as to our probable destination this summer coming, but nothing definite is known yet. Some say that we are going with Lieutenant Mullen, who is to construct a wagon road from Bitter Root Valley to Fort Benton on the upper Missouri River. If so we are going to get fit.

Jane Hall, an Indian woman who has lived much among the whites and assumes this name from former connections with a white man, came to our quarters and remained quite awhile. She speaks English indifferently well, plays on the accordion poorly, casts her jokes and amorous glances well, and much pleased our men. Salmon are being sought after by the Indians. They build a stage out over some deep rapid place and standing on it use a net about the shape of an egg cut in the middle through the length of it. This net is fastened on a bent sapling of the required shape, then made fast to a long pole some 20 ft. long. A rope or line about 13 or 14 ft. long is then tied near the scoop or net and platform. The Indian seizes the pole and sets the net in the water up stream as far from him as the length of the line will allow. Lets it go down with the current as far as the line will admit, if he gets a fish good, if not the same operation is repeated. The Indians have a great fandango over the first salmon of the season, consequently some old fellows were to be seen throwing their nets day after day, all day long, for a long time before any fish were taken. But upon the first one being caught, all business was suspended and preparations made for a great feast and dance.

Their music consists chiefly of a long pole suspended from the roof of the hut, punched against a board at irregular intervals, accompanied by some hideous howls and dance or gyrations of anything but a pleasing nature. These performances are conducted by the medicine man under sacred devotions. There are other occasions upon which they have these same, or nearly so, maneuvers. For one, when a boy shall have become 17 years old, he gives a feast and is taken through all of the scenes he will likely encounter in the chance of fight, and if he goes through all he is pronounced a man of the tribe. These scenes occupy seven days and nights and are accompanied by these fantastic maneuvers. During the entire time the subject must fast at his own feast. There is a festival at which a dog is killed, roasted and eaten by them, and several other occasions upon which pole, medicine man, and howling are brought into requisition. There seems little sense or entertainment to their services. Gratitude is a sentiment unknown to them, much as they have received from them. We find out that they have salmon. We pay more than those who have lived here longer and know more of their customs.

Fort Cascades, April 23rd.

Fine weather continues. Levee and Wilson left here last night and won't return. Upon being informed, Lieutenant Houston said he was darned glad of it.

Fort Cascades, April 30th.

During the last few days we have been on the road. All hands out working like the devil in order to finish it and have nothing to do. The guard duty is dispensed with. The weather is good and the men enjoy it much. There is an order from General Harney assigning us to duty with an expedition to the City of Rocks near Ft. Hall, about 200 miles from Salt Lake City, under the command of Captain H. Wallen. We would much prefer any other man, as we have had sufficient of his administration already. We went to the lower landing to muster this forenoon and returned at 12 M. Our road is finished at last and, if we haven't gained laurels by our labors, we have got many a wet jacket and the officers many a curse. An unnecessary amount of disagreeable duty has been put upon us and rendered as unpleasant as possible by our Lieutenant or some other.... (8)

May, 1859

Fort Cascades, May 1.

We were inspected by Lieutenant Robert after which few were to be found in quarters. The weather is fine and one enjoys it doubly for having been through so much wet. I spent portions of the day and evening writing home.

Fort Cascades, May 2nd.

Sergeant Wheeler, Corporal Walsh and Artificer Smith are gone to Ft. Vancouver to overhaul the pontoon train.

Fort Cascades, May 5th.

We have been drilling under Lieutenant Robert at skirmish drill the last two days and today. The party came from Vancouver yesterday much pleased with their visit. large train of mules passed by here for Fort Dalles for use on the different expeditions the coming summer. Two of our fellow passengers from San Francisco are with the train.

Fort Cascades, May 8th.

We were inspected by Lieutenant Robert in the morning. The day is wet and cold. Snow is falling a little way up the mountain. We have been drilling the past day, the weather has been fine. A few days since Corporal Supplee, while in charge of the guard, got on a drunk and is under arrest at the lower landing. Private Livermore is also in durance vile for the same offense and under the same circumstances.

Fort Cascades, May 10th.

We commenced a new drill this forenoon immediately after breakfast. Started for the lower landing. Arriving here took out the pontoons and took them to the slough, inflated them and launched them. After drilling four hours we repacked them, took [them] to the garrison and returned to our quarters about 2 o'clock P.M., having marched 13 miles and drilled four hours.

Fort Cascades, May 11th.

We were again down to the lower landing drilling with pontoons. Returning there was a general race and the five miles from block house to block house was accomplished in forty-five minutes by myself and one or two more.

Fort Cascades, May 13th.

We continue to go down to the lower landing to drill with pontoons. The band belonging to the 9th Infantry arrived here enroute for the Dalles and are staying with us by invitation. We procured a couple of barrels of lauger [sic] beer and some cigars [and] provisions and done the best we can towards entertaining them. They are pleased and discourse sweet music, which is most agreeably listened to by not only ourselves but the citizens here.

Fort Cascades, May 15th.

Inspection at ten o'clock A.M. I spent a good portion of the day writing home. The weather continues very fine and vegetation is coming forward very rapidly, much more so that it does at home in the spring. Salmon are becoming quite plenty, and one thinks he could spend the summer here much more comfortably than the winter, but we will soon be away. The water in the river is rapidly rising and the river presents a far different appearance than when the water is low.

Fort Cascades, May 20th.

We continue the drill with the pontoons daily at the lower landing. The weather continues fine and is growing warm. General Harney was up here today. Private Horton took the boat for Portland this afternoon, and will not return. The Lieutenant stood on the gang plank as he went aboard looking out for him. More will follow him. I think, only for becoming an outlaw in my own land, I would go too. We have passed a most disagreeable winter tyrannized over by our own officers and dealt unjustly by [what] was insufficient. We must fight among ourselves and in this way add to our miseries.

Fort Cascades, May 21st.

Our duties remain the same and the weather good. Supplee and Livermore arrived here last night from the lower landing, released. Supplee is fined three months pay and reduced to the rank of Private. Livermore is acquitted and returned to duty. So much for whiskey.

Fort Cascades, May 22nd.

We turned out for inspection in white hats and Hudson's Bay shirts, which looked fine, and the boys could not look better equipped for comfort on an expedition. We received a final order to march on the 26th of the present month.

Fort Cascades, May 25th.

For a wonder we have done no duty during the last four days, which greatly astonishes us. Privates Schilling and Gray took their final departure this morning, so we have six men deserted from us already. Tomorrow morning we take our leave of Fort Misery, as it is called by our men, and some of us may never come back. we are going into hostile country with, I very believe, an old coward for a Commandant. The Indians call him an old woman. The mail arrived tonight and is all the more welcome as it may be some time ere we get another. These times bring to one's mind home and its surroundings quite forcibly. After tattoo [bugle call] (9 o'clock P.M.) Ralph Write and myself received an order to report to Lieutenant Houston at lower landing. We arrived there at half after eleven, found him waiting for us and gave us a good mule to return with. We arrived home at about one o'clock A.M. after a ten mile walk, but had the consolation of lowering his whiskey bottle well before we left.

Tattoo

TRADITIONAL   Arr. for this book by Lauren Thomas Webber, Lynn, Mass. 1993

Traditional Bugle Calls of the British and American military, and some European armies, included "First Call" followed by "Reveille," "Assembly" then "To the Colors" in the morning for flag raising. If there was a band available, the National Anthem followed. During the day there were numerous calls designating various duties or field movements including "Mess Call" – time to eat. Evening calls included "Assembly" then "Retreat" for lowering the flag. "To the Colors" or the National Anthem followed. In late evening were "Call to Quarters," "Tattoo" and finally "Taps." The bugle call declared the most melodic is "Tattoo." For this book, the music for "Tattoo" and "Retreat" are included as these bugle calls are mentioned by Peck in his *Journal*. —bw

Fort Dalles, May 26th-

We left the Cascades at 9 o'clock A.M. on the steamer *Hassaloe** and arrived here at 6 P.M. and made our first camp. After leaving the Cascades, the country maintains about the same appearance as before for a distance of about 30 miles. The banks of the river are high and precipitous in many places, and covered with a heavy growth of what is termed Oregon Pine, but during the last 20 miles one sees some clear country, and upon immediately nearing The Dalles, one sees very little timber at all.

The ground is covered with a growth of fine grass, which is said to be very nutritious and animals do well upon it. It was indeed pleasant, to us who have so long looked at the sides of the mountains opposite our block house, to be once more allowed to extend our limits of observations a little. Then the open country near here made me imagine I was again nearing civilization once more, for I have so long looked at trees. Probably no sight that I have ever met has produced such a mixed feeling of familiarity, strangeness, and welcome as this has done.

We were hardly landed at the wharf before a deputation of men from the 9th Infantry Band were on hand to invite us to their quarters to partake of refreshments. Accordingly, after getting our camp pitched, all hands repaired thither, where we found a true German repast, except the sausages and My Goot. They said they were not to be had. We partook of the good cheer set before us, and amid music instrumental and vocal, smoke and beer, we spent the evening, returning to our camp at about 11 P.M., some of us so full of the delicious beverage as to require a guide to the tent, luckily I am not one of the number.

Camp No. 1, White Oak Grove, May 27th.

We broke camp at about 9 o'clock A.M. with orders to march to 3 mile Creek to rendezvous and await two companies, "E" and "H" of the 1st Dragoons, who with Co. "H" of the 4th Infantry and ourselves, who now number 21 men, are to comprise the strength of our expedition, (9) according to orders. Sergeant Wheeler inquired for 3 Mile Creek and the Walla Walla road being pointed out to him, we took our course with it. But upon arriving there, no indications of a camp were visible and we ascended the bluff and followed the bank of the creek,

---

* Peck's spelling of the ship's name was as he pronounced it however, this was the 135-feet long *Hassalo*, a stern wheeler built at Cascades, W.T. in 1857. —bw

65

expecting every moment to come to our camp.

Some of the men were in poor marching condition from their night's revelry. The day was warm and every mile is tedious. Riley at last fell back. I waited for him and finally found him unable to proceed. I put him in the shade, gave him a swallow of good water and he went quietly to sleep for half an hour. I woke him and found him so refreshed as to be able to proceed accordingly. I relieved him of his accouterments and followed on in the others trail. At last we overtook them and found several tired out completely.

At one time we came upon an Indian camp about 500 strong. They were Washoes returning from an incursion on the Snake and had two prisoners. Upon seeing us they mounted their horses and commenced some of the most ludicrous antics imaginable, ending with a war dance, all to the great alarm of the poor devils of prisoners. At last, after marching until 4 and one-half o'clock P.M. we found our camp, and to our chagrin, found that we had been traveling about six hours to get less than three miles from our starting point, all from not having proper instructions. During the last portion of our march, being in the rear through stopping for the purpose of giving others water.

Livermore came staggering to me, and begged me to remain with him until he died, and I should have all his money. Upon which he threw himself down and prepared for the bitter end. I told him that he must think I was a damn fool to spend my time looking at him die for six bits (75 cts.), that if he had enough to make it an object, I would stay. his so enraged him that he jumped up and it was with difficulty [that] I kept with him, for he has money. But I thought he was not near as bad as he thought himself to be, and only wanted a little resolution to get on well enough,-and he went into camp well enough.

Now commences our camp life in earnest, and this our final meal is gotten up in a style not altogether ala mode. The Dalles is a small town on the right bank of the Columbia River. It contains about two or three hundred cutthroats, who depend mostly on government for emloyment, and nearly all derive their support from government, either directly or indirectly from this source. There are now three expeditions fitting out here, and business is intensely lively with all.

A portion of the town in inundated, the water being unusually high, and still will not reach its highest point for some 12 to 15 days yet. There is little timberland immediately in this place. The soil is of a sandy nature and the land rolling or undulating, being inside the mountains. There is far less rainfall during the winter and the animals can in almost every instance live outdoors through the winter. I think some portions of the land suitable to agriculture, but not the uplands, for there is a dry wind [that] prevails a considerable portion of the year, which would so parch the earth as to destroy most crops. But these uplands grow a wild fine grass not entirely unlike our redtop at home, which is very nutritious and upon which stock does well.

White Oak Grove, Camp No. 1, May 28th.

I find Livermore in excellent condition this morning and he says it was and could be nothing but his mad that got him into camp last night, so I am also a good surgeon.

Our camp derives its name from a grove of timber in which it is situated, but unlike our White Oak at home, it is stunted and sparse, looking more like an irregular apple orchard than a forest of oaks. The day has passed in camp and shooting gophers, a species of ground squirrel very plenty here, but it is almost impossible to get the cunning little fellows, for on the approach of any person they scamper for their holes and disappear in the ground. Presently peeping their heads above the ground, offer a tempting shot. But if one succeeds in shooting one, which is not at all certain, he will lose his game, for upon being wounded, they instantly drop into their burrows and are lost to the gunner.

White Oak Grove, Camp No. 1, May 29th.

Today being Sunday, there has been little doing, only washing. The Dragoons arrive at our camp at 12 M. They are Co's. "E" & "H" of the first, and number 120 men. It surprised us uninitiated ones to see how quick they made themselves comfortable. We were hardly convinced that they had their camp made before they had their horses picketed out, dinner eaten and the week's washing done, and it has been a theme of speculation among us if we will ever arrive at the state of excellence that they have attained. We will undoubtedly move soon now.

White Oak Grove, Camp No. 1, May 30th.

Myself and some others have been at The Dalles overhauling some pontoons there and found it tiresome work in the hot sun. Returning to camp, each individual was served with his 18 ounces of raw flour, and then we were situated something like the man who drawed the elephant, for what were we to do with it? Soon messes were formed and things began to assume some shape. Some laughable little incidents occurred. Old Wright took his flour mixed with water and fried it into slap-jacks and ate them all, swore there was no room for splits in that deal. Horse dealers, Indians, settlers and some few camp followers are plenty in our camp right now. The soil in this bottom is good and grows fine crops, but on the uplands it is, or will be, so dry nothing could thrive.

White Oak Grove, Camp No. 1, May 31st.

I have been at The Dalles today again getting necessary articles for our march. The weather is quite warm and sun is getting to quite a familiar sight to us. There was a gray wolf in camp last night, but went off without injury to himself or us, was seen by the guard and one other.

June, 1859

Camp No. 1, White Oak Grove, June 1st.

Another pontoon expedition to the Dalles has occupied myself today. Mules and horses are constantly arriving and preparations being pushed for early departure.

Camp No. 1, White Oak Grove,. June 2nd.

Weather is quite warm today. I have done little during the day, came near purchasing a horse but wasn't sure of being allowed to ride.

Camp No. 1, White Oak Grove, June 3rd.

Everything is being organized for a start tomorrow, teams being selected, pack trains being organized and order being brought about. The transportation for the command is to consist of 60 wagons drawn by eight animals (and 500 pack mules) mules or bulls, they are termed here (oxen). There is to be a beef herd of 50 fat bullocks. About one hundred citizens are employed as packers, teamsters and herders.

Camp No. 2, June 4th, distance 3 miles.

We were up and stirring this morning for an order had been promulgated for us to move this morning, but we did not finally move until about 11 o'clock A.M., it being that hour before the trains were in starting order. We left a large number of citizens, Mexicans, Indians and squaws in the camp and are now comparatively free from camp followers. We have a settler in the train, a species of shark, almost always to be found where soldiers are. There is also a Mexican woman or two, dressed in male apparel, following their umbras [*sic*], either for love or money. We have only moved about two miles, just enough to straighten our train.

It has been an amusing sight to me, these wild mules being saddled for the first time, as well as being hampered, and they cut up some curious antics, and indeed one cannot well blame them for there are Americans, Dutchmen, Englishmen, Frenchmen, Irishmen, Indians and halfbreeds, all swearing in their own peculiar tongue, creating a perfect bedlam enough to craze a much wiser animal than a mule. It is also amusing to see the entire train following the monotonous rattle of a cow bell attached to the what is termed "bell horse," which is ridden at the head of the train.

We took a southeast course from our camp on Three Mile Creek and passed over a country rough and uneven, with no timber and little vegetation besides bunch grass. We are camped in a fertile valley. The land is of a sandy nature. one or two settlers having taken up claims here and might do well here, were it not for a strong dislike to work and equally strong affection for whiskey, so prevalent among frontiers men.

Camp No. 3, June 5th.

Distance about 8 miles, as determined by the odometer. We left camp at 8 A.M. and arrived here about 12 M. We are not over tasked in marches thus far, but we do not seem to get exactly the knack of camp life, our mess being in anything but a desirable condition. I was entirely unconscious of this being Sunday until evening. The men were also surprised, and some think our devotions anything but devout. The essentials of camping are wood, water and grass. e have plenty. We find settlers on this creek.

Camp No. 4, Tygh Valley, June 6th.

We left camp at 7 A.M. and arrived at 1 P.M., distance 18 miles. The country is very poor, affording little vegetation except bunch grass. we keep about a south east course bearing toward the Cascade range of mountains, with Mount Hood on our right, and getting a beautiful view of it nearly to its base today. The scenery is grand. The breeze from the snow capped mountains cool. We descended about 800 feet to get into this valley.

**The Wallen
Expedition of 1859**

70

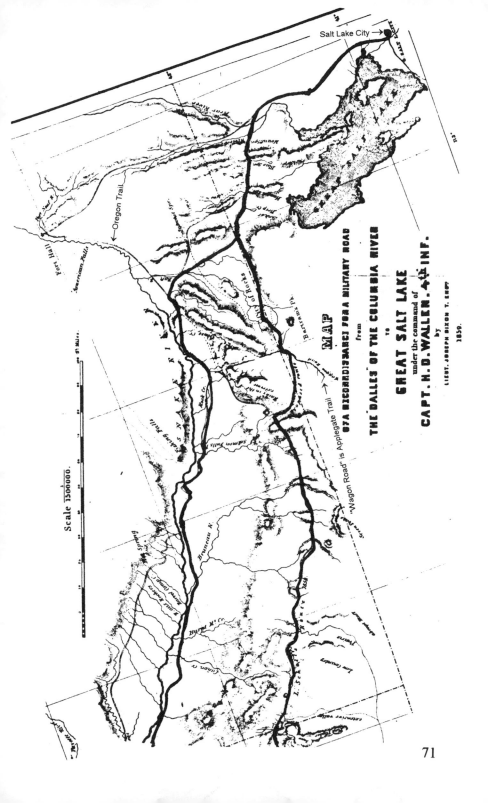

Salt Lake City →

Oregon Trail

Fort Hall

American Falls

Shoshone Falls

Salmon Falls

Scale 1/500000.

Bruneau R.

L. Schanlin Fork

Goose Cr.

Rock Cr.

City of Rocks

Barrams Pa.

"Wagon Road" is Applegate Trail

MAP
OF A RECONNAISSANCE FOR A MILITARY ROAD
from
THE "DALLES" OF THE COLUMBIA RIVER
TO
GREAT SALT LAKE
under the command of
CAPT. H. D. WALLEN. 4<u>th</u> INF.
by
LIEUT. JOSEPH DIXON T. ENG<u>r</u>
1859.

Camp No. 5, June 7th.

We are still in the Tygh Valley, still only about three miles from our last camp. We left the last white habitation that we will see yesterday. today we left camp at 8 o'clock A.M. and came to the banks of the White River after traveling about one and one half miles. It is a mountain stream about 40 to 50 yards wide and fordable at some points at this season, which is the time of highest water, the snow melting on the mountains raising the streams and rivers. The current is strong and water very cold. Here the pontoons were unpacked and a flying ferry constructed which occupied about three hours, at which time the train had found a ford and crossed, so that there seemed little to do but repack the boats.

Talk about snakes. There are any quantities of the reptiles here. Rattlesnakes and adders. Our camp is about two miles from the crossing and at the foot of a rocky bluff, which looks anything but passable for teams. Everything smells snaky and one can imagine a much pleasanter bedfellow than one of these forked tongued devils without any great stretch of fancy.

Camp No. 6, June 8th.

This has been a very hard days march, not that the distance has been great, for we made but 15 miles, but upon arriving in camp or on the ground, the Lieutenant ordered us to duty, but we finally slid out of it. In pitching his tent a little scene occurred by which the lieutenant is betrayed into expressing his feelings towards the 4th Infantry in the shape of a damn and I get a good horn of whiskey by it. We are in a beautiful pine hemlock grove.

Camp No. 7, June 9th.

Most of our detachment and a number of the 4th Infantry left the command and came forward to this place exploring and marking out a wagon rout through more timber than we have met before. We are in a fertile valley of a richer and more attractive nature than any we have met before. The whole surface of the ground bears evidence of mineral deposits and many fine specimens of rose quartz are to be found. Shirts shot a jack rabbit this afternoon, the first game for the trip. Corporal Walsh, who is purser for a mess comprised of Wheeler, Damerest and himself is with us, the others remaining with the train, mixed and fried into an imitation of griddle cakes the entire ration of flour (3 lbs. 6 oz.) for the three and by jove, ate it at one set-to. Some capacity, that. Besides the bean soup he took aboard.

Lance Sergeant McEnaney is evidently trying to put himself exclusively into the good graces at the disadvantage of Wheeler.

Camp No. 8, June 10th.

The command arrived at our camp at about eleven A.M., when we joined it, and moved about two miles and camped in an extremely barren valley. There are indications of gold in this section and the color has been found. Wheeler and McEnaney had a regular set-to and all ended in an entirely new mess arrangement, which it is hoped will be more pleasant than the living has been heretofore. One can now learn about how selfish his comrade is, and in fact, see everything in his character without much trouble, for with our very disagreeable manner of living the men try very little to cover their real dispositions.

Camp No. 9, June 11th, dist. 10 miles.

We left camp at 4:30 A.M. and passed through some of the roughest country yet encountered. One canyon in particular whose width seemed no more than 20 yards, with rocks towering up for 200 feet on either side, presented a grand appearance, a capital place for an Indian ambuscade. We are now camped on Warm Spring Creek and have visited the springs from which the river derives its name. There are two whose water is literally hot enough to scald and scarce two feet from them is an ice cold spring. Dutchman who had become dry stooped and dipped his lips in one of the hot ones in anticipation of a cool draught, but jumped suddenly to his feet declaring that the devil was in it. we seem to have gotten about as far as the law allows in this direction, for there seems no passable outlet unless the one by which we entered this den of rattlesnakes, which pets are quite plenty. Our beds tonight must be on round cobblestones in what seems the bottom or bed of a river of some [near] date.

The Express came in tonight bringing letters from home, which are read with more than usual interest. Imagine myself seated on a round stone about the size of my head perusing a letter from my sister Caroline, informing one of and describing her marriage and wedding tour to Niagara, where I guess they did not get a meal on the trip, so essentially enjoyed as our bean soup was by us, sitting around on stones in the boiling sun, no tents. Lieutenant Robert left the Command and subsequently got lost and only arrived in camp at 11 P.M. without coat, vest, pants, horse, saddle or shoes, and to use Lieutenant Houston's words, a hell of a looking Lieutenant.

Description of Pontoons and How They Were Used

EXPEDITION FROM DALLES CITY TO GREAT SALT LAKE.

Lieutenant Houston to Captain Wallen. FORT CASCADES, W. T.,
October 29, 1859.

CAPTAIN: In accordance with your direction, I submit the following report concerning the means used, on the recent expedition to Salt Lake, to effect the crossing of rivers.

The detachment of engineer troops under my command were provided with India rubber pontoons or floats, which were used in the construction of bateaux. These pontoons, when inflated, are cylindrical in form, with the ends shaped somewhat like the bow of a boat. Each pontoon is twenty feet in length, twenty inches in diameter, and is in three compartments. There are loops on each side of the pontoons for the purpose of fastening them together, and loops on the top to which poles may be attached to stiffen the bateaux. The following figures will show the construction of the pontoons, and the method of joining them together:

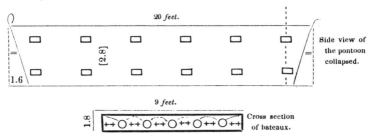

The pontoons are fastened together either by straps or ropes. Straps are the best. The poles are also strapped on, being fastened to the outer loops. Notches are cut on the poles, or staples driven in to prevent the straps from slipping. Poles are run through the loops at the ends of the pontoons, which assist to stiffen the bateau. A canvas deck is stretched over the bateau to protect the India rubber cloth. The weight required to submerge a bateau is about 2,600 pounds for each pontoon. A bateau intended to transport a wagon requires five pontoons. These will safely bear the wagon, its load, and as much more of ordinary freight as there is room for. In a perfect arrangement, a platform would be used to support the wagon ; but where transportation is limited, three or four short planks placed transversely and two placed lengthwise are sufficient. These, with two planks to run the wagon on and off the bateau are all that are absolutely necessary. Much time, however, would be saved by a more perfect arrangement. In crossing streams with a moderate current paddles may be used, but where the current is swift a rope is necessary.

At the crossing of the Des Chutes river, which is about eighty yards wide, a rope one inch in thickness was securely fastened to a tree on the opposite side of the river. The other end of the rope, the length of which was considerably greater than the width of the stream, was attached to the bateau, which was connected with our side by a smaller rope. In this way, by paying out the small rope, the loaded bateau was carried over by the force of the current alone. The empty bateau was hauled back by a yoke of oxen. With one bateau the whole command of nearly three hundred men, thirty wagons with their loads, and a large quantity of additional freight, were ferried over in three days, with frequent interruptions from the swimming of animals at the ferry. One accident occurred—the upsetting of a wagon. The cause of this was, that the bateau, as at first used, consisted of only four pontoons, and was found to be too narrow to afford the requisite stability. An additional pontoon was added, and, for greater security, part of the load taken from each wagon and placed beneath it. The wagon-covers were taken off, as they presented a large surface to the wind. After this no difficulty was experienced. The arrangement was intended originally to be used with a pack train, in reference to the contemplated expedition against the northern Indians last fall; but in the hands of one who has used them, wagons can be crossed safely and rapidly.

The average weight of a pontoon collapsed is ninety-six pounds, and with the straps, a pair of bellows, and the canvas bag in which it is carried, about one hundred and six pounds. The entire weight of a batteau of five pontoons, with its platform and the plank for running the wagons on and off the bateau is about 1,350 pounds. This, with the necessary rope, is, in ordinary circumstances, a light load for one wagon. If this pontoon equipage were to be prescribed for general use, one wagon should be used exclusively for its transportation, and this wagon would be so constructed as to admit of its being taken apart and used as a platform.

With a pack train, four pontoons are sufficient for one ferry, and can easily be carried on four mules, with all the appurtenances, rope excepted. The engineer detachment was also provided with two India rubber boats, each ten feet long. These consist of India rubber covers stretched over extension frames. On each side is a cylinder, which, when inflated, gives great buoyancy and stability. They were not used on the expedition, as it was found that the pontoon bateau answered the purposes of a boat much better than they. Three pontoons make a very excellent boat. Two of them in the hands of an Indian are equal to a canoe.

The pontoons were also used to construct a bridge over a slough about twenty feet wide, which was too deep to be forded. As we had not sufficient plank for a flooring, the poutons were covered with willows and grass. Earth was thrown over them, and the bridge answered every purpose. The pack-mules went over it loaded; one horse jumped off the bridge, being frightened by the undulating motion, which is inseparable from bridges of this kind. All the other streams that we crossed during the expedition were fordable at the season of the year when we reached them.

I am, sir, very respectfully, your obedient servant,

D. C. HOUSTON,
Second Lieutenant Engineers.

Captain H. D. WALLEN, *Fourth Infantry,*
Commanding Wagon Road Expedition to Salt Lake.

Camp No. 10, June 12th, distance 10.

After an immense amount of hauling, lugging, packing, unpacking, the wagons were at last got around the bluff, which seemed so effectually (to] bar our progress, and we reached this camp, which is on the DesChutes River about one P.M. and made a reconnaissance for a crossing. The country on the opposite shore rises very abruptly and it is difficult to find a desirable place. In ordinary rivers of this size it would be nothing, but the water is now about 20 feet deep and runs like lightning. The width is only from 25 to 35 yrd., but it being Sunday we do nothing further towards the crossing. Corporal Walsh, who claims to be something of a geologist as well as a linguist, avers that there is quantities of limestone about here, and in truth, the rocks do bear great resemblance to limestone. Beaver must be plenty, for they have left their marks quite plainly, having cut down trees which grow on the river banks, some as thick as six or seven inches. Some smaller ones are cut off in such a scientific manner as to lead one to almost believe the work was done with an ax, but as probably white man never trod this soil before, there can be little doubt of the workmen engaged at the timber.

In addition to rattlesnakes, scorpions have been found since our arrival. Delightful country, this. Our Supplees, who is detailed with the Topographical Engineers* in company with Reynolds, have failed to find camp thus far and some conjecture that they have become lost. Others think that by some means they have got hold of the top of a whiskey barrel and can't let go, both having a weakness that way.

Camp No. 10, June 13th

The pontoons were unpacked at an early hour this morning, and the entire day has been spent in establishing a communication with the opposite bank. Lieutenant Houston met considerable opposition from Captain Wallen in his endeavors to find a suitable crossing. We have finally succeeded in constructing a flying pontoon bridge and will be ready to commence our work in the morning.

Camp No. 10, DesChutes River, June 14th.

Today has been spent ferrying the train and swimming animals across the river. The current is so rapid that in crossing a heard of

---

* Refers to the U. S. Army Corps of Topographical Engineers. Explorers and map makers. In 1855, a command of these officers and men surveyed Central and Western Oregon for a suitable location for the main north-south railroad. Today's Southern Pacific line, as well as Interstate 5 freeway, generally follow the selected route. –bw

animals, they will reach the shore full half mile below the point of starting, and still be doing their utmost to gain the other side. We had some fun in getting the herd to take the river, and much excitement.

Camp No. 10, June 15th

We were out at 4 A.M. and at work at the crossing, and now 10 P.M. have only just eaten our supper and got through our work. Such days of work I have never seen before. Our cook has contrived to get whiskey from that curse of a Sutler and [it] would trouble a devilish smart geologist to determine whether we were eating sand cakes or bread from flour. But it must be very substantial and stick to our ribs well. A wagon was thrown from our raft to the stream today, and went tumbling down stream about 30 or 40 yards, but finally lodged against a rock. It was freighted with company property belonging to Company "H", 1st Dragoons, and much destroyed, which causes them to curse deep and loud. Don't blame them. (10)

Camp No. 10, June 16th.

We have been as yesterday working hard at crossing the train. Muggings and myself slept on the east side of the river last night, and contrived to get a pull [raid] on the commissary during the night, which caused bacon, potatoes and an addition to our flour ration to make its appearance in our mess.

Sergeant Wheeler blames us for our tardy appearance at duty, but the subscriber opines that his displeasure will vanish in time to get a good feed at the bacon.

Camp No. 11, June 17th.

After a vast amount of lugging and finally killing some bullocks, we succeeded in getting our entire train across the river at 2 P.M. and were met with the welcome intelligence that our mess wagon was gone and our dinner with it, and we must go ten miles before we could get anything to eat. Agreeable news, as we broke our fast at 4 A.M. The first two miles was an almost perpendicular ascent. The mule teams had to be doubled to get up an empty wagon, making 16 animals to haul one empty wagon and the freights were taken up by the pack mules. Our route lay along what seems a dividing ridge and was quite pleasant for ten or twelve miles, but at this time we commenced looking for a prospect of camp. The country widened into prairie and seemed as fine as any we have yet seen, but to us who had fasted from twelve to fourteen hours, nothing but a prospect of camp could look

> We were 19 hours without food and doing the
> severest kind of duty. There were oaths uttered
> which if properly recorded will sink Captain Wallen
> so low into perdition that he will never get out.
>
> —June 17, 1958

attractive. For myself, I confess to being completely tired out.

The incidents were too numerous to mention, but finally a party of six found camp at 11 o'clock and received a supper of tea and bread from Company "E" of the Dragoons. And should I live a thousand years, I shall never forget that meal. Never could foot taste so sweet under any other circumstances. We were 19 hours without food and doing the severest kind of duty. There were oaths uttered which if properly recorded will sink Captain Wallen so low into perdition that he will never get out. The train isn't one fourth in, and the devil only knows if it ever will be, and he won't tell. (11)

Camp No. 12, June 18th.

Lying in camp. Thermometer indicates 93°, Fahrenheit in the shade. Men weary, some not getting into camp until near morning, and then our bed didn't suit, being what was once the bottom of a river. There was one convenience, however, pillows were plenty, for the cobblestones were so large and numerous that one is troubled to get even standing room. Mounts Hood, Jefferson and the Three Sisters raise their hoary heads high in air, their covering shining brilliantly in sunlight and forming a decided contrast to the atmosphere we are not inhabiting. The country passed from the DesChutes has been undulating prairie covered with bunch grass and some cedars. The soil is light and dry, completely parched by the arid winds and sun's rays We are completely idle. I am to do my first guard duty since the expedition commenced tonight, and much I dislike it. We thought we would get out of it, it not being our legitimate duty, but no.

Camp No. 13, June 19th.

We took up our line of march at 4 o'clock A.M. and passed over a country similar in most respects to all that we have met. one exception being one fertile and lovely valley, more so than any we have met. We also passed through the valleys of death, so called from the fact that the last of 300 emigrants perished here in 149 form starvation in trying to get to Oregon by John C. Fremont's reports of his surveys across the Rocky Mountains. After great sufferings, these poor wanderers finally laid their bones to bleach in this desolate wilderness, where nothing cheerful meets the eye and everything around is of the most somber and forbidding hue. We did not remain long in the

> I found a small potato some days since in our train, and today watched it in the burning sun 2 hours, knowing if I left it for a moment it would be confiscated by some party and I should only get my labor for my pains. Did I ever dream that a potato would be valued so highly?
> —June 19, 1859

valley, but enough to see some of the remnants of wagons and cooking utensils, human bones and other evidence of the truthfulness of the story. Our camp is at only two miles distance from our crossing of the DesChutes River. Sitting on an elevated place, one is reminded of the snow drifting on the lee side of a high fence being whirled into piles of every imaginable form, so is the country cut up here.

And in following the [tortured] valleys or canyons through the hills, one is compelled to travel a much greater distance than the actual length by air line, in this instance nearly 20 time. We are camped on the confines of a vast sage brush prairie at one of the finest springs I ever saw, it supplying the entire command with water, our only wood being sage brush, which is about as good as dry grass.

I found a small potato some days since in our train, and today watched it in the burning sun 2 hours, knowing if I left it for a moment it would be confiscated by some party and I should only get my labor for my pains. Did I ever dream that a potato would be valued so highly?

Camp No. 14, June 20th

This has been one of the most tiresome marches experienced since we left The Dalles. Our route winding among canyons has been dusty and unendurably hot. But we are camped in a pleasant cedar grove near a high bluff, in which there stands a big boulder near 60 feet high, surmounted with a curiously shaped stone so nearly resembling a man in size and shape that the officers have termed it the old man of the prairies. This morning was very cold, water froze last night, and one felt the want of mittens quite sensibly while performing camp duty. We are now meeting alkali prairies in abundance. The water is impregnated with it and consequently great danger of sickness. (13)

Camp No. 15, June 21st.

We find ourselves camped on a beautiful stream. After a march of 20 miles, most of the way between huge masses of rocks, the train has been very much exposed, for a marauding party of 100 or even less Indians would have found little trouble in picking us off and we could have offered little resistance, a dangerous order of march in a hostile country. Our camp tonight is one of to me, indescribably beauty. The valley is fertile and runs out into deep prairies on every side, skirted on the north and east by fine pine timber, with the range of snow capped mountains stretching far away to the south and west, with here and there scattered over the rich prairies herds of horses, oxen and mules.

Make a grand picture for a painter's pencil. We have constantly borne southeast since we left Fort Dalles, consequently are nearing the Cascade range fast and are now fairly entered into that portion of country termed by Fremont "The Wilderness," and are constantly gaining in altitude. And as a consequence, getting nights colder than one would believe unless actually experienced.

Camp No. 16, June 22nd.

Indians are constantly seen hovering on our flanks and rear, but none venture among us as yet. The strictest vigilance is now necessary at night, and the command seems fully awake to the danger constantly about us. Should our arsenal be stampeded in the night by the red devils, ours would be a severe lesson. The march today has been very pleasant, being through timber mostly. The change is most agreeable, for the eye tires of constantly looking at those dry prairies covered with that eternal bunch grass or sage brush. Indians have used this same ground as a camp very recently, and their never coming into camp is a bad omen for their intentions. Still, we are strong and maybe they will not attack us. Game has been seen during the day but none captured, it being extremely wild and at great distance. Elk and antelope are found here, or would be, was hunting the object of our expedition, for there are plenty of signs of both. Pheasants and jackass rabbits are also her, but not plentiful.

Camp No. 17, June 23rd.

Today has been a long and hot march, but a great portion of the day was on good prairie land. Found one covered with alkali to the depth of 1/2 inch as pure white as the snow. One's eyes must be of good stuff to stand the bright sunlight reflected from so light a ground. And the effects of the alkali on the skin and lids of the eyes is great and painful. The water is also full of the same villainous dust, and one is compelled to imbibe what he is sure would kill him were he not tough as a boiled crab. (14)

We are encamped on the banks of a pure limpid stream. The view is magnificent, if it weren't for the mosquitoes, which are about as large as (well) can be and be classified insects. one can find plenty of enjoyment for body in mind in resisting the combined attacks of swarms of these birds of prey. I must confess to have never seen [such] mosquitos before today. One can study human nature to advantage on a march of this kind, for men so completely jaded care little to cover up their faults. On starting in the morning, everyone is lively and in fine spirits, jokes and songs are rife and everybody is funny. At 9 A.M. conversation lags at 10 mums the word, and at 11 all is grim; 11:30, if you speak be sure to get a short reply; 12:30, don't speak. If you do, you look out for a damn. At 2:30 be sure of a curse if you touch your neighbor, and at 3 P.M. everybody is full of fight. And camp at 4:30 coffee down, pipes lit and little feeling for fasting, 6:30 all down and asleep.

> **Rattle-snakes, red ants, mosquitoes and scorpions. Bad rations. Damn the expedition.—June 25, 1859**

Camp No. 18, June 24th

For the first time since we left The Dalles my ideas of Oregon are realized. We are in the edge of a fine pine grove, a vast prairie stretching off to the north and east of us. The ground gently sloping to a river about half a mile in front. Luxurious grass, something like blue grass in Connecticut, makes the scene grand and still peaceful. The march has been pleasant, air cool, and tonight water good. Antelope were seen today for the first time, but at a safe distance for themselves.

Lieutenant Bonnycastle threatened to shoot Sergeant Davis of "H" Company, 4th Infantry, but failed to scare him.

Camp No. 19, June 25th.

Enough toting for one day, I reckon, for we are tired out. Crossed, recrossed, and crossed Crooked River eight times. Alkali in abundance, everybody ugly. Country tamer and rough cold nights. Rattlesnakes, red ants, mosquitoes and scorpions. Bad rations. Damn the expedition. (15)

Camp No. 20, June 26th.

More Crooked River. More mosquitoes, more swearing and less rations. One of our factitious members has christened this Mosquito Rendezvous, sublimely thought of. Must have been inspired (by bite, I mean). If anything the country is more rough. And I can chronicle nothing I find pleasing and attractive. Some are in a quandary how the night is to be got over, for the mosquitoes won't let a fellow sleep.

Lieutenant Dixon lost his Indian guide, two horses, one rifle and saddle today.*

Camp No. 21, June 27th.

We are still on the Crooked River, with all in. Some of the Indians of the Shoshone Tribe are in camp tonight, undoubtedly in the capacity of spies. They are half starved looking thieves, old and useless. There is to be some division of our command, a portion continuing under Captain Wallen, the balance to try to find a route direct to John Day River. We are on the confines of an extensive prairie. In front, or to the north, the prairie stretches away for miles until it finally seems lost in the horizon. In the rear, the mountains rise abruptly at least two thousand feet, frowning down on us most gloomily. Considerable interest is felt in regard to who will go on and who will return, for the Lieutenant's command will work slowly towards The Dalles and probably be in as soon as the middle of August. (16)

Camp N. 21, June 28th.

We have been busy turning over property and preparing for the division of the command. The party to proceed to Salt Lake City are Sergeant Wheeler, Corporals Damerest, Artificers Smith, Hackell, and Shirts. Privates Rhodes, Gilbert, Whelon, Maken, and H. O'Donoghue. The balance are to accompany the return with Lieutenant Robert. Half of Company "H" Dragoons, "H" of the Infantry return also. I suppose the return is called the most desirable billet, but for a choice I would sooner have gone on through the trip. I dislike our amiable Lance Sergeant too much.

Camp No. 21, June 29th.

We continue here preparing for the final start. The days are very warm but the nights cold. Water froze an eighth of an inch thick last night. We captured prairie chickens enough for a good potpie for our dinner and relished it much. Our amiable sutler will sell us whiskey at 50cts per drink if we wish, and warrants a good drunk for the small sum of one dollar. An Express is now looked for daily from Fort Dalles, and of course with it letters from home. Considerable dissatisfaction is felt at our party being split, it only consists of 21 men and it

---

* Lt. Joseph Dixon, a member of the U. S. Army Corps of Topographical Engineers, was a keen surveyor and cartographer. He prepared the official map of the expedition that appears in Executive Document No. 34, 1st Session 36th Cong. 1859-60. A portion of his map appears in reduced size (to fit the pages of this book) on pages 70-71.—bw

seems as if we might be left together.

Camp No. 21, June 30th.

Must we was the first order for the morning. Lieutenant Houston and party took themselves off this morning and camp about 3 miles above us. I shot a noble rattlesnake this morning, the largest of the season. I am sorry to see the boys go and would much like to have gone, but would not apply to go. No Express yet.

July, 1859

Camp No. 22, July 1st.

We are occupying the camp ground vacated by the Wallen command. Lieutenant Johnson and detachment of Dragoons are gone for a scout and we remain until his return. Confounded uncomfortable days for heat and more so of nights of cold. Lieutenant Dixon of the Topographers sent in an Express from the Malheur River, where he is staying waiting for his party to join him. I hope some Indians may join and meiniluse [sic] him before I am ever with him again.

Camp No. 22, July 2nd.

We spent today exploring among the mountains looking for game or anything curious that might turn up. The mountains seem to rise in regular form and intervals. One finds after climbing up an almost perpendicular ascent that he is on a level plateau. And crosses it, ascends another mountain and finds himself again on a plateau, and again climbs the third mountain, finds himself at the top, has climbed three distinct mountains, which at a short distance appears entirely like one mountain springing from one base only. Being divided into three distinct rises or divisions. The soil is dry and bears nothing but bunch grass, rattlesnakes and sage brush.

Camp No. 22, July 3rd.

How often have I looked forward to tomorrow on the eve of July 3rd with bright anticipation of pleasure, and how little we anticipate tomorrow. Nothing is anticipated that I am aware of. Weather very warm, cold nights.

Camp No. 22, July 4th.

Old Fourth found us bright and early. The day has come and gone. I spent the day in the mountains and alone. Could well imagine myself treading ground never trod by white man, but could find little game. Found indications of Indians, in fact it is well known they are and have been on our flanks for some time. I arrived at camp and found the boys had gotten a lot of the sutlers villainous whiskey and pretty drunk. Anything for an excitement. I dipped of course. They paid $9.40 a gallon, and I consider it cheap at that. Makes drunk come quick. Am on guard tonight and must close for parade.

Camp No. 22, July 5th.

The spirit of 176, or the sutlers, is visible today. The valiant Chief of the Spaniards speaks of mortal combats as fluently as yesterday. A sure indication that fighting whiskey is in, for in its absence he never mentions such dangerous subjects. Water froze last night over an eighth of an inch thick. We were blessed with one drunken Dutchman on our picket last night who managed to keep what sleep we otherwise would have got from us. We were compelled to not quit our rifles, as it is confidently expected the red devils will give us a call. Corporal Walsh and myself were out making some observations and gained an altitude of 6,348 feet above the level of the sea. A difference of 1,348 feet between our camp and the highest point. We only traveled about 2 and 1/2 miles to get this difference, showing a very steep ascent. On the plateaus we found some fine and elegant pine groves. More so than any yet met by us. There is very little indication of game met around here. Sickness begins to show itself, and it were well for the Command to get where the water contains less alkali. He proposed route to John Day's River wholly impractical for a train such as ours. It being composed entirely or wagons, the pack mules are all with Captain Wallen. We are to continue our route back to Trout Creek and from thence to DesChutes Bridge, which shortens the distance to The Dalles. (17)

Camp No. 22, July 7th.

We remain in our camp but leave tomorrow with our faces turned westward. We found quantities of stone like pumice stone, soft and light. Most of the men are carving pipes from it. I have one which I intend shall go to the States as a present to George. As a memento of my journey on a Tom fools errand through the mountains of Oregon.

Camp No. 22, July 8th.

We left camp at 4 o'clock A.M. and this start was the most joyous one I have yet seen. Everyone now fresh and anxious for the trudge. Even the animals partook of the joyousness of the occasion. And the bulls swing along with a vigor rarely witnessed in bull teaming. We passed tow of our old camps and now on the crookedest of all rivers, but the crossings are all ready, hence they give us Engineers much less uneasiness than upon our first encounter with them. I am for guard and must close for the night.

Camp No. 24, July 9th.

We left our camp at an early hour and tramped off 15 miles before noon. am confoundedly near used up for being in charge of a picket over the herd of mules and done my regular sentry, so is double duty. Then the night was intensely cold. One could not keep warm with overcoat and mittens. I suffered more with the cold than I ever did a night in my life, I believe. Then we are doing long marches, so that one must be tough to stand it. Everyone else rides but us.

Camp No. 25, July 10th.

We left camp at 3 A.M. and camped on the Achea [*sic*] River at 2 P.M., tired, hungry and ugly. We have seen the last of the crookedest of all rivers and feel immensely relieved for it.

Camp No. 26, July 11th.

Ours has been a short tramp today, having camped at 9 A.M. in a very fine pine grove about 5 miles from our yesterday's rest. Lieutenant Bonnycastle has gone with an escort of Dragoons to look for a route direct from here to the DesChutes River, and we are to remain until he has determined upon the practibility of the road, if he finds one. It is a fine place for a halt, and we are reconciled to the delay wonderfully. Deer were seen as we entered the timber, and unless they get a good distance off, we will get some of them tomorrow. Corporal Walsh and myself went out after camping, but as I am on guard tonight, I returned early.

Camp No. 27, July 12th.

Remain in this place still. Wild currants and gooseberries are abundant on the banks of the streams. There are three varieties of currants, black, yellow and red. The two first being wholesome and of much the same flavor as those raised home. The red is dry, with little flavor, and very unwholesome. The gooseberries are small, but much the color of those in Connecticut. I tramped at least 25 miles after game and saw nothing as large as a squirrel.

Camp No. 27, July 13th.

Last was an extremely cold night, more so than any we have had. I was on guard. Water froze near 1/4 inch thick. Corporal W. tried his luck and fowling piece today. Came in at night with two <u>black birds</u> and them only, whereupon Kendall has displayed his wit to the best possible advantage ever since. Nothing is heard from the Lieutenant as yet, and uneasiness is felt, for we expected to communicate with Lieutenant before now.

Camp No. 27. July 14th.

Thunder showers this afternoon, the first rain since leaving Fort Cascades. The men, myself included, have been indulging in current jellies of our own make. Who would have imagined it. We undertook pies, but failed for want of shortening. An Express arrived from Lieutenant Bonnycastle. He left the Lieutenant only about three hours after they left us and had not got over 10 miles when the route was considered entirely impracticable for wagons. And he was sent to inform Johnson and order him to proceed to Trout Creek par our trail. he contrived to lose himself and has made a three hours ride into two days, threw away his ammunition to lighten his cargo. His horse is entirely jaded and himself too, I guess. Lieutenant Johnson told him that he was morally, physically and intellectually a damned fool. We are under orders to be on the march at 3 A.M. tomorrow and must push through in a hurry to join Bonnycastle. We may look out for a ram by our great Sergeant. My expectations are fully verified thus far on this march. (18)

Camp No. 28, July 15th.

We were turned out as soon as daylight and struck camp. Our cook [made] some coffee, but we were not allowed to drink it. An act or tyranny that will be remembered long by us. We pushed on and camped at Cedar Springs. Arriving at least 4 hours before the train, completely jaded out by the rapid march. Here two men were discharged by the Quartermaster on the outward march. And we now find the entire country for miles around black, it having been run over by fire, probably set by those two men. Water is short and the animals must suffer tonight from the want of food and drink. I am on guard tonight and in no kind of condition to do it, never having been so completely tired. I have seen enough of Oregon and would not live in it for all of its Territory, if the penalty were to never leave.

Camp No. 29, July 16th.

Commenced our march at a very early hour and halted at a distance of 12 miles to give the animals grass; again pushed on and camped at Trout Creek at 4 o'clock P.M. I never passed such a thoroughly tough night before. It was only by the most strenuous efforts that I contrived to keep my eyes open at all, while walking my tour of guard. I think our Sergeant only knows three names of ten in our party. They are Peck, Wright, and Livermore. We are the first called for every duty in camp and the march. We are now to pursue a different route into The Dalles, striking Columbia River some distance above where we left it.

Camp No. 30, July 17th.

Well, I am in for a mess, it seems, and don't care a curse for it. our devilish Sergeant contrived to get a report to the Lieutenant against me to screen his own shoulders. Our tramp today has been long and tedious, passing through a fine valley occupied by Indians not over three days ago. The Sergeant received some order from the Lieutenant, and failing to comply, put the blame on Peck, Wright and Livermore. Of course we were hauled up. myself first, and I must say I had about as many complaints to make as he had and got about as much satisfaction, I think. We seem to have got about as far as we can go without train. Are in a deep canyon with only one outlet and that the one by which we entered and no chance to go around.

Camp No. 31, July 18th.

A reconnaissance found an outlet from our last night's camp. But tonight finds us fixed for certain. We arrived at our present camp at noon and all endeavors to get a passage for our train amounts to failure thus far. Lieutenant Bonnycastle is ugly as the devil. The guide, after being imposed upon so long, gets obstinate and cares not how long we remain, for he can take a horse and get home when he thinks $5.00 per day does not pay well enough to remain. And us, well what are we: cost only $2.00 and plenty more to be had. But if the boy

87

knows himself, he won't get caught here again. Some say, let her rip, we are all right.

Camp No. 31, July 19th.

We remain stationary. As yet, all efforts to get away do not avail. he officers have been out all day and find no possible outlet for the train. The country is rough, ragged, and barren. Coyotes abound in large numbers.

Camp No. 31, July 20th.

I was on guard last night and although we have begun to feel pretty secure from an attack by Indians, the command turned out in anticipation of one. I was on post and a yell sudden, deep and loud as from ten thousand devils burst on the still hours, sometimes called most-witching. I cocked my rifle and as fully expected to see a pack of those devils of red as I expected to live. But it finally ended in a million coyotes' yells. Some of the bull drivers have been out and found a route by which the train can get from this hole.

Camp No. 32, July 21st.

Left camp at 5 o'clock A.M. and keeping the divide found tolerably good route to a miserable camp ground. We are on a high bluff about 3 to five hundred feet above the creek and all wood and water must be carried up this bluff. Our camp ground got afire and was near consuming the [place]. Luckily it was at a time when we were all in and subdued it in time to save our property. We are greatly inconvenienced for want of wood and have to substitute slapjacks for bread.

Camp No. 33, July 22nd.

Our march goes merrily today and the country has been level and pleasant. Tonight for the first time since last fall we saw the sun set, not drop behind a mountain, and it was a welcome sight. All hands are in the finest possible spirits and look to the time when we shall be in The Dalles, at not over three days at longest. Mount Hood looms up in the west. And we saw, or fancied it, the smoke rising from its summit.*
Today the Dragoons leave us for Walla Walla in the morning.

---

* According to geological records, Mount Hood erupted a few weeks later.

Camp No. 34, July 23rd.

We are at last on the Columbia River again and only about 20 miles from Fort Dalles. We left camp at 3 A.M. and understood we were to make 28 miles of a march, instead of which it is lengthened into 45 miles. About six P.M. and 12 miles from here we met a small stream and drank from it. But the water went through most of us like a shotgun. For myself, I was made quite sick but contrived to peg my way, being one of three only who done the entire day. Upon arriving in camp, most of the men, myself included, took a drink of the Sutler's whiskey and one drink only upon a stomach so entirely empty produced about as drunken a lot as is often met. Some fighting occurred, and to use the words of some great ass, even me was jolly drunk. For myself, I acknowledge to have been about as far along as I ever intended getting. Slept among the sand hills without tent or other covering.

Camp No. 35, July 24th.

This has been the most tedious march of the season, probably from yesterday's traveling and drinking. We are now on Three Mile Creek and in full sight of the town of The Dalles. And the sight of civilization has a most welcome and soothing influence. Tomorrow we hope to be in there. Probably none ever stood in sight of happiness and longing more to grasp it more than we now long to enter, that small frontier town and behold some new faces and get a square meal and diverse other things, of which we are much in want.

At Fort Dalles, July 25th.

Probably men were never much more humbugged than we have been, and as a consequence, more glad to get at what may be considered the end of it. We partook of our evening meal in a building, the first in two months. To eat without finding ones food seasoned with sand and take it form a table, rude although it be, is a luxury to ones like us. and then the anticipation of sleeping in quarters is perfect paradise, to be free from rattlesnakes, scorpions, ants and mosquitoes for an entire night, and we hope months, is really pleasurable. A delicate individual would have been astonished to see the amount of eatables destroyed by each of us at supper. Fresh salmon vanished before our admiring gaze with wonderful rapidity. Small stores stood no possible show on the table. A white woman is about the most interesting sight I have ever met. I could almost kiss a toothless old hag I saw this afternoon, and I mentally promised to make wife hunting my first business after arriving in the States. But I must close for now, for there is some corn juice to be disposed of and none too much time for the amount of business to be done.

Fort Dalles, July 26th.

Rumors has Captain Wallen and command annihilated by the ferocious Snake Indians, but it cannot well be so, for an Express could hardly have got in with such intelligence after our leaving them.

To change from camp to quarters is most gratifying and one is disposed to indulge in the conveniences of a bed to the very fullest extent of the law. Lieutenant Bonnycastle is gone to Fort Vancouver for orders for our final disposition. We found considerable mail accumuated here for us, and of course enjoyed the finding more than those friends who wrote could possibly imagine we should. Books and papers are being read with an avidity rarely witnessed among the literate.

Fort Dalles, July 27th

We are still doing nothing except in indulging in copious draughts of ye lauger, commissary food, etc. One feels like giving himself plenty of sea room after so long a shore tact. Weather continues warm, indeed.

In looking through the details of our summer's march, one finds little of real advantage gained to himself or man-kind. We have passed through some fine bottoms, but a majority of the country traversed is sterile, and if anything, poorer than our most barren portions of New England. And then to find oneself freezing of a July night, with rattlesnakes huddling under one's blankets to share their warmth with you is not so very fine. Good bye tents, rocks for beds, and rattlesnakes for bed fellows. (19)

Fort Dalles, July 28th-

Today finds me fit for nothing, being almost sick. The weather is warm and we indulge in old Morpheus embraces to an extent rarely indulged in.

Fort Dalles, July 29th-

I am entirely sick today and so reported, went to see the Doctor and have been using his pills. Wrote to friends in afternoon.

Fort Dalles, July 30th

Weather continues quite warm. I am still among the sick ones, but I feel somewhat better tonight.

Fort Dalles, July 31st.

We remain doing nothing, expecting to get our orders daily. I am slightly improved in condition and begin to consume my ration, a good symptom. The men are getting restless and begin to complain of The Dalles, thereby showing their soldier propensity. They are never easy when moving, they growl about their hardships. And when in quarter, about the monotony. I opine General Harney will find employment of some kind for us.

August, 1859

Fort Dalles, August 1st.

August comes with a cooler and more agreeable air causing everyone to feel more alive than for some time past. For myself, I am much improved. We get all kinds of rumors concerning the different columns in the field. Today Lieutenant Mullen and command are [rumored to to be] completely annihilated; only a few days since, Captain Wallen was in the fix.

Fort Dalles, August 2nd.

We received our orders today to proceed to Fort Cascades and repair the road. I wonder if that devilish road was ever in repair. I learn by the letters from home today that Sherman has made another fool in the family by running away with old Perkins and going whaling. But concerning this road business, only for the name of deserting, I surely would not go there to remain under our present administration, for our Sergeant, taken in connection with the Corporal, are two cursed fools.

Fort Cascades, August 3rd.

Again we are at our old stamping ground. Citizens and Indians welcomed us quite cordially, and although we are billeted in a wharf boat, we feel a certain homelike feeling in the atmosphere. A detachment of Company "G" 3rd Artillery, furnished supper for us, for which we were very grateful, not being situated as to cook it ourselves. Whiskey is plenty, of course. For me, I am in a more fit condition for sleep and shall soon stow myself on a friendly pile of oats.

Fort Cascades, August 4th.

We are in camp about one and a half miles from the lower landing, and our camp is dignified with our commanding officer's names (i.e.) Camp Robert. Our duties are to repair the portage road and rebuild the bridge across a branch of the Columbia River. The Lieutenant very kindly orders that there will be no work on Sundays, among a number of equally pungent edicts. If we survive the work and mosquitoes, we will do well.

Camp Robert, August 5th.

We are indeed fortunate and favored individuals. The elements extend their greetings and give us a real Cascades rain. So much of it as to thoroughly infiltrate everything and render us exceedingly uncomfortable. It is the first rain that has fallen since we left here in May. We commenced work, but were compelled to desist for the storm. An agreeable episode was turning out for the storm and ditching around our tents to avoid being washed out. I am inclined to think were some of the good people of Connecticut to see our sleeping accommodations tonight, they would deem us in great danger of getting cold from the dampness of blankets and ground whereon we must sleep, but ignorance is bliss. And I am sure mother sleeps more sound for knowing little of our real conditions that if she was thoroughly informed regarding it.

Camp Robert, August 6th.

Rain has fallen in torrents all day. our cooking is done in the open air, consequent it amounts to no cooking at all, for who can cook with a drenching rain pouring on the fire. Our situation can only be described as more miserable.

Camp Robert, August 7th.

This has been a real soldiers Sunday. The day came in and remained fine. We were paraded for inspection at ten o'clock A.M., after which the day has been spent in visiting Indians, sleeping and other such recreations as the place affords.

Camp Robert, August 8th.

We found our proper sphere this morning and commenced work once more with pick and shovel on the road. Nothing of importance occurring today.

> **Rumors of troubles concerning the rights of ownership of the Island of San Juan in Puget Sound are going the rounds. The case, simply stated, is General W. S. Harney, in behalf of the Government of U.S., claims and has taken possession of the Island per contra Governor Douglas of all the British Columbias [who] insists upon it as property belonging to Hudson's Bay Company, and as General Harney has already sent U.S. troops there, it is feared a collision will occur.**
> **—August 9, 1859**

Camp Robert, August 9th.

Weather continues clear and warm. We are on our very intellectual duties and in the absence of food, were humbugged by damn fool Wright and myself found some buckwheat flour at the store and bought it. Such destruction of buckwheat cakes was never witnessed and still the rations are all consumed. Rumors of troubles concerning the rights of ownership of the Island of San Juan in Puget Sound are going the rounds. The case, simply stated, is General W.S. Harney, in behalf of the Government of U.S., claims and has taken possession of the Island per contra Governor Douglas of all the British Columbias [who] insists upon it as property belonging to Hudson's Bay Company, and as General Harney has already sent U.S. troops there, it is feared a collision will occur. (20)

Camp Robert, August 10th.

Weather continues clear and warm. We continue our work on the road. Wright and myself luxuriate on our buckwheat cakes in grand style. n attempting to make our sleeping more comfortable by stealing boards, we have imported fleas enough to eat us alive, and are somewhat sick of our bargain. One cannot get an accurate idea of the annoyance of these vermin without actually experiencing it.

Camp Robert, August 11th.

The portage road is once more pronounced in good repair, and we are to commence on a new bridge at the slough. Commenced repairing tools for the work. This afternoon the steamer arrived from Vancouver confirming the reports of trouble at San Juan Island. Troops are being sent thither and we may look for an order at any time sending us to the scene of disturbance.

Camp Robert, August 12th.

We are now engaged in cutting timber for the bridge, but the general opinion is that its progress will be slow, as Supplee, the only carpenter in the party, is thoroughly drunk and undoubtedly purposely so. However, we are as indifferent as he can be, and his drunkenness makes some sport for us poor devils.

Camp Robert, August 13th.

We are literally doing nothing today and much wonder thereat. Were furnished bedsacks and straw today. Don't believe so much luxury will last long.

Camp Robert, August 14th

Sunday has been spent as usual. Inspection in the morning and balance of day spent writing, among the Indians, and asleep. Two good wholesome rows occurred during the day, both occasioned by our very amiable non-commissioned officers.

Camp Robert, August 15th.

Today found us [working] on the road once more (it isn't finished). I went on pass in the afternoon, hoping to get some intelligence of the boys who left here on the *French,* but could find nothing concerning them. Horton was in Portland a short time since, but upon our approach left.

Camp Robert, August 16th.

A general order assigning the detachment of Company "A" Engineers on duty on the portage road at the Cascades came yesterday, so the speculations concerning going to San Juan are less numerous tonight.

Fort Vancouver, August 17th.

We started for our work as usual this morning, but were overtaken by Lieutenant Robert and ordered to return and strike our camp and be ready to leave from here in the afternoon. We are ordered to the island in dispute. Four companies of Artillery have already gone. An Indian came up during the night from Vancouver.

Fort Vancouver, August 18th.

We have been as busy as mortals can well be in preparing for work at San Juan. Tools have been brought and put in order and preparations made for a siege with Mr. John Bull. The steamship *Northerner* is at Portland, Oregon, and to convey us to the seat of (if not war) disturbance. Serious apprehensions of a collision are entertained, and in such case, we are almost sure of a whipping.

Fort Vancouver, August 19th.

If this hasn't been a day of immense humbug and hard work. The detachment of Engineers never saw me grinding tools, overhauling boxes, running in every direction, and I may add, damnfooling has been the order of the day. However, the steamer is at the wharf and we will embark tonight and sail for our destination. Fort Vancouver is beautiful at this season and we imagine a few days stay would be very agreeable for there are some few signs of civilization here.

On Board Steamship *Northerner*, August 20th.

We embarked at eight o'clock P.M. yesterday and left our wharf at about eleven. All hands but myself and one other were drunk as lords. Understand, for myself, I was too tired to indulge and went aboard to sleep as soon as possible after arriving at the landing. There was some fine playing sick to avoid coming on this trip, but it would not do.

We arrived at Astoria at 11 o'clock A.M., took aboard the U.S. Mail and crossed the bar at 12 M. The day is delightful, and we enjoy the sail immensely. We have an immense amount of commissary stores aboard for the island, and if John Bull should capture us and it, he would be well paid.

Aboard *Northerner*, August 21st.

This morning we are running [east] up the straights of Juan De Fuca in fine style. Arrived off San Juan Island at 12 o'clock M. Some settlers seemed to have found a home on the coast of the straits, as we noticed a number of farms, and the lands are said to be fertile. We arrived at Port Townsend at 3 o'clock P.M., discharged freight and cast off our mooring at four. This is a small town of 20 or 30 buildings, a good farming country and plenty of heavy timber, which furnishes considerable trade along the sound. We see now and then a vessel laden with lumber outward bound. And sailing up the sound of Puget is not wholly unlike Long Island. It is really pleasant, this pleasant Sunday afternoon, gliding along among the islands and by the numerous inlets and bays. It is also the anniversary of my advent in Company "A", U.S. Engineers. How many scenes and changes we have passed through during this one year. We have endured more real hardship than one would commonly endure in a lifetime in Connecticut, and now are on an expedition of some danger, for the representative of John Bull is said to be as ugly, nasty, and mad as our own Harney, and trouble is looked for. I am not sure, but with all of our humbugging and hardship, it will be a good school for me and I will learn more than I could otherwise have found out. (21)

Arrival At San Juan Island

Aboard Steamer *Northerner*, August 22nd.

We arrived at Olympia at 12 o'clock last night, discharged and received freight, and sailed at 4 A.M. today, bound [north] down the Sound and to San Juan finally. Arrived off Steilacoom at 8 A.M., sent the mail ashore, and steamed down the Sound. Weather beautiful. Touched at Port Townsend and at 3 o'clock P.M. run for our final destination. A high wind having sprung up, we got it plenty rough crossing the straits. Run into the harbor of San Juan at about 7 P.M. While coming, saw Chips engaged putting heads into hermetically sealed cans containing meats, and now bolt heads, nuts and other small missiles, for the purpose of returning the *Satelite's* fire should she open on us. M. French, our first Officer, is a brick and swears he will hurt them a little bit with his signal guns, while they are sinking him with their heavy ones. I fear we will get the worst of it, should it come to blows. Captain Dalls says they can never have his ship.
While coming, saw Chips engaged putting heads into hermetically sealed cans containing meats, and now bolt heads, nuts and other small missiles, for the purpose of returning the *Satelite's* fire should she open on us. M. French, our first Officer, is a brick and swears he will hurt them a little bit with his signal guns, while they are sinking him with their heavy ones. I fear we will get the worst of it, should it come to blows. Captain Dalls says they can never have his ship.

In Camp on San Juan Island, August 23rd.

We transferred aboard the U.S. Store Ship *Massachusetts* last evening and remained until morning. The *Massachusetts'* 32 pounder cannons are ashore, 8 in all. We came ashore at 11 o'clock A.M., preceded by Company "I" 4th Infantry. While they were shoving off in their boats, the men pulled directly under the guns of H.B.M. Sloop of

97

War *Satelite* and the musicians played "Yankee Doodle" for dear life. We find 4 companies of Artillery, of Infantry and ourselves, numbering officers and men, 500 all told. We are to maintain the honor of the nation and lick the British, no matter what odds [are] brought against us. There is a Hudson's Bay establishment on post here and the British officers draw many of their luxuries from it. The two national flags wave about 60 yards apart.

Drills are thoroughly enforced and Colonel [Silas] Casey, the Commandant of our forces, is bound not to be caught napping. The island is under martial law and two men have been appointed constables against the time when we withdraw. After landing, we were compelled to make room for ourselves and received a detail to assist in moving the logs and rubbish, which of course caused considerable grumbling. The soil seems good and unless the dry season affects it too much, ought to produce well. In addition, we have the 8, 32pd. guns on ship carriages, 6, 6pd. light pieces and one 12pd. mountain howitzer. John [Bull] has five ships and sloops of war and can put 2,000 sappers here in 48 hours. (22)

Major General Silas Casey was a Colonel when he served in Washington Territory.
—U.S. Military Academy

San Juan Island, August 24th.

Today has been spent getting tools ashore, putting them in order and general duty. The Colonel is kind to us and inquired for his son Tom. It seems the present difficulties all arose from an unruly hog, of which there are plenty here. One [Mr.] Sawyer, who claims to be a citizen of the United States, had a piece of land enclosed and planted with potatoes. The hog is or was the property of the Hudson's Bay Company. Sawyer claimed to them that the pig was unruly and destroyed his vegetables, and finally threatened to shoot his pigship unless he was kept at home, which he was not, and consequently got shot.

Whereupon the company agent got British officials from Victoria to arrest Sawyer, but failed to do so, he couldn't be found. General Harney was informed and sent Company "D" 9th Infantry to protect the American settlers. Governor Douglas, governor of all the British Columbias, ordered Captain [George Edw.] Pickett, the Commanding Officer, to leave, giving him 3 days to do so. General Harney has reinforced the island to about the extent of his command, and now we are waiting the attack.

The British Governor claims the Straits of Rosario as the boundary line; Harney, the Straits of De Haro. Should the question come to a

Brigadier-General William S. Harney, Commander of U. S. forces in the Northwest.
—Bert Webber Collection

contest with arms, with the present forces concentrated, we will undoubtedly get used up, for ours is nothing, compared with what they can bring against us, and probably will whip us beautifully.(23)

San Juan Island, August 25th.

We have engaged in laying out works for a fort all day. Lieutenant Robert seemed pleased and the men take an interest in the work before them. For myself, I am better satisfied today than any previous day since joining the Company. The weather is fine, the prospect delightful, and we feel that we can enjoy ourselves well here. Mount St. Helens rears her show capped head in the east and Rainier north. Hood looms its towering peak far above the clouds in the south.* The beautiful Straits of Juan De Fuca on the one side of the island and the Bay of San Juan on the other, dotted here and there with a sail or Indian canoe with the surrounding islands covered with their heavy pine timber, all add to the enchantment of the scene, and make this one of the most beautiful locations imaginable.

—————
* Relative locations of mountains.

San Juan Isl ⚬ ————————— ✸ Mt. Baker

✸ Mt. Rainier

Mt. St. Helens ✸

(Not to scale)

Mt. Hood ✸

George Edward Pickett served as Captain, U.S. Army (above) in Washington Territory and was the first officer to land American troops at San Juan Island. He resigned and became a Major General in Confederate service (left).
—(top) Bert Webber collection.
(lower) U.S. Military Academy.

The island itself is about 18 miles long by an average width of 6 miles. Blackberries and red raspberries are plenty and the timber of the same species as is found in the other parts of Washington Territory I have visited, comprising mostly of pine, cedar, and low lands covered with black cedar.

The Hudson's Bay Company have large flocks of sheep here, numbering in all 8 to 10 thousand, from which the British ships get their mutton. There is one tribe of Indians camped here pursuing salmon fishing. There is an abundance of these delicious fish in these waters. (24)

San Juan Island, August 26th.

The detachment has been laying out work on the fort all day. A peculiar feature of this country is its heavy dews. I thought during the night we were getting rain, the drops came on the tent so often from the trees overhanging it. This is to be known in the future as Camp Pickett, after Pickett of Company "D" 9th Infantry, who came here first with his company. We are a busy party now, laying out work,

101

making and repairing tools and everything pertaining to building defenses. (25) *

Camp Pickett, San Juan Island, August 27th.

Weather continues beautiful and most inviting. We finished our fort and everything is in readiness for operations next week. The fort is laid out of an irregular form 425 feet long by 125 feet wide; parapets 20 feet thick and at one face 22 feet above the natural ground; ditch 20 feet wide, not less than 8 feet deep. If ever completed, will be good work. (26)

Camp Pickett, San Juan Island, August 28th.

This, our first Sunday on the island, has been a fine one. The usual Sunday morning inspection was made at 8 o'clock A.M., after which, in company with others, took a ramble over the island. Saw the renowned white squaw, who is like in principle, I should think, the albino. Excepting color she is Indian, but unusually white for white persons of her habits brought from Russian America He also visited the camp of Indians and their fish flakes where tons of salmon are being dried for winter use. Their mode of living differs little from other tribes we have seen. they have brown instead of black hair, or many of them at any rate, and belong to a tribe in British America. We went ashore about 12 miles from camp, stopped at settlers ranches and shepherds hamlets, saw fine lands and good timber. (27)

Camp Pickett, August 29th.

Weather continues fine. We have been making some alterations in the fort and more are to be made.

Camp Pickett, August 30th.

We are still engaged on the fort and also procuring good water for the camp. Nothing new or strange has taken place. I may mention, however, that by neglect of some one, our mess chest was left at Fort Vancouver and we are without cooking utensils, plates, knives, forks, or spoons. Some of us have made wooden ones and use boards for

* George Pickett graduated from West Point in 1846 but resigned from the U.S. Army to join the Confederacy in 1861. As a Maj. General, he led the famous charge at Gettysburg's Cemetery Ridge July 3, 1863 but was defeated with extreme casualties. He again engaged the Union Army at Battle of Five Forks, Virginia but lost to Gen. Sheridan in April 1865. He died in 1875 at age 50. —bw

> One [Mr.] Sawyer, who claims to be a citizen of the United States, had a piece of land enclosed and planted with potatoes. The hog is or was the property of the Hudson's Bay Company. Sawyer claimed to them that the pig was unruly and dest-royed his vegetables, and finally threatened to shoot his pigship unless he was kept at home, which he was not, and consequently got shot.
> —August 23, 1859

plates, borrowing cooking utensils, as far as we have been able.

Camp Pickett, August 31st.

Today being muster, the day was mostly spent on that duty, so much so as to prevent other duties. We are now six months behind in pay and need the money badly. The alterations in the fort are all made and tomorrow we are to commence work with pick and shovel. We will see about the sandbag battery, then the laugh may be on the other side.

September, 1859

Camp Pickett, September 1st.

A detail of 100 men from the command here reported to Lieutenant Robert for duty on the fort this morning and were put to work under the immediate charge of our detachment with pick and shovel. The work went on well until afternoon, when they began to murmur whiskey. The Lieutenant took no heed of their hints, but it is thought he will be compelled to do so. A camp rumor says that Governor Douglas [British] has given Colonel Casey [U.S. Army] two weeks to move his command from here in. It may be and probably is mere rumor. At all events, no one imagines the Colonel will accommodate old Douglas to that extent. The sentences of a lot of prisoners who have been tried by Court Martial was read last night. Most of the charges were for drunkenness and absence without leave. And they were generally fined five to ten dollars and released.

Camp Pickett, September 2nd.

Weather continues as fine as could be asked for. We are or have been during the day in charge of working parties on the fort. The non-commissioned officers [of the borrowed troops] growl very considerably about taking orders from privates of ours, but seem to avoid it. Lieutenant Kellog [*sic*] of Company "A" 3rd Artillery was

Henry Martyn Robert, Corps of Engineers, U.S.A.
Class of 1857 U. S. Military Academy, West Point New York
—U. S. Military Academy

relieved from duty with his company and put under arrest for drunkenness on duty. And by all reports, it will not be difficult to sustain the charges, for a private conducting in the same manner as he has done would be under punish-ment continually.

Camp Pickett, September 3rd.

Weather unpleasant, no work on the fort today. The Coast Survey Steamer *Active* came down the sound from Steilacoom, but no orders have come ashore from her as yet. It was expected there might be some from Head Quarters. There are about 200 Indian women assembled here, almost all of whom are prostitutes, which causes considerable trouble in camp. The men absent themselves often, sickness is very prevalent, and the discipline of the command is materially injured by their presence. (28)

Camp Pickett, September 4th.

Weather very unpleasant. It being Sunday, we were inspected by Lieutenant Robert at 8 A.M., spent the remainder of the day on pass and out of camp. Sergeant McEneney is drunk and absent. Our Kendall says the popular comedy entitled "The old soldier's downfall, or the lost towney found" will be performed with great eclat by the original of disobedience of orders. At all events, the Sergeant is a devilish fool.

Camp Pickett, September 5th.

Weather continues unpleasant. The Lieutenant has gone to Victoria on the *Active*. The Colonel is in charge of the detachment. Sergeant McEnaney continues on his spree. I am off duty today, being slightly unwell. The men seem inclined to take advantage of the Lieutenant's absence, as Kendall, Carmichael and Thompson were out all night and came home drunk this morning.

Camp Pickett, September 6th.

We continue operations on the fort. The non-commissioned officers of the line refused to obey orders given by us today, and were taken in hand by the Colonel, who succeeded in convincing them of the practi-cality of his arrangements, and that an Engineer soldier must be sustained when in charge of defenses. Whiskey was issued to the men today for the first time since work commenced on this fort.

Reports of Indian troubles at Whatcom* came to the island today and a detachment of Infantry are under orders to proceed there to quell the disturbances. Lieutenant Scott goes in command.

Camp Pickett, September 7th.

Weather continues cloudy and unpleasant. The detachment continue at their duties on the fort. A squad of 25 men left for Whatcom today to garrison and protect the place against Indians. Rumors of the defeat of Captain Wallen's expedition are still in circulation. Our grand Sergeant in charge has recovered his usual irritable equanimity and declares he will never drink more. But we know that the first towney who comes along will cause him to forego his good resolutions and get drunk.

Camp Pickett, September 8th.

Weather warm and pleasant. Men [working] on the fort. Mail came in, the first since our arrival. I received letters and papers from home.

Camp Pickett, September 9th.

Weather has finally settled beautiful, and we could not be better situated than now, for duty is the kind Engineer Soldiers take pride in, and although constant, is not laborious. The men growl and we make slow progress on the work. Recommendations for promotions were sent off to Headquarters today. I am included in the lot, I believe.

Camp Pickett, September 10th.

The detachment employed on the fort. The men detailed became almost mutinous and done little work during the day. Lieutenant Robert was compelled to report to the Colonel, who although a mild and kind officer, is strict in enforcing discipline. We get little outside of our daily routine of duty of interest.

Camp Pickett, September 11th.

Sunday, being a day of rest, inspection at 8 A.M., after which we disposed of ourselves as best suited the individual fancy of the men until four P.M., when the long roll was beat [on a snare drum] and the entire command mustered to check the advance of a fire. It was known

---

* Whatcom was a village on the mainland on the site of present day Bellingham. —bw

to be burning some six miles from camp yesterday, but run so rapidly as to be almost on our camp this evening at a point opposite our tents. It reached to within three or four rods of the tents, running in the small dry brush and leaves so fast as to cause us to remove our ammunition and property.

Camp Pickett, September 12th.

Weather continues fine. Work has continued on the fort, notwithstanding the men growl and that an extra detail of fifty were watching and keeping the fire in check. Lieutenant Robert shows considerable energy in the prosecution of the work in his charge. (29)

Camp Pickett, September 13th.

There is no change of duty here, men daily engaged on the fort in charge of working parties. The expected amount of growling, swearing and joking occurs daily. We get an unlimited share in as much as we are immediately in charge of the work.

Camp Pickett, September 14th.

Weather cool and cloudy. The new pantaloons and uniform hats were issued today and the hats worn at retreat by us. They are generally liked as being something new, and have already received the name Plug Hat from the men, but are known as the Pattern of 1858 and suggested by Secretary Floyd. The black pants will be put on as soon as the company tailor gets them altered.

A new order of work is established on the fort, the detail going out only after dinner call and remaining until night. We will be compelled to go out in the morning with prisoners. A line of defense around the camp has been begun, composed of logs forming a breast high wall and put up in such a manner as will resist all rifle and other small missiles. The timber is here and little trouble to build it.

Camp Pickett, September 15th.

Today the rain is pouring. The detail was turned out for work, but ordered back by the Colonel, considering the weather far too wet for men to be out. The men are making preparations for winter quarters. Floors are being laid in the Silby tents. Stoves [are] being issued and preparations for a winter in Latitude 48° 30" going on. The stoves add very materially to our comfort, not only affording warmth, but with the little kettle belonging with them, we heat water to make tea with, giving a good opportunity for hot whiskey also. Sergeant Rapalle, the Commissary of this camp, came tonight with a bottle and paper of sugar, declaring we could afford warm water if he furnished whiskey and sugar.

Camp Pickett, September 16th.

The weather continues bad and rainy. We have been engaged around our camp the entire day making such conveniences as we require, bunk benches, tables and wood boxes. I was out with the prisoners in the forenoon. The Sergeant in charge related the stratagem the Colonel [played] on the John [Bulls] on his arrival here. First, four vessels of war were guarding it, and the Colonel with four companies of Infantry in the little steamer, *Julia,* crept down in broad daylight under cover of a fog and landed without molestation or the British having knowledge of it. Sent the [ship] *Massachusetts* to sea and returned after night, and in the morning all of her guns were on the hill overlooking the bay. (30)

Camp Pickett, September 17th.

Detachment at its usual duties. Most of the boys were at the town of San Juan* last night attending a ball or dance, where were congregated soldiers, citizens and squaws. Sergeant McEnaney is drunk and disgraced himself again. It is extremely fortunate that he is about the worst man in the detachment, otherwise it would be difficult to get along. Invariably, upon going to the town he meets with some person from his portion of Ireland and comes home drunk upon the delightful acquaintance of a towney formed, so that it is becoming a common subject of ridicule among the men, and "the old soldier's downfall, or the lost towney found" is a common subject of discussion among Infantry and Artillery, as well as us. It is also time for Supplee to break out and show up the Chief of the Spaniards.

Camp Pickett, September 18th.

Another delightful Sunday has passed and gone. Inspection at 8 o'clock A.M., after which Corporal Walsh, others, and myself procured a boat from the Quarter master and went aboard H.B.M. Sloop of War *Satelite*, attending service, and were shown over and

---

* The name Peck uses for the village, "town of San Juan" stems from the informal name given to the village that sprang up on the island. According to Hitchman (see bibliography), the name "Friday Harbor" was officially charted by the British Navy in 1858, a short time before American forces landed. —bw

around the ship, and well entertained. She is a screw vessel carrying 64pdr. guns, and a better regulated vessel would be hard to find. The crew seemed mostly young men, were very clean and the ship itself a model of cleanliness. The officers seemed to take pleasure in letting us go through the ship, and we returned pleased with visit. (31)

Camp Pickett, September 19th.

Weather cloudy and unpleasant. The men got on a spree last evening and continue it today. Work continues around the camp on the breast work of logs, and on the fort.

Camp Pickett, September 20th.

The weather is bad today. None of the men except the prisoners are at work today. Lieutenant Robert promulgated orders prohibiting drunk-enness tonight. The thing has gone so far as to greatly interfere with the duties of the men, and none could be depended upon for duty. A Marine form the *Satelite* visited us in our camp today. Seems quite a fine fellow, but awfully salt.

Camp Pickett, September 21st.

Weather continues bad. Detachment engaged on the fort. Supplee continues drunk and actually insulted the Lieutenant on the work this afternoon.

Camp Pickett, September 21st.

Today has been clear and fine, all but Carmichael and myself were on the work. We were out with the Lieutenant running a line for the government reserve, and only reached camp at 7 P.M. The Lieutenant was quite familiar and sociable, and I conversed more with him than ever before.

Camp Pickett, September 23rd.

Weather continues fine, the detachment employed much as yesterday. Carmichael and myself in the survey, the balance engaged about as usual.

Camp Pickett, September 24th.

As winter approaches we get more and more rain and clouds. Today is very uncomfortable. I have been inside all day cleaning my gun accouterments and washing my clothes. The Lieutenant is very kind and considerate to us when we deserve it and, notwithstanding his hum-bugging, a good officer.

Camp Pickett, September 25th.

Rain all day. Inspection at 8 o'clock A.M. by Lieutenant Robert. Spent the day rambling and sleeping. The steamer *Shubrick** arrived here with the States mail tonight. I received two papers from Sister Jennie Frost, quite an acquisition. I can assure any person disposed to doubt it, one has only to place himself outside the limits of civilization to appreciate anything with the smell of home upon it.

Camp Pickett, September 26th.

Weather cloudy and rain in the afternoon. The entire detachment was out with the Lieutenant surveying in the forenoon. I was in the Lieutenant's tent in the afternoon getting instructions from him in surveying, and find him willing and anxious to impart all of the knowledge he possesses on it or any other subject.

Camp Pickett, September 27th.

The sun shone clear and bright in the forenoon, but the afternoon has been rainy. The detail went to the fort, but returned for the rain. Nothing of importance transpired today.

Camp Pickett, September 28th.

Weather clear and cool all day, the detachment employed much as usual. Wright and myself at work trying to plot our work. The Lieutenant was with us for a time. I feel considerable interest in learning all that I possibly can concerning the duty and think it will not be my fault if I am kept on it as long as there is any of it to do.

---

* The *Shubrick* was the first steam-powered lighthouse tender built and was completed in November 1857. It was staunchly armed and qualified as a fighting ship. Gibbs (see bibliography) wrote: "So as not to be tampered with by hostile Indians on her west coast assignment, the *Shubrick* mounted a 24 pound Dahlgren cannon in the forecastle and two Dahlgren 12 pounders at the sternposts. Further, she had an ingenious apparatus for throwing scalding water from the boiler onto unwanted intruders who might try to capture the vessel." One of *Schbrick's* voyages, after planting the first buoys at the mouth of the Columbia River, included an epic trip up the Columbia River past Fort Vancouver through rapids, barriers and obstructions to Fort Cascades. Going back downriver, the skipper shot the rapids in his 140-feet long ship – a feat nothing short of remarkable – with such break-neck speed that guest army officers, badly frightened and distressed, leaned over the side and "fed the fish." —bw

Camp Pickett, September 29th.

Rain is pouring down in good earnest. The men are all inside. Wright and myself plotting our survey during the forenoon. Kendall and Carmichael in the afternoon. They seem to care little for the work and the Lieutenant is not over pleased with them.

Camp Pickett, September 30th.

The weather continues unsettled and disagreeable. I am detailed for surveying the entire Government Reserve, a job which, with a reasonable amount of stretching, will keep [me] from [guard duty and on t]he fort survey for weeks.

Most common public access to the San Juan islands is by the Washington State Ferry System's boats from Anacortes, Washington. .–Photographed June 1993 by Susan Eyerly

THE SAN JUAN ISLANDS were claimed by The United States and Great Britain and laborious discussions had been going on for a considerable time with efforts to resolve the boundary matter. On June 15, 1859, an American settler, Lyman Cutlar, tired of having British pigs from adjoining Bellevue farms, raid his potato patch, shot a pig that was raiding his garden. After threats by the British, Captain Pickett, U. S. Army, was ordered to land his troops on San Juan island "to protect the interests of American settler." British authorities promptly summoned their men-of-war to the off-shore anchorage. After sabre-rattling on both sides, the two nations agreed on joint-occupancy. Finally, in 1872, German Emperor Wilhelm I decided the issue in favor of the United States.

Artist's concept (top) of the pig incident. Charles J. Griffin (right) who operated the Hudson's Bay Company Bellevue Farm on San Juan Island. The standoff between Cutlar and Griffin was instant after Cutlar volunteered to pay for the pig but Griffin demanded an unreasonable price and said that the garden of potatoes should not have been there in the first place.

—Bert Webber collection

112

Bellevue Farm, on San Juan Island, was formed eight years after the Hudson's Bay Company formally took possession of the island in 1845. The farm was put there to establish British residency. The farm was primarily a sheep raising venture with large acreage's in pasture but there was also a vegetable garden. The farm community had "...7 small houses, a barn, outhouse and shed." —Bert Webber collection

The first American campsite was near San Juan Village. It had no fresh water supply and with the British Navy watching every move, Captain Pickett moved his presence to the other side of the island. This second site was near a spring but was heavily buffeted by winds off the Strait of Juan de Fuca. After Lt. Colonel Silas Casey assumed command from Pickett, he moved the camp beyond a hill which afforded protection from the wind and was out of sight of the British. —Bert Webber collection

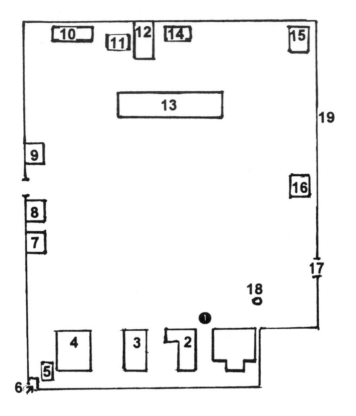

American Camp
The major buildings in the compound:
1) <u>Viewing position for visitors</u>; 2-3-4) Officer's quarters; 5)
Adjutant's Office; 6) Telegraph Office; 7) Orderly Room; 8)
Quartermaster and Commissary Office; 9) Company store-
room; 10) Bakery; 11) Non-commissioned officers mess hall;
12) Mess hall for the men; 13) Barracks; 14) Wash house; 15)
Carpenter shop; 16) Guard House; 17) Gate; 18) Flag Pole;
19) Wooden perimeter fence four feet high. (Not to scale)

American Camp

American soldiers lived in tents until make-shift barracks were constructed. Although officers requested materials for improvements they received only whitewash and brushes. After the post closed in 1874, some buildings were sold, some moved, some carefully dismantled to reclaim the lumber. Only two survive.

–Bert Webber collection

(Left page) Magnificent Mt. Baker (elev. 10,778 feet) looms on the eastern horizon across Griffin Bay. View (center) from Early Encampment site. View of Griffin Bay (lower) from American Camp. (This page) Prairie at American Camp. (Inset) Men from both camps gathered here for races and games. Captain Pickett's horse, far in the lead on one occasion, suddenly bolted for the spring to the delight of the British. The post cemetery was also located on the prairie. Men buried here died of disease, accidents and a large number from suicide. After the post was closed, the bodies were reinterred at the cemetery at Port Townsend.

—Photographed June 1993 by Susan Eyerly. Inset: Bert Webber collection

Memorial to Lt. Henry Martyn Robert the 22-year old Engineer who supervised construction of the Redoubt as his first major assignment after graduating from West Point. He spent his life in the Army retiring as Brig. General and Chief Engineer in 1901. He died in 1923. Picture on page 104.

–Photographed June 1993 by Susan Eyerly

Robert became an expert in parlimentary procedure and wrote *Robert's Rules of Order.*

American Camp – Officers Quarters.
—Photographed June 1993 by Susan Eyerly

(This page) American Camp – Porch (top) of Officer's Quarters with view toward Redoubt. (Lower) View toward Parade Ground. (Right page) Laundress Quarters, Officer's Quarters and post flag pole at head of Parade Ground. (Inset) Laundress with her children and her soldier-husband. The job of laundress was sought after by many married soldiers as the money and housing, extra rations, fuel and free medical benefits provided sorely needed additional support for the family. Each unit had a laundry day when garments were deposited for washing. The work was very hard and often required more than 12 hours a day. Laundry charges were deducted from each soldier's wages on pay day. (Lower) Laundress' quarters.

–Photographed June 1993 by Susan Eyerly. Inset page 121 from Bert Webber collection.

Sir James Douglas, Governor of Vancouver Island. He assertively opposed the American "occupation" of San Juan Island. The Kaiser's decision to award the islands to the United States was a blow to the British but was good news to the Americans. Had the islands been handed to the British, U. S. military planners were concerned that British guns along the south and west sides of the island might block access to Puget Sound ports. However, once the decision was announced, each side packed up his armies and went home. Since that episode, the entire American/Canadian border has been unfortified and stands as the world's model for international border cooperation. –(top) Bert Webber collection. (Lower) Photographed June 1993 by Susan Eyerly.

ENGLISH CAMP

In 1859 the killing of a pig on San Juan Island brought England and the United States to the brink of war over the issue of territorial rights here.

By agreement, both nations' troops were permitted to occupy this area while the problem was studied.

British soldiers established camp at Garrison Bay, just west of here, while American troops camped at the southern end of the island.

Peaceful arbitration of the dispute in 1872 placed the San Juan Islands within the territorial United States.

In October of that year the British garrison was abandoned.

Erected by the Washington State Highway Commission, in cooperation with the State Parks and Recreation Commission.

English Camp – Building, as seen today, believed to have been infirmary
–Photographed June 1993 by Susan Eyerly

English Camp – Warship at dock and formal garden that started out as a vegetable plot for the Royal Marines. The garden separated the garrison from the officers' quarters which were on a bench of land from which this rare photograph was made. (Lower) View of the garrison and **blockhouse from end of the dock** – Bert Webber collection

English Camp – Royal Marines stand inspection. (Lower) Early English Camp. —Bert Webber collection

English Camp – Formal garden; blockhouse; flag pole with Union Jack; commissary building seen from hill on which, years ago, the Officers' Quarters were located.
–Photographed June 1993 by Susan Eyerly

English Camp – Block House
–Photographed June 1993 by Susan Eyerly

127

English Camp – Commissary (top) and Commissary and Marine Barracks (rear). –Photographed June 1993 by Susan Eyerly.

English Camp – British Marine Barracks, now occupied by the Visitor's Center.

–Photographed June 1993 by Susan Eyerly

During the years of joint occupation, the troops from each side got along well and neither side felt in danger of attack from the other.

October, 1859

Camp Pickett, October 1st.

Today is fine and warm. The detachment employed as usual. Wright and myself surveying in the forenoon, cleaning up for Sunday in the afternoon. There is the usual amount of transgressions committed and consequently the guard tents are full of prisoners, all of which have done not-enough to subject one of them to incarceration were they civilians, but must answer for their crime before a military tribunal.

Camp Pickett, October 2nd.

Weather beautiful. Inspection at 8 o'clock A.M. In company with a few others, I spent the entire day in a trip down the island, visiting a number of ranches and running over some fine country, visioning some good farms, and took dinner at one. We came in camp at night tired and hungry.

Camp Pickett, October 3rd.

The fine weather continues. I['ve] done very little today, was out a while during the forenoon, found some fine specimens of quartz rock, with which the Lieutenant seemed considerably pleased. Also done some plotting on the survey we have been running.

Camp Pickett, October 4th.

A frost covered the ground this morning, the first of the season in the locality, followed by a fine warm day, and much resembling one year ago today. We were then on the eve of starting on this western trip, and were full of hope and bright anticipations for future joys, but have been sadly disappointed in some of them. Yet we have seen much that may be useful in future and learning something of Oregon and Washington Territories. We have done everything but our duty as Engineer soldiers and are only now performing such duties for the first time. I have been on the breastwork around camp with the entire police and prisoners force today, constructing that defense.

Camp Pickett, October 5th.

Weather fine. The detachment have been employed on the work. Wright and myself on the survey. One year ago we left West Point amid good wishes, tears, good byes and whiskey, and finally slept among the guns of Castle William, Governors Island, New York Harbor, feeling a vast amount of grumbling, swearing, etc., and it was a most appropriate beginning for this most miserable of campaigns. Who wouldn't sell a farm and be a soldier?

Camp Pickett, October 6th.

Rain came down in good earnest during a portion of today. Wright and myself with our party were out at surveying a portion of the day. One man cut his knee with an ax. We['ve] run through a growth of vine maple, blackberries and alders so thick it was impossible to penetrate it without axes.

Camp Pickett, October 7th.

Rain continues. We are doing nothing in consequence. The Colonel and Major Haller are both absent, and Captain Maloney in command. The men look for a respite from duty on this fort during this administration, but I fear the Captain will so far regard the Colonel's wishes as to continue the work during the absence of his superiors. I have spend the day reading and sleeping in our cloth hut, or tent. Our detachment seem in a remarkable degree of quiet at present; may it continue.

Camp Pickett, October 8th.

Another fine day is just over. The detachment has been employed at the defenses as usual. Wright and myself on the survey for the government reserve. I dream of home every night of late, and fully expect letters on the arrival of the mail, now fully due.

Camp Pickett, October 9th.

Weather quite cool. Inspection at 8 o'clock A.M. by Lieutenant Robert, after which I spent the forenoon in rambling out among the claims of settlers, and wrote to Jennie in the afternoon and evening. Land is being taken up quite fast on the island, but when the troops leave, I imagine there will be a clearing out of them.

Camp Pickett, October 10th.

Fine weather and fort building the order of the day. Wright and myself finished the survey on the reserve today and dismissed our party. Have now to put it on paper. (32)

Camp Pickett, October 11th.

Raining like the devil in the forenoon, but cleared up in the afternoon. Wright and myself out with a field level at work in the afternoon. We got the first intelligence from the balance of the detachment under Houston and Wallen. They are returned to the Cascades to build that bridge. Strange, none of us can get by that bridge or those Cascades without a pull at it.

Camp Pickett, October 12th.

Weather unpleasant in the forenoon, and no work, but the party out during the afternoon. I am detailed to superintend the construction of a road from the well to camp, a distance of about half a mile. The Lieutenant seemed immensely pleased if any of the party evince a desire to learn anything connected with the use of instruments. (33)

Camp Pickett, October 13th.

Weather cool. Wright and myself were out getting the depth of water in the harbor. Went on board the *Massachusetts,* she having arrived during the afternoon. Colonel Casey, the Paymaster, and several other officers came by her, also the mail from the States. One gun is in the fort and will be mounted tomorrow.

Another one of those improbable camp stories is going around that the entire command is ordered off the island before 12 M. tomorrow. Files of the *New York Herald* gives anything but a correct view of the situation here. It represents the forces, land and naval, of each side about equal, whereas the British have at the very least four ties as much as much in either land or se force as ourselves, and in case of an encounter, will whip us like the devil, and we shall have the pleasure of being told we did not fight when we get home. Indeed, if we should be so fortunate as to get there at all.

Camp Pickett, October 14th.

The detachment mounted the first gun on Fort Harney this morning, and considerable rejoicing and enthusiasm. The Paymaster is industriously counting out the gold to the men. Our turn will come tomorrow, and right glad will we be, it being almost 8 months since such an even transpired to us.

Considerable excitement is occasioned by the war steamer, *Satelite,* shifting her anchorage and her crew cutting a trail through the woods and onto the hill commanding our camp.

Camp Pickett, October 15th.

Weather delightful. We received our pay and continued our work today. There will be a high old spree tomorrow it being Sunday, and we may expect a demonstration from the great Mogul, also from the Chief of the Spaniards.

Camp Pickett, October 16th.

Weather fine. Inspection at 8 o'clock A.M. by Lieutenant Robert. The detachment all on pass down town and most of them on a spree. Kendall and Carmichael, in particular, they being the Sergeant's pets, would of course be. Supplee hasn't commenced yet. Livermore begins to show his too frequent libations. Thompson is so taken with his clutchman as to not feel inclined over indulgence in whiskey as yet, and the balance are not given that way.

Camp Pickett, October 17th.

Weather is wet and unpleasant. The detachment are idle or not out at work. Thompson found too much good stuff last night, or at all events was drunk this morning. This really a fine place for one inclined to look upon human nature as bad, for in the entire command one sees but few who have not been more or less drunk since pay has been received by them. Our Sergeant McEnaney is and has been drunk, and there is no fooling in the matter, for he gets so thoroughly pickled that there is no room for argument.

Camp Pickett, October 18th.

The unpleasant weather continues. I have been on the fort today. Nothing of importance occurred except Uncle Mark has finally got enough poor whiskey down to make him the most intolerable nuisance in camp, and finally get him in the guardhouse. The *Massachusetts* came down the sound and is to proceed to Fort Vancouver at once. Colonel Casey goes in her to attend a Court Martial to be [held] at that place. We constantly look for the States mail, and I, for me, as unusually impatient.

Camp Pickett, October 19th.

We are getting quantum sufficio of storms these days and nights, for they continue without abatement. [The men in the] detachment were out on their usual duty in the forenoon. Uncle Mark Supplee has found his proper level tonight, (i.e.) the guardhouse, and upon getting sober, will have a long list of grievances to relate.

Camp Pickett, October 20th.

The god of rain seems disposed to favor us with a goodly share of liquid element, for it continues to fall much, to the discomfort of us poor devils who have only a few threads of cotton to protect us at night from too copious an external application of that invigorating element and are compelled to be out during the day, come in at evening to endure the inconveniences of wet clothes, damp tents, damp beds and dampened spirits, unless it be of the ardent nature. Or one is easier persuaded to imbibe under these circumstances, than some others. I paid the moderate price of two and one-half dollars per pound for smoking tobacco today.

Camp Pickett, October 21st.

We have a clear day at last and the fort has been pushed ahead with redoubled vigor all day. A man of the detail work left it during the afternoon, and a great commotion is the result.

Camp Pickett, October 22nd.

The old sort of weather made its appearance today, only less rain than was its wont. The detachment employed as usual. I have been on the road from camp to spring with a party of men repairing it. The Chapman family are on the island and will erect a large pavilion tent, and give theatrical entertainment for the amusement of ye soldier and all others who may be willing to give one dollar for a few hours annoyance looking at the murder of some play. Still, we will all go, for it helps pass away the time and changes the current of one's thoughts for a time.

Camp Pickett, October 23rd.

A beautiful Sunday is just over. We were inspected at 8 o'clock A.M. by Lieutenant Robert. Sergeant McEnaney is or has been off on a drunk all of last night and today, only returning tonight under arrest in

134

Thompson's charge, he being next in rank, Corporal Walsh being gone to Victoria on pass. Upon arriving in camp, the Lieutenant ordered that he, the Sergeant, should go to the Lieutenant's tent, but he would not obey the order, and as a consequence, is under arrest and probably [will] be tried by Court Martial.

Camp Pickett, October 24th.

Today is exceedingly wet and disagreeable. The detachment has been busy, myself at the breastwork around camp. Came in with my clothes saturated with rain. That uncertain mail is still looked anxiously for, and unusually so, for we have not received letters very recently. Who wouldn't be a soldier?

Camp Pickett, October 25th.

Another fine day has passed. The detachment employed as usual. Corporal Walsh arrived from Victoria last evening full of improbable yarns and good tobacco He took charge of the detachment at once. I visited the theater last evening to see Jack Shepherd's play, but it was not produced, and a comedy enacted in its place. one must use his imagination extensively to enjoy such theatricals, and on returning to camp, I overheard a pair of non-appreciative Hibernians criticizing the merits of the entertainment most severely, and one finally put the finish upon the matter by declaring we could have got a bottle of poor whiskey for the dollar that would put you asleep till morning.

Camp Pickett, October 26th.

Today is fine and warm. We have no frost up to this time, an unusual thing for these latitudes in the States. The detachment employed as usual. Sergeant McEnaney was tried for absence without leave, disobedience of orders and drunkenness today. Result unknown as yet. The States mail came by the steamer *Julia*. I get nothing. General Scott is on the coast and expected here tomorrow per the *Massachusetts* to settle existing difficulties. Probably after the great Pacificator shall have conferred with British powers at Victoria, the trouble will be referred to the home governments and finally an amicable settlement.

Camp Pickett, October 27th.

Weather continues fine. Detachment employed as usual with the prisoners as a working party with Infantry. Colonel Norman, inspector of Artillery, reviewed and inspected the Artillery here today.

Camp Pickett, October 28th.

Weather continues pleasant. The detachment and other troops engaged as usual. General Scott does not arrive. He is undoubtedly investigating the merits of the troubles in this case and looking at the situation of affairs before coming here. We hear of his being at Vancouver, then up to Steilacoom, Olympia, Bellingham Bay, and other points on the sound, and this will probably be the last place he will visit before returning to San Francisco enroute for Washington. (34)

Camp Pickett, October 29th.

A dense fog has pervaded the atmosphere all day. The usual employments occupy the garrison. The sentence of Sergeant McEnaney was read tonight at dress parade. The court found him guilty of all the charges and specifications, and sentenced him to be reduced to the rank of first class private and forfeit to the United States ten dollars of his monthly pay for one month, exhorts him to behave (or the equivalent of it), so his foolishness costs him but the ten dollars his family much need.

Camp Pickett, October 30th.

The penetrating fog has disappeared, leaving a cloudy sky. We were inspected at 8 o'clock A.M. by Lieutenant Robert. This Sunday has been spent like many previous ones, rambling over the island in the forenoon, reading and sleeping afternoon.

Camp Pickett, October 31st.

Weather very pleasant. Detachment and working party out on the fort in the forenoon. The command turned out for inspection, muster and review at two o'clock P.M. and were put through the minutia of such an occasion by his Royal Highness Major Haller, who takes much pride and pleasure in the pomp and circumstance of war, albeit, he has been court martialed for cruelty to enlisted men within the last twelve months.

November, 1859

Camp Pickett, November 1st.

A change for the worst in the weather occurred during last night, and today is cloudy and uncomfortable. the detachment are engaged as usual. I am to superintend the revetting party. Do not like in, inasmuch as I never done any of it until now, whereas some of the men have done it for years. One year ago tonight we slept in the Presidio Barracks.

Camp Pickett, November 2nd.

Weather fine. Detachment at their usual duties on the fort. Lieutenant Robert complimented the detachment for the manner in which they conduct themselves on the work, and expresses himself greatly in our favor-

Camp Pickett, November 3rd.

A heavy frost covered the ground this morning and today has been like fall in Connecticut, making one feel more at home than any preceding one. We have been employed about as usual. General Scott has not arrived.

Camp Pickett, November 4th.

We have had an extremely unpleasant and windy day, a real old Northwester, from which we get our very worst storms. They correspond well with our easterly storms on the Atlantic Coast.

Camp Pickett, November 5th.

Weather cloudy and cool Detachment as usual on fort. I am permanently in charge of the revetting party.

Camp Pickett, November 6th.

A conglomeration of weather prevailed today: rain, hail and sunshine. We were inspected at 8 o'clock A.M. by Lieutenant Robert.

Sergeant McEnaney is drunk again, in spite of all of his promises of good behavior, and it will go rough if the Lieutenant finds it out.

Camp Pickett, November 7th.

Today at morning the weather was fine, but at 10 o'clock A.M. a black cloud came down bringing a severe wind storm which raged furiously a few moments. The weather grows cold constantly since, and in our cotton houses [tents] we feel the change quite sensibly. At about ten o'clock the *Massachusetts* came into the harbor bringing the Commander in Chief and Staff. A salute of thirteen guns were given, and Colonel Johnson of the staff with Colonel Lee came ashore, but the General did not leave the ship.

Operations on the fort are suspended, and the troops ordered to their former garrison, except one company, which remains. A joint occupation is agreed upon until the home governments have time to act. There were great rejoicings at the orders to suspend work on the fort. The tools were collected quicker than ever on a former occasion and brought to their proper repository, with many shouts and much confusion, and to us it is a sad disappointment, looking for considerable credit, as we did, for our services here. Again, it may be looked upon as an act of disapproval of General Harney's conduct in the matter, and of course, be censured by his friends. There is already considerable ill feeling between the two generals.

Camp Pickett, November 8th.

Considerable snow fell during last night, and today has been uncomfortable and cold. The troops are preparing for an early departure from here. The detachment [is] putting tools in condition for transportation. One year ago today we were trying the strength of the good ship *Columbia* on Umpqua Bar. The Lieutenant thinks possibly General Harney may send us home to West Point.

Camp Pickett, November 9th.

Today is cold and blustering. Walsh, Carmichael and myself have been out surveying. The remainder of the detachment preparing to leave this gay and festive [place] as soon as may be, and if this cold weather continues, we will be much better with something more substantial for protection from it than cotton cloth. It was with considerable difficulty we kept alive in our tent last night.

Camp Pickett, November 10th.

The cold continues and ours is decidedly the wrong latitude for the present state of life (48° 30").

Camp Pickett, November 11th.

Weather continues the same. I am still surveying with Walsh and Carmichael. he mail came today and I rejoice in letters from George and Mother. Colonel Casey arrived also. Lieutenant Robert is going up the sound per the *Massachusetts*. We also rec[eived] information from the detachment under Lieutenant Houston. They are arrived at the Cascades and building that bridge we did not build. One of them, Shirts, gone home on furlough.

Camp Pickett, November 12th.

Weather continues cold and our surveying around the shore of this island exposed to winds is anything but agreeable. Uncle Mark is once more in durance vile for a too great indulgence in spirits. Lieutenant [Lie-?] Dandy is in charge of the detachment in the absence of Robert. Carmichael and Kendall went up the sound with the Infantry, four companies of them having left for Steilacoom and Port Townsend. Captain Hunt of Company "C" 4th Infantry is in command of the island now.

Camp Pickett, November 13th.

Weather of the moistest possible order. We have done nothing, of course. [A. J.] Price, the expressman for Captain Wallen, came on the island and called on us, informed us that the boys are at the Cascades and all well.

Camp Pickett, November 14th.

Like yesterday, rain is pouring down. Lieutenants Scott and Forcyth got into an altercation. And from high words, they loaded their pistols and were about trying their courage when Lieutenant informed them he would place them under arrest unless they desisted. Undoubtedly they were glad of the opportunity to do so, one of them, at least. The trouble arose from a dispute about [the] Quartermaster's animals. The *Massachusetts* might soon return and take us off from here. When she does come, the four companies of Artillery and ourselves embark for Fort Vancouver.

Camp Pickett, November 15th.

Weather continues decidedly moist and uncomfortable. We are reinforced by one recruit, one John Coughlin, having joined the destinies of this invincible detachment today. I would like to exchange with him and become a citizen.

Camp Pickett, November 16th.

Weather continues unpleasant. We finished the survey tonight, and now there seems little for us to do until we leave here. I am glad for a few days respite from duty, for we have been so constantly engaged.

Camp Pickett, November 17th.

The weather continues drear [dreary]. Almost all of the men are off on pass today. I spent the day in my tent writing, plotting, for the rain seems to have commenced in good earnest and there will be little of pleasure to be taken out of doors until spring.

Camp Pickett, November 18th.

Weather as usual, dull. Detachment doing nothing. These are really halcyon days of our soldiering, utterly idle, a thing almost unknown to an Engineer Soldier, but we are kept quite busy at nights in the vain endeavor to keep warm.

Camp Pickett, November 19th.

Last night was one long to be remembered by occupants of cotton domiciles in these parts. A perfect hurricane prevailed. The American citizens of this island met and agreed to adopt any resolutions drawn up by one of their number sustaining General Harney in his actions here. No doubt he will be gratified.

Camp Pickett, November 20th.

Weather pleasant during most of the day. I am on pass and out hunting. No inspection. Corporal Walsh is in durance vile for firing his pistol in the vicinity of camp, there having been a general order against it published. He was very foolish in doing it and was caught in the act.

140

Camp Pickett, November 21st.

A delightful day is passed. Captain Hunt released Corporal Walsh from arrest, and to pay for his condensation, detailed the detachment to put an addition on his quarters, the same occupied by the Colonel not being large enough for him, so the Engineers must do it. If he waits for us, I guess he will go without some time. At all events, we are not disposed to pay for the leniency bestowed on Walsh.

Camp Pickett, November 22nd.

Weather continues cool but pleasant. We are engaged on Captain Hunt's quarters. Today is Thanksgiving Day at home. There is a decided difference in the fare of the two boards, I opine. I shall have to remember that I dined from bean soup and pork, while they will undoubtedly fare quite sumptuously on turkey, chicken, etc. Mountains Rainier and Baker loom magnificently far above the clouds, their snow covered summits shining like monuments of burnished gold in the bright sunlight. Surely nowhere can grander or more beautiful scenery be found than here among the mountains and rivers of Washington Territory.

Camp Pickett, November 23rd.

There is no change in the weather, clear and cool. Detachment employed on Commanding Officer's house. If he does not find some wet blankets before spring, it [will be] curious, for the men took delight in putting the shingles on the roof in such a manner as to make it most certainly leak. Uncle Mark has been confined and released again. He got sober and the Captain found he needed a bookcase, and as in Corporal Walsh's case, released him and set him to work. But Mark could not be induced to promise better behavior in the future, declaring himself unreliable. Confound him. I nearly went into the guard tent for his fault, being sent to take him to the guard. He went into his tent and the Officer of the Day insisted that I gave him the opportunity to do so in order to let him get a bottle of whiskey. But I was just as firm in asserting that I knew nothing of it, and by the dint of a hard cheek got clear. I certainly knew that he had a bottle of liquor on his person when I arrested him, but did not consider it my duty to take it from him. (35)

Camp Pickett, November 24th.

Weather continues the same. The detachment doing nothing. I

spent the day in washing my clothing and doing other domestic duties, such as repairing clothing, fixing sleeping apparel, etc. The [ship] *Massachusetts* is reported in the offing, and if so we may soon be on board of her and bound for Fort Vancouver and probably the same old Cascades.

Camp Pickett, November 25th.

Weather cool and pleasant. The *Massachusetts* arrived down from Steilacoom at night and has gone to Bellingham Bay for coal. Kendall and Carmichael came by her. They were greatly pleased with their visit, but give doleful accounts of the accommodations for passengers aboard. The Lieutenant came also. We are doing nothing today. Otherwise on duty.

Camp Pickett, November 26th.

Today is a beautiful one. The detachment at work on the Captain's house. Corporal Walsh and myself are on pass and at McKay's ranch. We brought out provisions and our rifles, bound to kill something before we return. Thus far, nothing has lost its life by our deadly aim and we are snugly strewed around the fire in McKay's cabin, listening to his exciting yarns. The cabin is built of logs, the cracks plastered over with mud. One small room inside and here he lives all alone except for the cheerful companionship of a solitary rooster, which regularly roosts on the bunk of its master and inhabits the room with him.

Camp Pickett, November 27th.

Weather clear, but extremely cold. We passed a much more pleasant night than we would have done in camp, and rose to a tolerably good breakfast. Went for game, but after remaining three hours came in with only a couple of poor ducks, which McKay made into a kind of stew, putting onions, turnips, cabbage, carrots and potatoes into it, and although it looked decidedly Gaelic, it relished well. Wright arrived out in time for dinner. We had arrived home at retreat, and had enjoyed ourselves hugely.

Camp Pickett, November 28th.

Today is cloudy and damp. The detachment employed as usual. The *Massachusetts* arrived in port this afternoon, also steamer *William G. Hunt*. We will soon be off for Fort Vancouver, and if not going home, we are certainly going to join our comrades, from whom we have been separated five months, and we will have a pleasant reunion, I am sure.

Camp Pickett, November 29th.

Weather of the very gloomiest kind. Detachment employed on the Commanding Officer's house, the rain notwithstanding.

Camp Pickett, November 30th.

Weather cold. Detachment employed in moving tools, etc. to the wharf and making general preparations for embarking aboard the *Massachusetts* in the morning. Almost everyone is more or less drunk, and all but myself off [duty] this evening. I am obliged to remain in charge of the camp. Sergeant will be drunk as a lord.

Retreat

TRADITIONAL   Arr. for this book by Lauren Thomas Webber, Lynn, Mass. 1993

December, 1859

On Board Transport *Massachusetts*

Weather cool and cloudy. We were astir at daylight and putting our camp and garrison equipage on wagons and finally transferring our property from wharf to ship. At eleven o'clock we had everything aboard and moved away from the wharf, the vessel crowded to its utmost capacity, having on board four Companies of Artillery and ourselves. We have a portion of the ship known as the boiler deck assigned to us and it is the most desirable portion of the ship. The main deck is entirely covered with sleeping Artillerymen, and all of the hammocks are occupied.

Many of the men came aboard drunk, and of coups, our foolish Sergeant among them. He must [have] abuse[d] and insult[ed] Lieutenant Robert, and is now under arrest and will undoubtedly be tried by Court Martial on our arrival at Vancouver. So after three months and eight days duty and excitement in the teeth of the British Lion, we leave with few laurels added to those already decorating our fair brows. Yet we have been doing our legitimate duties as Engineer Soldiers, and I, for one, am pleased with the part I have borne while on the island. It is a pleasant spot, and some day will be a favorite resort for pleasure seekers. We steamed from the bay at two o'clock P.M. and are now running down the Straits of Juan De Fuca in fine style.

On Board *Massachusetts*, December 2nd.

Weather stormy. A strong north west wind accompanied by rain is driving down the coast in fine style, and at this rate will be off the Columbia River tomorrow.

On Board Ship, December 3rd.

This morning was clear, cool and really delightful. We arrived off the mouth of the Columbia at ten o'clock A.M., fired a signal gun for a pilot, but before one came out to us, a strong north wester struck us and we are, and have been, running before it all day. The wind whistles through the rigging and the sea runs very high, larger waves than I ever before saw are rolling up, and altogether it is a wild time. The boys aver that it is all occasioned by the presence of a French Romish Priest who is aboard. On thing is certain, no sooner did he go on deck than it began to blow big guns, and has kept up the tune. Captain Fauntleroy (our Captain) was the first man who took a steamer over the Bar at all. (36)

On Board Ship, December 4th.

Weather continues boisterous, but cool. Last was the night for the soldiers on this ship. She got into a trough of a sea and gave a lurch to the port side, which dislodged many of a poor devil of a soldier. For us there is a sail hung up dividing the boiler deck room and one-half occupied by our detachment, the other by the married people. The first grand lurch she made precipitated us down among these married people and mixed us most curiously. I found myself being most lovingly embraced by the legs of another man's wife, and many a curse from the men and screams from women were the result, but sleep was out of the question during the remainder of the night. Uncle Mark had considerable trouble with an empty barrel, imagining it some intruding artilleryman, and Livermore was ready to surrender life at once, in his terror. The day and night has been spent in getting back over the course run on the day before.

On Board *Massachusetts*, December 5th.

We continue to get cool weather, with a high wind. Not much amusement, unless that growing out of the crowded condition of the ship, and fun made by Johnie Morton, a stowaway taken aboard by us and being smuggled to Vancouver. We arrived off the mouth of the river about eleven A.M. and crossed the bar in safety at noon, and are now at anchor in Baker's Bay, awaiting for daylight to run up the river. While I am writing, Johnie is amusing all hands with song and joke, making time pass lively by.

On Board Ship, December 6th.

Weather foul indeed. Snow, sleet and rain has fallen all day. The wind so furious as to make the ship drag anchor and a vast amount of discomfort. In fact, it is by far the worst storm I have witnessed on the coast.

On Board Ship, December 7th.

Weather fine and pleasant. All hands were at the brakes this morning, heaving lustily and slowly bringing the anchors from the mud, the chorus of the sailors and roar of breakers making wild music. We passed Astoria at eleven o'clock A.M., and the old ship is steaming up the river, finally. The prospect of being off this old ship in the morning gives new life to all, and cheerfulness and pleasant faces are met today, in place of grumbling and discontent yesterday. We expect to be in Vancouver at six A.M. tomorrow.

On Board Ship, December 8th.

Weather beautiful. We are tied to a stump fifteen miles below the fort, having encountered ice to such an extent that it was feared would cut the copper on the vessel. She was laid alongside the bank and made fast to trees. The banks are bold and high, so a plank is shoved ashore and the men are all of them ashore. There are rumors of a march in the morning. We, Wright and myself, went about two miles, found an old couple at a ranch, and bought pumpkin pies at four bits each (50 cents) and enjoyed them hugely, they being the first we have seen since leaving old Connecticut.

On Board Ship, December 9th.

Weather beautiful. The four companies of Artillery left the ship at eleven o'clock A.M. and marched to Vancouver. Kendall, Carmichael, Wright and myself obtained leave of absence and went on foot to Vancouver also. After arriving we found that Sergeant Wheeler and Artificer Smith of the detachment at the Cascades were at the Allen House, being down on leave and detained in consequence of the ice in the river.

We spent a pleasant evening and night with them. They seem to have had a severe march, but speak highly of Lieutenant Houston. They describe him as having turned around completely and is now a very indulgent officer. Only two of the detachment succeeded in getting to the City of the Latter Day Saints, and they doing the duty of servants to the officers, so that had I been with them I should most finally have succeeded in entering the gates of that far famed city where plurality of wives is part of the church creed. I had a great desire to penetrate into that kingdom of Brigham's, and have regretted being compelled to join our portion of the detach, for that reason as well as any other. From their description of their march, they did not have so hard a time as they anticipated and seemed to [have] enjoyed it far better than we did our portion of it. After the Lieutenant found the quality of material his men were made of, he was a much different person and done all in his power for their welfare and well being, so says Wheeler and Smith.

On Board Ship, December 10th.

We spent the forenoon in Vancouver and started on our return about noon, arriving at one of the settler's ranches at 7 o'clock P.M. We had a good supper prepared, and after dispatching it, proceeded to the ship, a distance of 2 miles, and spent the remainder of the evening with the balance of the detachment. We enjoyed our visit to Vancouver immensely, and none the less for meeting our old comrades.

Last night was the most sleepless one I have ever passed. lay in bed with sheets and pillows, a thing I have not indulged in for fifteen months. They felt so strange and soft, I could not get a moment's rest, and did not shut my eyes until six o'clock A.M., and then after getting out on the side rail to the bed. How much of a heathen I must have become, certainly.

On Board Ship, December 11th.

We remain ice bound still, which is anything but pleasant, and were it not for mother Lambert's pumpkin pies, should be disconsolate indeed. Mrs. Lambert is the man's wife who lives near the ship. And Wright and myself go daily and regale ourselves on her pies at fifty cents apiece. Wheeler and Smith returned to Vancouver today.

On Board Ship, December 12th.

The weather continues fine and cool. We are still tied to the bank.

On Board, December 13th.

Condition same as yesterday. Our only amusement is of our own making.

On Board Ship, December 14th.

Weather continues fine, and we remain tied to a tree.

Fort Vancouver, December 15th.

Today has been very wet. Our rations having run out, the Corporal deemed it proper to send me to this place to get a requisition approved by Lieutenant Robert, who is here, and I was detailed for the duty. I found a fifteen mile tramp in a drenching rain on a trail through low meadow land a more serious affair than I anticipated, even. I arrived at the garrison at one o'clock P.M. and at once entered the orderly room of Company "B" 3rd Artillery. Sergeant Downing wanted to know what damned fool compelled me to come fifteen miles in such a rain, and ordered a good dinner to be prepared for me, sent out and got a bottle of brandy and done all in his power for me. After getting my dinner and somewhat dry, I found Lieutenant Robert, and after he had approved the requisition, I asked permission to remain over night, which was readily granted, and I remain. It was worse than folly sending me.

Fort Vancouver, December 15th. [*Sic*] (There are two "Dec. 15th" entries. –bw)

Weather continues very rainy. I reported at the Lieutenant's quarters at guard mounting and spent the remainder of the day around the garrison.

Fort Vancouver, December 16th.

The rain continues. Again reported at guard mount and got orders to report tomorrow at the same hour. Spent the day in garrison, as yesterday.

Fort Vancouver, December 17th.

A thick fog and rain has prevailed all day. I reported to the Lieutenant at the usual hour and received orders to get an animal from the Quarter Master and proceed to the ship and return. Accordingly, I was mounted at 11 o'clock A.M. on a mule and laden with a note from the Lieutenant to his servant and a bottle of brandy from Mrs. Tolan for her husband, started on my journey. The rain for the last few days has rendered the trail soft and mirey, and my mule early discovered that I was spurless, and mulelike, would not perform his part of the burden at all satisfactorily.

At length, I found a place that afforded a good opportunity to secure a persuader, and availed myself of the opportunity to do so. There ensued a serious argument on the practicability of a galloping mule asserting his aversion to the measure and myself in its favor. My persuasive powers, being [a] good four feet long and of hose, finally convinced him of the utility of the motion. And all went well.

Arrived at the place where the ship was supposed to be and found it gone. Returned as far as Lambert's ranch and made inquiries. They knew nothing concerning it. Made a detour of some miles, arrived at Hathaways, a point some three miles below where the ship was moored when I left, and upon questioning him, found that the ship had dropped down to a little town of St. Helens, some 35 miles below and impossible to reach it by my means of travel. It was now 3:30 o'clock P.M. and I had fasted since six A.M. I had preserved the brandy at great inconvenience, and determined to carry it no further.

Accordingly, I drew the cork and invited Hathaway to join me in a drink. He took hold freely of the really good liquor and after a few moments we repeated the maneuver. I wished to get him good natured, for I was hungry, and all of the money I possessed was twenty-five cents, and no one thinks of giving a meal for less than fifty. After the brandy began to loosen his tongue, I stated my case simply: hungry, no money. He sent me into the house, and the Madam furnished me a good meal. I inquired the price, she said nix. I gave my 25cts to her little girl and took a good pull at the bottle, gave the remainder to the old man, and mounted.

It was now four o'clock, and I was 18 miles from the fort, a heavy fog, and rain, a difficult trail, in fact a dangerous one under the circumstances, but I had great confidence in the powers of my mule, it generally being difficult to lose them in the night on a trail once traveled by them. After three or four miles, I found the mule fast failing in strength, and was compelled to ride qt the slowest pace.

Soon a night of pitchy darkness came on. The mule and me differed again, he insisted on keeping more to the left than I thought right. Felt sure I was right, but at the same time had great confidence in the animal. At last, I determined to give way and allow him his head. I had not ridden more than one half a mile before I found myself on the brink of a deep slew, washed by the high water of the river, this being the danger to be avoided by pursuing the right course. I saw I had been right and the mule wrong. I had my way after [all] and arrived at 11 o'clock in safety.

Fort Vancouver, December 18th.

Weather pleasant. I turned out at six A.M. and while feeling of myself and trying to straighten my sore legs after yesterday's hard ride, I got an order to proceed to the wharf, that the little steamer had come around from Portland last night and reported the Willamette slew free from ice, and had been chartered by Quartermaster [Rufus] Ingalls to go down to St. Helens and get the property and men aboard of the ship and bring it to Vancouver.

I at once went aboard, notwithstanding I had not broken my fast since 4 o'clock P.M. yesterday at the ranch of Hathaway and had ridden 18 miles after and then passed the night, and now off without anything to eat, was coming close to the times that try men's stomachs, if not souls. Arriving at the ship at two P.M., we commenced transferring camp and garrison equipage at once to the steamer. Leaving the ship at six P.M. and arriving at Fort Vancouver at ten, we continued discharging freight and finished at 12.

The night is extremely cold, but we must remain on board until morning, and I have not eaten since 4 P.M. on the 17th. This being Sunday, we could not procure anything at the one or two restaurants near the wharf, and we have no place to sleep unless on the deck of the steamer, and no place where the air is broken from the outside circulation, and taken with yesterday's ride and experience, [it] is one of the hardest tours of duty performed by me since I entered the service. There was no particular necessity for my going down with the steamer.

Fort Vancouver, December 19th.

Weather very pleasant. The detachment turned the tools belonging to the Quartermaster's department over to that department this morn-ing and proceeded to the garrison, and are quartered with Company "D" of the 3rd Artillery, where we are to remain until the ice breaks up and gets out of the river, so that we can proceed to the Cascades, there to winter and build that bridge. I broke my long fast at 9 o'clock A.M., making forty-one hours of a fast.

Fort Vancouver, December 20th.

Weather continues fine. Detachment idle.

Fort Vancouver, December 21st.

Weather continues good. Detachment got under way and went as far as the wharf enroute to the Cascades, but after remaining some two hours, learned that the steamer would not go. Returned.

Fort Vancouver, December 22nd.

Weather fine. Detachment at garrison, as usual.

Fort Vancouver, December 23rd.

Weather dubious. We were surprised during the afternoon by the arrival of a detachment of twelve men commanded by Lieutenant Thomas Lincoln Casey from West Point direct to reinforce the detachment here, and Casey to relieve Houston of the command of the detachment doing duty in this department. We spent the evening at the Vancouver House. A supper and festivities made the evening pass quite pleasantly.

Fort Vancouver, December 25th.

Weather rain. We partook of a good Christmas dinner with Company "D" today, and with it and inquiries concerning home matters of the detachment just arrived, passed the day quite pleasantly. Considerable whiskey has been drunk today by the soldiers, and some fighting done, but on the whole, it has been passed quite pleasantly.

Fort Vancouver, December 26th.

Today, like others preceding it, has been dull, nothing in particular occurring.

Fort Vancouver, December 31st.

The weather during the few days since the 26th has been dull. We were mustered this morning and spent our time around quarters. Sergeant McEnaney released by Lieutenant Robert at the request of Lieutenant Casey and promises good behavior again. The men are impatient to go to the Cascades. They will be equally impatient to leave before spring, I think.

> This is the beginning of another year, and if we are
> called on to pass through so much unpleasant duty
> as during the last, we will be in bad luck indeed
> —New Year's Day 1860

January, 1860

Fort Vancouver, January 1st.

Weather of the very moistest kind. Raining and freezing all day.
Our detachment furnished a dinner for Company "D" and ourselves,
which was no mean affair for this country, and it passed off in good
style. There were only two who got so much invigorating down as to
show it in their behavior. The Sergeant, who invariably of late finds a
towney on every occasion of merriment, met with his usual success
today and got tight. What a town that must be. This is the beginning of
another year, and if we are called on to pass through so much unpleasant duty as during the last, we will be in bad luck indeed.

Fort Vancouver, January 2nd.

A severe ice storm of sleet and ice prevailed during the entire day,
preventing us from leaving the quarters. A very disagreeable circumstance occurred in the quarters. Sergeant Barr of company "D" missed
from his orderly room a gold watch. It is a good one, and doubly
valuable to him inconsequence of having been the property of his
wife's father. A search was made [by] the men of both parties, but no
trace of it found. The Sergeant made a very liberal offer for it, and we
hope he may finally recover [it]. We feel it more perhaps than is
necessary, being strangers and in strange quarters. We have had men
capable of the act, and perhaps there [are] some among us still.

Fort Vancouver, January 3rd.

The weather is more endurable. No change in life. The Sergeant
recovered his watch this morning. It was found hanging on a nail
under his window on the outside of the building, and could not have
been long there when found. At all events, we are greatly pleased that
it is found.

Fort Vancouver, January 4th.

Rain continues to pour down and we look for an opportunity to stretch our legs without getting wet in rain. So we must depend on cards and sleep for pastime. Reading there is none. A recruit belonging to Company "H" 4th Infantry was buried this afternoon. It is reported that he went on the sick report and that Doctor Hegar, who is a Hungarian who came to America with Kossooth, sent him to his quarters, informing him he was drunk, and that on the day before he died. But then he was buried with military honors.

Fort Vancouver, January 5th.

Weather continues rainy. The Paymaster disbursed today. The river is so far free from ice that we are under marching orders tomorrow morning, and expect to reach Fort Cascades.

Fort Cascades, January 6th.

The [Engineer] detachment left the garrison at Vancouver at 9 o'clock A.M. with the kindest expressions of respect and friendship from the men of Company "D" and proceeded to the government wharf and embarked on the steamboat *Carrie Ladd* for here at 12 o'clock M. We enjoyed the trip much. The scenery is grand and equals that of the Hudson, and in some respects is finer. Cape Horn shows immense palisades [that] tower far above with their moss covered sides broken here and there by a small rivulet or cascades running down the side. Arriving at the Cascade landing, we found all of the men there awaiting us and a good supper prepared by our old comrade, Ned Gibert. The men are quartered in a Quarter Master's building outside the garrison. Lieutenant Houston turned over the property to Lieutenant Casey and left for Vancouver and the States by the return boat.

Fort Cascades, January 7th.

We find about the same old rain here that we had all of last winter. The day has been consumed in getting ready to leave. We are much crowded, but contrive to squeeze in somehow. We of us who came out here last year feel that we are home once more, and for myself, to feel that I am to be humbugged no more by that prince of humbugs, McEnaney (beats Barnum). The Indians welcome us again. Who will not now admit that our names are not great among the heathen. The men here have been engaged in getting out timber for the bridge we were to build on our leaving for San Juan Island, but they

Fort Cascades on the Columbia River

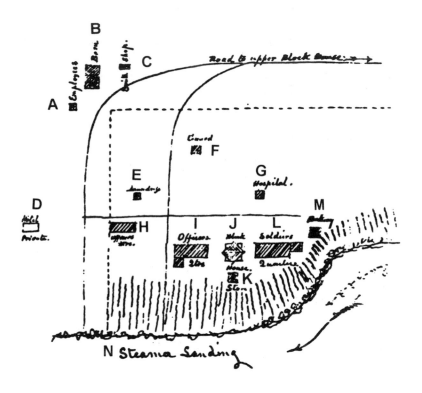

Fort Cascades (locations):	
A Employees Barn	H Officer's Mess
B Employees Barn	I Officer's Quarters
C Blacksmith Ship	J Block House
D Private Hotel	K Suttler's Store
E Laundry	L Soldier's Barracks
F Guard House	M Bakery
G Hospital	N Wharf

have done little beyond cutting some of the timber.

Fort Cascades, January 8th.

This, our first Sunday at this place, is an unusually stormy one. We were inspected by Lieutenant Casey, and afterwards all hands remained in quarters during the entire day. Paraded 32 rifles at our inspection parade this morning, and it would be difficult to find another squad of thirty-two so tall and good looking soldiers.

Fort Cascades, January 12th.

The weather has been very bad until today. The party remained inside also until this morning. We turned out and went into the woods to get out timber for the bridge. The day passed off pleasantly enough, although I think there are some malcontents that will eventually make trouble or endeavor to do so at all events. One can easily see [that] the spirit of some of the old soldiers is to run the internal affairs of the detachment to suit themselves.

Fort Cascades, January 14th.

The pleasant weather continued until today, when the old familiar rain appeared. But unlike last year, we do not as yet turn out in it. Captain Wallen represented the necessity of doing so to the Lieutenant, but he could not see it.

Fort Cascades, January 15th.

Weather very fine. Inspection by Lieutenants Casey and Robert at 9:30 o'clock A.M. and then most of the men were on pass for the remainder of the day. I went down the river as far as Mr. Hamilton's and took dinner. Arrived home at 3 P.M. When we do get a pleasant day it is like spring and far pleasanter than at the upper landing.

Fort Cascades, January 19th.

Weather has been pleasant until today. Since the 15th we have been employed on the bridge, five hours per diem, and the work goes on cheerfully. Much different from last winter. We contrive to get among the Indians evenings now and again, and life seems much more endurable.

Fort Cascades, January 22nd.

The weather has been bad most of the last three days. We have been engaged on the bridge when the weather would permit. Inspection in quarters by Lieutenant Robert. Nothing remained to be done. For amusement we lay around quarters in consequence of the rain.

Fort Cascades, January 29th.

The weather has been clear most of the past week. The men are engaged on the bridge as usual. Little of interest has occurred during the week. The usual Sunday morning inspection was had this morning. A number of us went to the upper landing and took dinner at Bushes.

Fort Cascades, January 31st.

Yesterday and today have been so pleasant – the detachment on the bridge. Lieutenant Casey remained on the work during the entire day and takes a great interest in everything pertaining to the work.

February, 1860

Fort Cascades, February 2nd.

Today came in stormy and disagreeable. The detachment doing nothing. Some of the Company "H" 4th Infantry went to the Indian ranch last night and kicked up a general row, nearly killing one or two of the poor devils, and one or more of the soldiers were hurt, to what extent I know not. A special order was read tonight prohibiting any enlisted man from visiting the ranch without special permission.

Fort Cascades, February 3rd.

The weather continues stormy and disagreeable. Rain, snow and ice are the component parts. The detachment have been employed on the bridge as usual, notwithstanding the storm. Our old friend, Captain Wallen, has made representations to the General commanding that finally have resulted in the promulgation of an order for us to continue our work, rain or shine. So we are again not so good as mules. We would very much like to be situated where the arbitrary, cowardly old cuss could not have an influence over us. But it seems our doom to be domineered over by him, and he seems to delight in annoying us.

McEnaney and Lieutenant had a good row today, in which much abusive language was used, and much of the meanness of both related by the contending parties, and only for the interference of others, they might finally [have] worked themselves up to fighting pitch. Lieutenant Robert continues the section nightly, and many of the men are interested deeply.

Fort Cascades, February 4th.

We are favored with fine weather once again. The detachment were out at the bridge at the forenoon, and everything and everybody was in the best possible mood and condition. We enjoyed ourselves much. In the afternoon, the usual preparatory cleaning took place. We seem to have been reinforced by a strong party of grumblers in the old lot of members, for never did the mania for fault finding run so high. What they would have said at last winter's treatment, I know not.

Fort Cascades, February 5th.

Weather continues fine. Inspection by Lieutenants Casey and Robert at 7:30 A.M. The remainder of the day spent reading, writing, fishing and sleeping.

Fort Cascades, February 6th.

Weather good. Lieutenant Casey has gone to Steilacoom to see his father and wife. Rhodes is gone on pass to Portland. Lance Corporal Schlag was broke by order and Artificer Smith promoted, vice Schlag reduced, which promotion raises our uncle to near the fourth heaven, and as we cajoled him into getting cigars for us, we are satisfied. There was more fooling over him than I have ever seen. All said something, and I verily think the old cuss is loony over it. Kendall expended more than a ration of his eloquence on the occasion.

Fort Cascades, February 7th.

The weather continues very good and the detachment have been employed as usual. Lance Sergeant McEnaney was broke to the rank of Corporal and ordered under arrest, charges of drunk on duty, absence without leave and neglect of duty put against him for his conduct on Sunday last, and I cannot see how he will escape punishment this time.

Fort Cascades, February 9th.

Yesterday and today are cloudy. The detachment employed in the usual manner. Rhodes returned from Portland yesterday. Nothing of importance transpired.

Fort Cascades, February 10th.

For variety we are getting rain. These constant drenchings must prove good seed for future rheumatic confinement. I am afflicted with the blues. We have been out at work constructing the bridge as usual. Corporal Walsh and the Baron von Mackett are gone to Portland on leave. The dames of that city must be seductive, or our party easily attracted, for a perfect mania seems to have taken hold of them for pleasure hunting.

Fort Cascades, February 11th.

The conditions of life remain as yesterday, except that more than the usual amount of water has fallen. We were out during the forenoon, but preparing for tomorrow's inspection in the afternoon. The usual amount of swearing at being compelled to work in such weather has been done.

Fort Cascades, February 12th.

Weather unchanged. Inspection was held in the rooms at 10 o'clock A.M. by Lieutenant Robert. The remainder of the day passed by, the men in quarters. Consumption of tobacco is the chief occupation on such days. A member of Company "H" 4th Infantry was found drowned at the bridge at Green Leaf Cottage today. He had been absent since Friday, supposed to have fallen from the bridge in a state of drunkenness.

Fort Cascades, February 13th.

Today has been a fine one. We were out at work as usual. Corporal Walsh returned from Portland per boat. The Infantryman (or his remains) were sent to Fort Vancouver accompanied by an escort of ten men. It is not known what will be done with him. [A] number of officers came here to attend a Court Martial, to be convened for the trial of prisoners here.

Fort Cascades, February 14th.

Weather continues fine, and when one can say this, we are really favored, for no place can boast of a more congenial atmosphere than this when it is fine. Sergeant McEnaney was brought before the Court Martial to answer to the charges brought against him. The findings of the Court are not known tonight, but little doubt exists but the verdict will be guilty. His adherents stoutly assert the injustice done him by Sergeants Wheeler and Smith, while the other faction as stoutly proclaims his unfitness for the position as Noncommissioned officer. Being one of the latter, I heartily wish him to the devil.

Fort Cascades, February 16th.

The weather continues fine. Detachment employed at bridge building.

Fort Cascades, February 18th.

Raining during the last two days incessantly. We did our usual number of hours without regard to weather. One is amused at the objects or subjects of arguments brought out here. Today there has been much warmth of feeling brought out about the merits of the Utah and Snake Expeditions.

Fort Cascades, February 19th.

Today has been a fine one. The detachment employed as usual. Nothing unusual occurred in our little world.

Fort Cascades, February 20th.

This is an extremely wet day, even in this land of rains. The detachment were out building the bridge in the forenoon, but were excused from duty in the afternoon. The men growl extensively, and at the present time blame Lieutenant Robert for being compelled to be out in the storms, but Sergeant Wheeler assures me that it is General Harney's order and none other that causes it.

But all things conspire to make this a very unpleasant way of living. The old hands who came out with Lieutenant Casey, are inveterate growlers and make more trouble than all the rest combined. The sentence of the Court Martial which tried Sergeant McEnaney was published today. He is thereby reduced to the rank of second class private. In my opinion, he merits the punishment, and I am glad he is so fixed that I shall experience no more of his little tyrannies.

Fort Cascades, February 21st.

Mountain mist fell in profusion during the forenoon, but the afternoon has been fine. We were out at the bridge in the afternoon. An order excusing us from duty tomorrow in honor of it being the anniversary of the birthday of George Washington was published at retreat.

Fort Cascades, February 22nd.

Weather today has been fine, as if the elements finally determined to be on its good behavior and favor in our celebrations. We were amusing ourselves in quarters and otherwise. An unusually good dinner was served and notwithstanding, some of the men are showing their feelings in the usual manner (i.e.) getting drunk. The day has passed thus far quite pleasantly. The States mail came up this afternoon, but I get no word from home, as usual of late.

Fort Cascades, February 23rd.

The weather continues fine. Work on the bridge. Quite an excitement prevails today in consequence of a number of our men being arrested at the Greenleaf Cottage by a patrol of infantrymen last night. There is an existing order for the arrest of all soldiers found outside of the garrison without a pass after tattoo. This patrol found our men at the Cottage without their passes and arrested them. It is undoubtedly a matter of spite on their part, but our men ought to have had their passes with them. All kinds of things are threatened to the infantry, and one challenge has been sent. Also, Lieutenant Robert is greatly censured by the men and all kinds of mean things said of him, such as that he did the thing, that is, being in command of the garrison, gave the men the passes and then sent the patrol to arrest them.

Fort Cascades, February 24th.

Weather continues fine. The detachment engaged on the bridge as usual. The affair of yesterday is about blown over and Artificer Latson has been the chief amusement. He insists that so soon as there is paper enough manufactured, he will write a book entitled, "the miseries and misfortunes of a poor old drunken carpenter."

Fort Cascades, February 27th.

Weather has been quite good. Detachment employed in the usual routine of duties. An altercation took place today between Kendall and Campbell. It ended in a great words and little fight.

Fort Cascades, February 29th

The weather for the last two days had been of the old Cascades kind – wet. Men on duty as usual and thus ends February of eighteen hundred sixty.

March, 1860

Fort Cascades, March 1st.

Rain and work on bridge as usual. A row about laundresses for a change. A memorial sent to Lieutenant Robert on the subject. The men don't like the way the squaws do the washing, and charge that it is only a game of the Sergeant to keep the Clutchmen for personal purposes. The memorial setting forth the matter was returned as not coming through the proper channel, so that another course must be pursued.

Fort Cascades, March 2nd.

Our condition and circumstances continue as ever. Rain continues to fall incessantly, and our duties on the bridge continue as ever. The growlers get no satisfaction from the Lieutenant concerning the matter of the laundress, and evidently, like other attempted reforms in high places, it will end in the discomfiture to the petitioners.

Fort Cascades, March 4th.

Yesterday has been much like all Saturdays and Sundays here. After inspection, myself and Wright went to the Upper Landing, partook freely of Old Bush's hospitality (i.e.) whiskey, principally. Listened to much talk concerning the newly discovered gold diggings on the Samilkamene River,* just where said river is located seems difficult to

---

* There does not appear to be a river "Samilkamene" in Washington however, in the general area Peck mentions, "Colville," there is Ghamokene Creek but this is south of the Colville with the creek being more-or-less between towns of Ford and Deer Park. —bw

find out, only it is generally understood to be in the upper country and above Colville. The citizens greatly excited over the accounts coming from the mines, and one is forcibly reminded of what the early gold excitements of California must have been. Those fellows, gamblers, whiskey peddlers and laborers, are preparing to go to the diggings, but some doubts seem to exist in the minds of the more cautious as to the genuineness of the accounts, and fear another Fraser River stampede, yet cannot resist the temptation to try their fortune in the new Eldorado.

Fort Cascades, March 10th.

Another week has passed amid storm and turmoil. Our work on the bridge continues, but the most disagreeable part of our life is made up from the continual fight among the men just from West Point. Old Gerber must have rid himself of an extremely noisy element of his company, if they are a fair specimen of the company proper. The fates preserve me from being sent among them.

Fort Cascades, March 12th.

This has been a fine and delightful [day]. The mail from the States came up this afternoon and rendered most of the men content by bringing letters from home. I get two, one from mother and one from Carrie. A person must be situated like unto us to fully appreciate letters from friends and home. Captain Wallen is ordered to Washington, and stories concerning our summer destination are beginning to circulate.

Fort Cascades, March 16th.

A change in the monotony of our life. Tonight, Johnny Morton, our old San Juan friend, has been among us during the last few days. Sergeant Wheeler, Corporal Wales, Kendall and Byron, assisted by Morton, gave an entertainment for Morton's benefit this eve. It consists in a regular negro minstrel performance. The parts were well taken, and the house well filled with the elite of the town, all of the squaws and gamblers were in attendance, and were satisfied with the efforts of our amateurs.

Fort Cascades, March 17th.

The state of the weather continues wet. Duties on the eternal bridge. Lieutenant Casey came up from Fort Vancouver by the steamer

Independence. He is returned from Steilacoom, where his father, Lieutenant Colonel Silas Casey, commands. There is more than the usual amount of speculation concerning our summer's duties. It [is] generally thought that they will be important from the fact of Lieutenant Casey being in command.

Fort Cascades, March 23rd.

Our duties and the weather have been about as usual, until this morning, when we were greeted by Old Sol with a countenance all smiles, and the forenoon was like May in Connecticut. Lieutenant Casey seems quite pleased at the progress made upon the bridge during his absence. He spends the entire day with the working party and promises that it shall be known in Washington of our work.

Fort Cascades, March 25th.

Sunday morning inspection by Lieutenants Casey and Robert. Yesterday and today have been as fine as could be. Campbell and myself procured horses and went to the Upper Cascades, took dinner with Bush and listened to much talk of the gold discoveries at Samilkamene River. Parties are going in considerable numbers, and our own party are somewhat afflicted with the fever. It seems hard to be so near such rich diggings as are there reported, and be unable to try one's fortune among the gold fields.

Fort Cascades, March 28th.

Weather continues good. The work on the bridge continues. By an order from General Harney, Lieutenant Casey and fifteen men leave here and proceed to Fort Vancouver for the purpose of exploring and opening a trail or road from Vancouver to some point on the Cowlitz River. The country to be passed through is a very difficult one to penetrate. Three expeditions fitted out for the same purpose have failed to get through, and it remains for the Engineers Detachment to finally open this country. The detail is not made yet, so it is unknown who is to be of the party. (37)

Fort Cascades, March 29th.

The detail for the Cowlitz River duty is Sergeant Smith, Corporals Walsh and Smith, with twelve artificers and privates. Fortunately, I am to remain to assist in completing the bridge, much to my satisfaction, for I disliked going into the mountains with the months of

April and May before us [—wet]. And further, I find with Sergeant Wheeler, I get humbugged around less than with any other non-com in the detachment.

Fort Cascades, March 31st.

Weather continues fine. The detail of Artificers to go with Lieutenant Casey are Campbell, Hackett, Schlag, Leese, Privates Krikser, Carmichael, Maher, O'Donaghue, Reily, Caughlin, McEnaney and Jordan, and most of them are in fine spirits in being selected to perform such a difficult task, and one that so many have failed in. However, we feel quite willing they should have all of the glory to be gotten from wallowing in the mud for the ensuing two months, at least. Lieutenant Casey is greatly elated at being selected for this duty and wherefore we of the common herd cannot conceive, for it is generally understood that the Commanding General sends him to get rid of the vexed question of rank arising between Lieutenant Mallory of the 4th Infantry and Casey.

April, 1860

Fort Cascades, April 1st.

Weather fine. The usual Sunday morning inspection by Lieutenants Casey and Robert. Day spent as Sunday usually is, when nothing in particular is done.

Fort Cascades, April 2nd.

Today opens encouragingly for the Casey party, it having rained in torrents the entire day. Lieutenant Casey and party left per steamer *Carrie Ladd* this P.M. enroute for Fort Vancouver, thence to the woods.

Fort Cascades, April 8th.

The weather has been bad the entire week. We have been engaged as usual. Unless the reduction of numbers makes our routine somewhat more pleasant, we have more room in quarters, which were crowded before, and our discipline less strict. The party are now at Fort Vancouver fitting for duties. The mail from home came, brought me papers but no letters. Our usual Sunday morning inspection was held by Lieutenant Robert this A.M.

Fort Cascades, April 15th.

Another Sunday morning inspection and the remainder of the day spent in quarters smoking and sleeping. Weather for the week has been bad. We have been at the bridge. A growl comes up from the detachment at Vancouver and discontent seems to be with them. General Harney does not seem overawed by the superiority of Lieutenant Casey, and they are finding that an Engineer Soldier isn't so much of a fellow in this department, finally. It is a noisy element gone from us.

Fort Cascades, April 22nd.

Sunday and its duties over again. The week has been spent at our usual duties. We cannot complain at the amount of labor we are doing, for it is small, but life [is] so monotonous and dull.

Fort Cascades, April 29th.

Inspection by Lieutenant Robert at 9 o'clock, A.M. Balance of day passed in and around quarters. There has [been] nothing of interest transpired in the detachment.

May, 1860

Fort Cascades, May 1st.

Yesterday and today were extremely unpleasant. We mustered for another two months pay yesterday and spent the balance of the time bridge building. The river is rising fast and fears are entertained that operations will necessarily be suspended in consequence. The steamer *Carrie Ladd* could not get to her landing today in consequence of the current having become so strong. And the wharf boat has been moved about 13 miles down the river from the usual landing place.

Fort Cascades, May 12th.

Since my last entry we have had the usual time of duty at bridge building, with a majority of unpleasant weather to perform it in. May seems about as unpleasant a month as any in the year. now, rain and hail, with sunshine rarely interspersed, has prevailed. Lieutenant

> Perhaps nowhere in the world are so fine salmon caught as in the Columbia River, and in such numbers that for the small sum of two bits (25cts) one can get a fish weighing from 25 to fifty pounds, and we avail ourselves of the opportunity.
>
> —May 20, 1860

Robert has become so ambitious to get this structure finished that there is no excuse on account of weather. A party of Royal English Engineers are here by the *Ladd* enroute for Colville and the boundary survey. They seem mostly ax men and display no very brilliant spirits in their profession.

Fort Cascades, May 13th.

Sunday morning inspection at 9 o'clock A.M. by Lieutenant Robert. Quite a pleasant day. Myself and some others went to the Upper Landing, received letters from Annie. Mailed others to Joe, Jan and Mother. We turned out to witness punishment. A foolish fellow, having deserted from Company "A" 4th Infantry, was apprehended, tried, found guilty and sentenced to be branded with a letter D, receive fifty lashes on his bare back and drummed out of garrison, which sentence was executed upon him today. Everyone connected with this garrison was compelled to witness the whipping. The culprit having been previously branded, was led under an open shed, stripped as low as his waist, his hands triced up, and the lashes given by members of his company, two [of] which were chosen by lot and administered 25 blows each. The lot fell on one old soldier and one recruit.

The punishment inflicted by the old soldier was light, but in the case of the recruit, was somewhat more severe. But in neither instance was blood drawn. This punishment is always performed by the musicians, but there are none at this post. It seems a barbarous custom to flog men in this manner and ought to be abolished. But the poor devil says now that it is over, he is right glad to become a citizen once more, at that rate even, and surely for the amount of punishment inflicted, I don't doubt it.

Fort Cascades, May 20th

Weather and duty continue about as usual. Still, we fancy summer is near. Salmon and strawberries have become quite plenty and add much to our mess. I have never seen wild berries in such profusion as grow on these prairies. Each of us go out every evening and gather sufficient for his supper, about a quart generally, and Chinese sugar and fresh bread have a supper worthy [of] any Lord. Even if the sugar does cost 50cts per lb. And for breakfast few fare so well. Perhaps nowhere in the world are so fine salmon caught as in the Columbia River, and in such numbers that for the small sum of two bits (25cts) one can get a fish weighing from 25 to fifty pounds, and we avail ourselves of the opportunity and are quite luxurious in our habits.

Fort Cascades, May 27th.

Another Sunday inspection. A pleasant day throughout. on the 22nd a thundershower, about the first since we came to this country. Heaven's artillery played with a vigor rarely excelled. The spectacle was grand and terrific, as the lightning flashed over and among the mountain tops and seemed running down their sides, followed by the thunder peals that made the earth tremble with its force.

I met John Wedmore today, a native of New Haven and brought to manhood by our neighbor, Mr. Elias Bishop of Cedar Hills, and although almost an entire stranger to me, the meeting was one of real pleasure to me, and to him seemed equally so. One meets a person that he has known once, or even known of, with far different feelings than would seem possible to those who have never been so entirely isolated from friends and home. Wedmore is fol-lowing the life of a frontiers-man working some, dreaming continually of making a lucky strike, securing his pile and then for home. He may succeed, as life here seems so en-tirely like banishment from civilization that one could not wish to remain for many years voluntarily.

Fort Cascades, May 28th.

Weather is becoming somewhat more endurable, less rain and considerable sun. General Harney came to the Cascades today to inspect our work, and although the bridge is a far different structure than he expected to be built, he seems pleased with our efforts. The general desire among the men is to remain here all summer.

Fort Cascades, May 31st.

The last two days have been wet, and in consideration of the progress made on the bridge, we were allowed to come in out of the

167

wet. Stories as concerning our destination this season are continually circulated. Probably we will join Lieutenant Casey and be in the woods all summer. All intelligence of them is of a nature not calculated to inspire one with the desire to join the party.

June, 1860

Fort Cascades, June 7th.

The weather is suddenly become like summer, and our life here is more endurable as we get out in the timber and on the prairie more, not being confined to quarters by the rain. For the last few days a perfect system of loafing has been adopted, since our bridge gets nearer completion, for fears of getting done and being sent to the mountains makes the men feel anxious to delay the thing, as all of the work done now shows the Lieutenant is deceived and thinks our progress is wonderful. Rumors of Lieutenant Casey and party returning to Vancouver are in the air, some think, for the purpose [that] the entire party will return to West Point.

Fort Cascades, June 13th.

Summer seems to have commenced in reality and it grows warm quite fast. Two of our men, Dan McGill and Jim Love, are discharged by expiration of service and started for the States today, and they so lately from there and us poor devils must remain. Uncle Mark returned from the lower country, having been in Portland, and had, according to his tale, a grand time, and comes home immensely satisfied with himself and greatly disgusted with soldiering. Generally longs for independence and cares little for the honors of the Spanish Chief.

Fort Cascades, June 17th.

Sunday morning inspection at 9 o'clock A.M. the day spent much as usual by the members of the detachment. Our duties at bridge building are literally ended, as the structure is now completed, and only now requires the filling in of the approaches on either side of the river or slew. And it is a work for which none of us much blush, as it is said to be the best built structure of the kind in the Territory, and some say on the coast. Built by citizens, the cost would have been so great that the outlay would have been unwarrantable, and nothing of the kind been thought of, but from having been done by us, who must get our pay at any rate, the expense will never be felt, and a few rheumatic twinges felt by us in consequence of some of the severe drenchings we have gotten on the work, will be nothing to the pikes who will be benefitted by it.

Fort Cascades, June 21st.

Today we finished entirely at and around the scene of our winter's work. By tearing away the old bridge, which all thought would have gone by the force of the current sometime ago, this structure was put up under directions of that humorous writer, Doestick [Derby], an officer, then of the Topographical Engineer Corps, and on duty in this department. And now what next, is the inquiry of everyone of the boys.

Fort Cascades, June 25th.

This has been the warmest one experienced in this territory since we came, 92° in shade, and drives us all thence.

Lieutenant Robert returned from The Dalles, where he has been to turn over property on his papers. Orders assigning us to some other duties are looked for daily.

Fort Cascades, June 25th.

Another quite warm day. There is a general upturning here tonight, for we are under marching orders and leave here to join Lieutenant Casey's party at Fort Vancouver tomorrow. There is a general feeling of gratification at being ordered to join them. Some think it is the first stage in a homeward bound journey, else why are they returned? It would cause every heart to leap for joy, should this prove true.

We shall leave this place with some pleasant remembrances at last, for the last few days have been so fine, and our work so much more pleasantly conducted than at any previous time, that it has been quite an episode in our soldier life. Then these greasy Indians seem to have some real regrets at our leaving and, impossible as it may appear, there is quite a friendship existing among us. I think at these times of home more than at any other. The contrast between the two lives seems greater at times like this, when we get ready and move with so short notice and little care as to our destination only, so we change.

Fort Vancouver, June 27th.

We left the Cascades per steamer *Carrie Ladd* at 3 o'clock P.M. and had the most delightful trip ever experienced by me. The scenery is grand, vegetation in its most attractive dress, with balmy atmosphere, made everything lovely. Arriving here, we find Lieutenant Casey and party awaiting us. The literal truth seems, after penetrating some forty or fifty miles, the Lieutenant backed out, returned, reported the route impracticable and, on being directed to return, has obtained sick leave and is going to his wife and father at Steilacoom on Puget Sound per the next steamer. Lieutenant Robert is ordered to continue the work with the entire detachment. Three military expeditions have failed to accomplish this object (i.e.) to get a route from the Fort to some point on the Cowlitz River, for the purpose of having land communication between Department Headquarters and the posts on Puget Sound during the winter, when the river is closed. Almost everyone in the party is on a spree, general jubilee.

Fort Vancouver, June 28th.

The men are generally on a spree yet. All of Lieutenant Casey's men are growling about him and give him any but a good name. Especially is it the case with the old hands, who came with him, and have said so much for him and against little Roby. They claim to have suffered untold hardships, say he is cross and impracticable in the field and generally bad.

Fort Vancouver, June 30th.

Weather fine. Detachment doing no duty. Were mustered for pay by Major Wyse and under orders to get out of this [place] on the 5th proximo.

July, 1860

Fort Vancouver, July 4th.

No one drunk today. I guess not. There has been an excursion from Portland, Oregon to visit the garrison. All of the companies on parade but us, and a general turn of all of the citizens around about, and has reminded one of the States. It is the only attempt at a celebration we have seen since our advent into this country. General Harney has been around as lively as a school boy, and almost everybody belonging to the government frisky.

Fort Vancouver, July 5th.

The detachment have been busy in preparing for marching tomorrow, getting rations from the Commissary and turning over surplus material, storing useless clothing, and finally getting paid by Major Rugan, and lastly, the indications are more than favorable for a general intoxication. A feeling of disappointment at not going home is felt by quite a number of the party. For myself, these times of change are particularly disagreeable in consequence of the men getting so drunk. One must either join in their carousals, else be continually annoyed by their drunken wit and sarcasm.

In Camp at Salmon Creek, July 6th.

The detachment, with a train of packed mules, left Fort Vancouver at about eleven o'clock A.M. and arrived here about 2 o'clock P.M., distance six miles. Our train consists of 36 pack mules, 5 citizen employees and 29 of our men, the whole in charge of Lieutenant Robert. John Corlis, pack master, [is] in charge of the mules. The country traversed is hilly, with a heavy growth of pine timber, good soil, and generally free from stones.

Salmon Creek, July 8th.

We have been inspected today, complimentary orders made, and due praise given us for the manner in which we performed our duties at bridge building. The plan of our summer's duty seems to be to divide the party at this point, one half of the detachment remaining here under the immediate charge of Sergeant Wheeler to construct a wagon road, the other half to proceed with Lieutenant Robert to the point where Lieutenant Casey abandoned the trail, and continue to survey and open the country, as is sufficient for the passage of packed animals. I am detailed to go with the latter party, and much as I like Sergeant Wheeler, do not dislike to go, for there is a prospect of too much pick and shovel duty in prospect. And it seems to me if 14 men are to build a wagon road 100 miles in a country of the nature of what is in view, government must change our term of enlistment from 5 years to life, for it is rough and hilly.

Camp N.2, July 9th.

Left camp at about 9 o'clock and arrived here at 3 P.M., the country traversed being extremely hilly, and after about three miles from Salmon Creek, through burnt timber, it having been fired about 20 years ago. The old timber is all dead, and a growth of vine maples and wild peas makes it almost impenetrable. We follow the trail made by Lieutenant Casey and only made eight miles.

Camp N. 3, July 10th.

We are camped on the South Fork of Lewis or Catapote River. Arrived at 4 o'clock P.M. Distance about 9 miles, and one of the most tedious I ever experienced. From having laid in a heavy dew without tent, I was awakened about eleven o'clock with a severe tooth ache, which prevented me from sleeping or eating until tonight. Caughlin, who is cook, drew me under a cedar bush and damned me into eating bean soup, the first mouthful of which stopped my tooth ache as effectually as would the sight of a dentist's forceps. There are a number of farms on this bottom land in a flourishing condition. The land is good, and only 30 miles from Vancouver per river trail, which furnishes a convenient market for produce. Since the War of 1856, the settlers have no trouble with Indians, and little further trouble is apprehended, as the Indians have been mostly removed from here to reservations.

Camp N. 3, July 12th.

Yesterday and today have been rainy, and we have been delayed in moving, in consequence. Casey cached a good portion of his supplies here on his return. We have been busy getting them out and preparing for an advance. We are to leave our tents and all baggage that can be possibly dispensed with here and move in as light order as possible. An old Indian, said to be over 100 years old, with his son, are to go with us as guides, and Lieutenant Robert is sanguine of success.

Camp N. 4, On Klamath* River, July 13th.

We struck camp at 10 A.M., and after crossing a very rough and mountainous country, arrived here at about 7:30 o'clock P.M., a distance of 18 miles. The men generally tired and hungry. Considerable difficulty was experienced in crossing the river in the night and darkness, but found a few small potatoes here left by Lieutenant Casey, which were quickly appropriated to our use, and made a delicious supper. It is reported by those of our party who were here before that they were considerably annoyed by wolves at night here on this stream, in prospecting. Gold in somewhat flattering quantities was found by Caughlin, but were the hills full of the filthy ore, we would be none the richer for its existence, for that is not the object of the expedition.

Camp N. 4, Klamath R., July 14th.

Weather very fine. After a thorough reconnaissance by our guide (the old Indian) we commenced the duty of opening the route, or continuing to open it, for it is here Lieutenant Casey left off. The old guide says a much better route thus far might have been followed had the guide with them been acquainted with the country. We worked about 4 hours and broke off. Artificer Latson cut his foot quite severely at the first stroke with his ax.

Camp N. 4, Klamath River, July 15.

This Sabbath has been one of the most pleasant since my entrance into the service. The weather is beautiful, and our camp is one of those [most] delightful retreats imaginable, far from civilization, situated on the bank of this fine stream, completely walled in by high mountains, lies [in] this beautiful little nook. An order from Lieutenant Robert directs me to be in readiness to go to Fort Vancouver with dispatches tomorrow morning, while himself and the two Indians, with one of the packers, start for the Cowlitz River at the same time. The detachment under Sergeant Smith continues to open a trail six feet wide in the

---

* The reference should probably be Kalama River as the "Klamath" River flows from Klamath Falls in Southern Oregon into California thence to the Pacific Ocean. This error is thought to be in transcription. The publisher regrets being unable to check the original diary.—bw

courses, marked by blazes on the trees by the Indians.

Camp N. 4., July 26th.

I am arrived from Vancouver this A.M., disposed of my cargo and find myself almost sick. I arrived at Vancouver after a very severe ride, delivered my dispatches, after which I was informed that Colonel George Wright now is in command of the Department, and has gone to Walla Walla, and I must remain until he returns. Accordingly, I returned to Salmon Creek and camped with our party there until the Colonel returns. When I started to rejoin our party, I had a large cargo on my mule, and in supplying myself with rations, endeavored to take absolutely nothing beyond my actual wants. I thought I would overtake this party yesterday, and had only provisions for yesterday's dinner. I camped at 7 P.M., having no supper, built a great fire, smoked, picketed my mule to my leg, and tried to sleep.

There are plenty of bear and other carnivorous beasts here, and through nervousness caused by exhaustion, I could not sleep. The constant howlings appeared ten times more hideous than ever before, and daylight was joyfully hailed, and the loss of my revolver, which I had broken, [made by situation] ten times greater. I was in the saddle before day was fairly begun, and found the boys in good condition, and was welcomed with enthusiasm, particularly the gallon of whiskey sent by Keef as a present to the men.

Lieutenant Robert and his escort of Indians have not returned yet from the Cowlitz, but are expected daily. I am suffering considerably with pains in head and back and symptoms of fever. Have used only the available medicines (i.e.) some rhubarb root. Tonight we are missing one man. Corporal Hackett started on the return from work with the party and has not reached camp. Fires are built, guns fired, and every means used to give him a chance to find his way in.

Camp N. 6, July 27th.

Weather cloudy. The entire force except Carmichael and myself are in search for Hackett. He was found about one mile from camp. Something attracted him a short distance from the trail, and in returning he missed the proper course, and finally, after a short time, he found himself so completely bewildered that he despaired of getting out, and had the forethought to remain perfectly quiet. Made a large fire, and after smoking, laid down believing that when the sun should rise in the morning, he could get the points of compass. But at sunrise he was so far down the mountain side that (the sun) could not be seen, and it soon became so obscured by clouds that it was of no avail and, although he had made a number of attempts, he had failed to find the trail and returned to his last night's bivouac.[He] was found near the place. We are following a dividing ridge of mountains, and one getting a short distance down the sides of the mountains might never find his way out again. My illness increases, and I am so unwell as to be unable to walk any distance. The mosquitoes are troublesome and I am generally uncomfortable.

August, 1860

Camp N. 7, August 4th.

I am and have been too sick to keep up my memorandum, but mention the arrival of Lieutenant Robert and Sergeant Wheeler's party.

In Camp on Goba* River, August 9th.

Latson again went to duty, and as before, with the very first blow with the ax, drove it into his foot and injured him[self] so badly as to have to be sent to hospital. I am a trifle improved, yet quite weak.

In Camp on Coweman River, August 14th.

The weather continues warm and the detachment pushing on. I am getting well quite slowly, and move only when the commissary [Headquarters unit with cooking equipment and foodstuffs] does. We have been in this camp since the 11th. The route and country encountered are as rough as is possible to traverse, the detachment having advanced less than 2 miles in 4 days. Caughlin has found the color of gold at this creek or river, which shows conclusively that the precious metal exists all along the rivers in this mountain range. We are led to believe that we are in the vicinity of some beautiful lakes, concerning which there is a legend among the Indians, which is related by them as follows:

> Once many suns ago an Indian boy went out to hunt for deer.
> He, after wounding one, followed him several days and finally arriv-

---

* The name of the river is spelled "Gobar," actually, "Gobar's River." This was an earlier name for the Coweman River which Peck mentions in his entry for August 14. —bw

ed in sight of these lakes in time to see his wounded game take (to] the water and swim to the other shore. Pulling off his clothes, he swam after him, but on getting in the middle of the lake he was surrounded by beautiful water nymphs and made captive by them, and finally their chief, and is now living with these most beautiful beings as such, and no Indians dare go near the enchanted water.

In Camp, August 20th.

We have been pushing through this miserably rough country as fast as possible. The timber for the last few days is alive, and we have made much greater progress than at anytime before. The weather continues good and warm. I have been on duty with the working party today, and excepting being quite weak, think I am [about] recovered. The malady seems to have been the mountain fever, of which I have had plenty. I am well tired tonight, but hope that after becoming more accustomed to the work, I shall feel less fatigue.

In Camp in pine under Brush, August 21st.

This has been an extremely vexatious day. Commenced work at 5 o'clock A.M- Met burnt country at about 9 o'clock, and immediately encountered dense pines from 4 to 10 feet high, as thick as they could possibly stand, besides immense piles of logs that required an effort of no mean character to remove. After laboring all day we camped on the ground. Water had to be packed in camp kettles. A vast amount of swearing at the situation has been done. This is the 2nd anniversary of my enlistment.

August 24th.

The same routine of chopping, lifting and swearing has prevailed. The young Indian cut his knee quite badly today, and we have found much more trouble in getting along today than at any previous time. The weather is very warm, our provisions scant and bad, the pork having been out of brine since April 10th, is soft and rusty, and having no fresh meat in two months, the men are somewhat reduced.

In Camp on Toutle River, August 25th.

And express arrived today from head quarters with orders for us to proceed to Fort Steilacoom for winter quarters, also relieved Lieutenant Robert from duty with the detachment and assigning 2nd Lieutenant Alexander to duty in his place, so that the Lieutenant is quite anxious to push through the work. In fact, it is expected that after reaching a point about 12 miles from here, an Indian trail will be met and no more cutting with the axes be done, and a march of one day will bring us to the Cowlitz River, then 100 miles more and we will be at Steilacoom and probably have an easy winter, as Lieutenant Casey's father commands the post. The drunkards growl at the prospect of wintering at Steilacoom, and prefer Fort Vancouver. Any place but the Cascades for me.

In Camp on Toutle River, August 28th.

The detachment arrived here today and found the work of getting here during the last two days less, in consequence of meeting and Indian trail and live timber. This, the river known as the Toutle, the camp of the 25th being on a smaller stream emptying into this river. We found a similar instruction as to a weir here used in the season for salmon fishing by the Indians, several ranches of whom are living here. Now it is expected we will reach the Cowlitz tomorrow, as only 15 miles intervene, and the trail is sufficiently open for pack animals. Sergeant Smith was left behind sick with Coughlin and Uncle Pete. They were expected up with the command tonight, but have not reported.

Surveyors Camp, August 29th.

I am with the surveying party. Upon leaving camp, one of this party reported sick, and I am detailed for duty in his place. Corporal Walsh in charge [who] forgot to provide rations for us, and only for meeting an Indian of whom we purchased a quarter of venison, we would have been entirely without provisions. We get on quite well by cooking the venison quite brown for bread, leaving other (parts] of it quite rare. Our surveying arrows are used as gridiron. The country traversed is rough and hilly and difficult to survey.

Cumlum* River, August 30th.

This has been an extremely warm day and we have worked hard. Our venison has diminished so much only enough for our evening meal remains. There is little of interest to record. A thunder shower threatens, our only comfort for the night is a huge fire that we intend shall be kept, that if possible we may dry our clothes after the rain.

---

* This river, or one similar in spelling or pronunciation, has not been located. —bw

Laton's Ranch, August 31st.

We were at work as soon as we could see this morning. Having no provisions, there was no delay waiting breakfast. The thunder shower of last night settled into a constant rain, and we were as completely soaked as had we been in the river. We pushed through the wet brush, the rain still falling, and arrived here at 11 o'clock A.M., and after getting dry clothes and food, done some good sleeping.

> We are well tired and weary from the extremely low diet of the day, a very small piece of bread and some coffee being the extent of our rations.
> —September 4, 1860

September, 1860

Laton's Ranch, Sept. 1st.

We carried our survey to the Cowlitz River, a distance of about 1 mile, which completes our summer's duty, the distance from Fort Vancouver to the Cowlitz being about 70 miles. Our detachment under Lieutenant Robert have opened 40 miles, the distance from the Kalama. The color of gold has been found on the Kalama and Coweman Rivers, and that is about all of value discovered, unless it be timber, some of which is fine. I measured a dead cedar trunk without bark and found its circumference 45 feet, and have seen pines still larger. The country east of the Lewis River offers fair inducements for agriculture, but after leaving that point, it has been of so rough a nature as to offer no advantages to the settler.

Gilbert and Gallagher were sent back to meet and assist in getting Sergeant Smith along. Uncle Mark has succeeded in getting drunk on Laton's whiskey. This man Laton has a fine farm, fair house, two good barns, blacksmith shop, all built by himself. Estimate his oat crop at 3,000 bushels, which finds a ready market at Portland, Oregon, [which] is reached by sending down the river to Monticello, and thence by a small steamboat. The bottom land here is good, and one or two more fine farms are near here. None so good as Laton's, who is so much pleased that the route overland to Vancouver is to go directly by his door, that he treats everyone to whiskey as often as they will drink. He is 60 years old and active as a boy.

Toutle River, Sept. 2nd.

Gallagher came in and reported Sergeant Smith quite poorly, and the force too small to get him further, and eleven of us were detailed to return here for him. The march was the most rapid one I have ever made, much of the distance done at double quick time, 3h[ours]-10m[inutes]. The Sergeant is almost unconscious, and must be carried the fifteen miles by hand on a litter or bearer.

In Camp on Cowlitz River, Sept. 3rd, 12 P.M.

At daylight our party were astir, and after a very light breakfast, were on the march. The morning was very wet, and all of our blankets required to protect the Sergeant from the rain, which increased his weight to about 200 pounds. In consequence of the extreme roughness of the trail, only two men could do duty at one time, and often they could carry him only about 100 yards without change.

The rain poured down, rendering the footing difficult. He was unconscious during the entire trip of 15 miles, which was accomplished at one o'clock P.M. He was taken to the river and put into a canoe, and the services of an Indian secured, who with Sergeant Wheeler and Artificer Campbell, started down the river for Monticello, hoping to get him to Fort Vancouver by the steamer from Monticello. Doubts of him living to reach that point are entertained. Immediately on our arrival, orders for a move were issued and the intervening time has been used in getting into camp here on the west bank of the river.

In Camp, September 4th.

It was found this morning that our commissary was running low, there being only one pound of flour to each man on hand and one hundred miles [yet] to Steilacoom. Chorlis, the chief packer, and the Lieutenant had an altercation in consequence. It ended in talk, and only delayed us in getting on the march, which we did at 8 A.M., and made 12 miles over a level trail, camping at about 2 P.M. Thus far, the soil is clay and seems well adapted to agriculture and stock raising. we are well tired and weary from the extremely low diet of the day, a very small piece of bread and some coffee being the extent of our rations.

In Camp at Mound Prairie, Sept. 5th.

We made 30 miles today over a good trail, and halted 3 hours at Skookumchuck River. There is a store kept by a rogue of a Jew. Three of us, Leese, Caughlin and myself, started in advance of the command on pretext of sore feet, and made excellent time, arriving at the store full three hours in advance of the others, and devoured all that the Jew had of crackers, and no small quantity of whiskey at Benjamin's expense. On the arrival of the train, Lieutenant Robert attempted to provide commissary stores for the command, but could only get a few pounds of salt beef, which upon being cooked, proved to be spoiled by age. Most of the men succeeded in getting full of whiskey, and at 2 P.M. we left the Jew, most of the command well filled with com [*sic*] juice. It was here at Skookumchuck that a nephew of I. I. Stevens, then Governor of Washington Territory, was drowned in attempting to cross the river.

Yellow Prairie, September 6th.

Weather is very fine. We got on the road at 7 o'clock this morning and made 20 miles, arriving at this place at 3 P.M. The country traversed principally gravel prairie and seems almost useless for farming purposes. Nothing of interest has transpired.

Fort Steilacoom, Sept. 7th.

We left camp at 7 this morning and marched over about 20 miles, mostly gravel prairie, arriving here at 2 o'clock P.M., and may consider our summer campaign ended. As Colonel Casey commands the Post, and the Lieutenant has established himself here, he is gone to Olympia today. There are quartered here "H" and "F" of the 9th and "C" of the 4th Infantry, many of the men on quartermasters and extra duty. Our summer's work seems to be considered quite a success and of great importance to the people on the Sound, as by it communication may be kept during the winter with Fort Vancouver and Portland. The garrison here is about two miles from the town of Steilacoom. It is in the form of a perfect triangle on the end of a prairie of several miles in extent. There are a number of small lakes or ponds near, and one ought [to] enjoy himself here as well as in any place in the territory. The country about here is considerably settled, and one sees much of civilization moving around here.

Fort Steilacoom, Sept. 8th.

Weather fine. During the forenoon we were busy about cleaning our quarters, took down the old bunks, and after renovating the building, we are to have new iron ones. In the afternoon I was in the town and find that there is less doing here than I had supposed. I had seen the place from the deck of the *Northerner* enroute for San Juan, and it then appeared much larger. There are a number of stores, and quite a trade is done with the surrounding country. I took occasion to invest $1.50 in a square meal, much to my satisfaction.

Fort Steilacoom, Sept. 9th.

This, the anniversary of my birthday, has been passed at work about our quarters. Lieutenant Casey returned and was among the men, seemed most anxious to make us comfortable, and is to have our rooms fitted in good shape.

Fort Steilacoom, Sept. 10th.

There has been some rain today. We drew our quarterly allowance of clothing today, and a detail made for quartermaster's duty. I am to drive a six mule team. Lieutenant Casey came to the quarters and selected myself first, then Thom Lease and Pete Schlagg for that duty. We will be paid 35 cents per diem extra and be excused from all garrison duty. I could smile to see me driving through the streets of New Haven astride the hindmost of six long eared devils. Still, I do not mind it here, and it will relieve the monotony of garrison life at this lonely point.

Fort Steilacoom, Sept. 11th.

I reported for quartermaster's duty this morning and soon found myself in full charge of my six mules. Commencing with the saddle animal, I find him a large, powerful fellow weighing about 1200 pounds, and a good specimen of muledom. His mate, Fan, is a coarse grained blue animal, would weigh about 1250 in good flesh, terribly given to stumbling. My left hand swing is a pretty red fellow called Jack, and has all of the virtues ever possessed by mule. His mate, Katie, is coal black, with an affliction of the head that renders her extremely restive in handling. She is active and pleasant in the team. White, my near leader, is a powerful gray, with a strong partiality towards his own wants, but generally a good leader. Rilly, his mate, is a powerful little black, very quick, and I found the green driver first of

181

any in the team. He is constantly looking for chances to loaf, and yet is not lazy. My first duty was carting camp and garrison equipage for company "C" 4th Infantry to the wharf, they going per steamer to Whatcom for duty. The first mule I struck was myself, having given my black snake whip a preparatory flourish, I let go for a tremendous blow on my off swing, but owing to some miscalculation, I received the full force of said blow on my devoted head.

There is a party going with Lieutenant Casey to survey Point Defiance, a promontory some thirty miles from here towards the entrance to the Sound. The object of the survey being a reconnaissance for a fortification for defense of Olympia and Steilacoom.

Fort Steilacoom September 12th.

Weather cloudy all day. A boat was sent to Point Defiance for the use of the going in and coming out. General Orders relating to the future duties of the detachment [are issued].

Fort Steilacoom, September 13th.

Lease, Schlagg, Carmichael, Supplee, Livermore and myself are the force detailed on quartermaster's duty. Lieutenant Casey and nine men are gone to Point Defiance.

Fort Steilacoom, September 15th.

Lieutenant Casey and party returned from their survey today, having finished.

Fort Steilacoom, September 18th.

The weather is very fine and beautiful. The mail steamer arrived last night. Lieutenant Alexander and Lady came by her. McEnaney is discharged and gone to the States. We also learn that Corporal Carter is discharged and gone to his home. Corporal Walsh and four men are gone to Point Defiance to try to find water more convenient for garrison use.

Fort Steilacoom, September 22nd.

Weather continues fine. I am driving mules yet. The paymaster visited us and payed off the garrison, and as usual, a general drunk is in progress. Almost the entire party on a spree. The effect on the few sober ones is anything but pleasant, for they are cross and fighting among themselves and everyone else.

Fort Steilacoom, September 24th.

Weather continues beautiful. Corporal Walsh and 13 men are gone to the post garden to assist the gardener in harvesting the crop. Colonel Casey adopts a plan of post garden to the work, of which the entire garrison contributes, and all troops stationed at the post share in the vegetables, and we find them most convenient, having had none for the entire season. And such vegetable soup and roasted potatoes as we indulge in I have never before eaten.

October, 1860

Fort Steilacoom, October 5th.

Weather not altogether pleasant today. Nothing of interest has transpired since my last. Uncle Mark has been on a continuous drunk for several days, and will finally make it an anniversary celebration, I believe, as this is the anniversary of our leaving West Point; the two years are gone by and the time seems short indeed. Still, look back, and we have passed through many trying scenes and undergone many hardships, more by far than is experienced by many, and I believe a majority, in an entire lifetime. Still, I often feel that it is the best possible lesson I could have. Of course, all of the fine things I expected from the service are not realized. I may say, none of them. But I have seen and traversed much of the country that I should never have done, and if I live to return to friends at home, I shall feel paid for all. There comes to us faint sounds of a fierce political contest at home, one that threatens much evil for the future.

Fort Steilacoom, October 8th.

Nothing different from the usual routine of duty has transpired until today. Another party are gone to Point Defiance to make some further search for water. The States mail came over from Olympia today, but I got no letters from home.

Fort Steilacoom, October 9th.

Steamer *Brother Jonathan* came around last night. Sergeant Wheeler, Campbell and Latson came from Vancouver in her. Latson has recovered from the effects of the wound on his foot. They report leaving Sergeant Smith quite low, but the crisis in the disease passed and it is thought he will recover.

Fort Steilacoom, October 18th.

The weather has been beautiful. The detachment are almost all engaged in getting vegetables from the garden, a duty they much like, as they get plenty of vegetables to eat and discipline is relaxed while in camp at the garden. The States mail came today, and by it a letter for me. Notice of the promotion of Gilbert, Krikser, Reily, O'Donoghue and myself to be Artificers, the promotions to date from the 23rd of March last, was received today. I am completely surprised, as I had no knowledge of having been recommended for promotion, so that is my first step upwards in this service, and the chances are against any further rise in this corps.

Fort Steilacoom, October 20th.

While coming from the garden today, my saddle mule became sulky at being driven faster than usual and fell on me. I was drawn about 25 feet with my leg under him, and that member severely injured. The bones are injured, and I am unable to walk unless I am assisted by a crutch. (38)

November, 1860

Fort Steilacoom, Nov. 6th.

Nothing important has transpired today. the men commence a course of practical instructions in SAR Drill, or in preparing siege material for such a course. Company "F" of the 9th Infantry give an entertainment tonight, at which considerable quantities of beer, liquors, etc., besides dancing, are indulged in.

Fort Steilacoom, Nov. 10th.

The steamer *Brother Jonathan* came around today and brought Sergeant Smith. He is almost recovered from his illness, but looks thin and delicate.

Fort Steilacoom, Nov. 19th.

Major Emory, acting Inspector General for this defense, inspected the garrison today. Our men feel particularly elated, thinking that they made a fine appearance. The quarters looked very clean, and our shooting was better than either of the infantry companies. The entire garrison building and everything pertaining to the post was closely inspected, the entire day

Fort Steilacoom, Nov. 22nd.

After inspection, Ralph Wright and myself procured horses and went to the Nisqually Indian Reservation. I find them quite well provided for, having good frame houses to live in and getting a great portion of their living from government. Some of them attempt some farming, but I judge from appearances that they do not get much crops, being too lazy to care for them. We also stopped at the trading post of the Hudson's bay Co. and bought such articles as we needed. The distance from Steilacoom to Nisqually is 17 miles, and makes a decent little ride, and I enjoyed the canter over the prairie very much.

December, 1860

Fort Steilacoom, December 1st.

The steamer *California* arrived here from San Francisco bringing newspapers and mail announcing the election of Abraham Lincoln as President of the U.S. The canvas has been an exciting one, and grave results may attend. Talk of secession by the southern states is indulged in, and war is most likely the end.

Fort Steilacoom, December 8th.

A party composed of Sergeant Wheeler, Corporals Walsh and Smith, Artificers Gilbert and O'Donoghue and Private Wright are gone to San Juan Island to make a different survey for a government reservation. They will remain away some days before completing it, I think.

Fort Steilacoom, December 25th.

The weather is much more mild than at the same latitude on the Atlantic coast at this season, but we get considerable rain and have had some frost. This Christmas has gone. We, some of us, took dinner with Company "H" of the 9th Infantry and enjoyed it much, as such dinners are generally enjoyed. It is a big thing, because it is an attempt at something social, and is appreciated as such.

January, 1861

Fort Steilacoom, January 1st, 1861.

Another year comes around and finds us as we have been, but if any reliance can be placed upon any of the great many rumors that come to us from the States, there is much to fear from the change of administration. We get no details, but rumors [are] that some of the southern states have already seceded and that Lincoln will not be inaugurated. This means war, if it means anything, and then where will it all end? Certainly not in division of the States, for then there would be constant strife between the two nations.

And then again, the North has more men and more money than the South has, and must in the natural course of events be victorious in the event of a resort to arms, and after that a subjected South. In the case of hostilities in the field, the war will be long and bloody. The South, with their prejudices, will contest the question to the bitter end, for they must finally yield to the North, who possesses the most men and money.

Fort Steilacoom, January 7th.

The weather during the past week has been dull enough. Rain fell for three or four days, and the last two, snow accompanied it in good quantities, but does not remain on the ground. The men, many of them, have been on a spree most of the time, and continue it. This is the most demoralizing place for the men that we have been in. The citizens of the town court the company of the members of the detachment. The troops stationed here are extremely friendly, and as a result, spree succeeds spree until it is becoming a continual debauch.

We get news from the States of a less alarming or more pacific nature. The men continue to be employed on making siege material, which labor consists in gathering hazel from the woods and forming fascines, gabons, sap rollers and sap fagots.

Fascines are bundles of small poles cut to a regular length of about 8 feet, and firmly bound together by withes made of hazel. The bundles are 8 inches in diameter and used for revetting the interior slope of an earth work, or that portion of it that rises above the gabion.

The gabion is a basket work barrel without heads, only the sides are straight, is made of hazel or some other small kind of touch nature, is used for revetting interior slopes of earth work and saps. It is placed along and directly in front of the sap, or trench, that is to be. The earth is first thrown into the gabion until filled, then over and beyond them, thus forming the parapet of the work. The gabion first protects the men from the enemy's fire, and afterwards forms a revetment, or retaining wall, and prevents the earth from falling back into the excavation. It is used also as a revetment in the check of embrasures and other places where the slopes are so great as to require a retaining structure to keep the earth in place.

Sap rollers are large basket work structures about 9 feet long and 3 feet in diameter, made of the same material as the gabion, and, filled with fascines, they are placed directly ahead of the men in the direction of the course of a sap, and are supposed to protect the working party and resist musketry and grape or canister shot.

Sap faggots are bundles of sticks cut to a regular length of about three feet, with one of their ends sharpened so as to penetrate the ground somewhat. They are used in connection with the gabion, and afford protection to the men along the line of work or sap, being set upon the end which has its sharp points directly against the gabions and in front of where two gabion sides meet, thereby strengthening the joints, as it were.

The object of the men being now so employed is merely instruction for the younger members and practice for the old hands. This work is principally for field or temporary use, and is one of the many legitimate duties of a sapper & miner, in fact, one of the most important ones. Lieutenant Casey harangued the men on the possibility of their being soon put into positive use in these duties, and at our first drill at sapping, complimented me on having proved myself the best sapper of the entire party, having gotten the quickest and best cover. He is very practical when at drill, and compels as much caution and the same care in all of its maneuvers, as [if] we were indeed before an enemy.

Fort Steilacoom, January 13th.

We have been occupied in practice at siege material. The weather has been snow, rain and sun, and our life corresponds with the elements. Continual broils and excitement agitate our community. The men have been on pass today, it being Sunday. This evening Sergeant McKanlus went to the house of McKibben and called for his wife, who had been stopped at the Lieutenant's house by reason of McKanlus's treatment to her being so unkind. Upon her appearing at the door, McKanlus deliberately discharged the contents of one chamber of a revolver at her, the ball taking effect in her breast. McKanlus is Orderly Sergeant of Company "H" 9th Infantry, and generally liked. He is now in the guard house. It seems he has been jealous of his wife, and through this cause [they have] not lived happily with each other for some time, which caused Mrs. McKanlus to finally go to Lieutenant McKibben's. It is thought the wound will not be fatal.

Fort Steilacoom, January 16th.

Weather and duties continue about as usual. Sergeant McKanlus was taken to jail by the civil authorities. Considerable excitement exists over the matter and numerous stories are circulated concerning his treatment of her, one of which is that he had compelled her to promise to get a divorce and then be his mistress; this promise was made with the muzzle of a pistol at her head.

Fort Steilacoom, January 21st.

There had been a light fall of snow each of the last few nights, but the next day's sun melted it away until today [when] the air is somewhat cooler an about two inches remain on the ground. Sergeant McKanlus had a hearing before a justice today, and in default of $3,000 dollars bail was remanded to jail to await trial before the superior court. There is great indignation felt at him for his behavior in court today, and the feeling is so strong against him that he would not be safe from the populace were he at large.

January 22nd.

More crises came. This morning Lieutenant Casey's servant girl did not get up and get breakfast in time, and an effort on the part of Mrs. Casey to arouse the servant in the room discovered the existence of a man in the bed, which turned out to be Maher of the detachment. The Lieutenant confronted the young man and wanted to know if he was married to that woman. Maher said: "No." Then said Casey: "You must be at once." The boy said: "Not if he knew himself," and away he went to the guard house, where he has remained all day. And now he has consented to marry, and preparations are being pushed forward for the ceremony to be performed this evening. Johnie Riley is the great mogul in the affair, and I believe was instrumental in persuading this gay* young Lothario to comply with the Lieutenant's demands.

Fort Steilacoom, January 24th.

Uncle Mark Supplee is in the Guard House, having hoisted aboard too great quantities of snake juice. Maher and wife are being serenaded tonight, and whisky being furnished in great quantities. In fact, one would almost think the parties had contracted an honorable alliance, but as I am not one of the interested parties, I need not find fault with the arrangement.

January 29th.

The abominable rain continues. Almost every day is wet, some portion of it at least. The detachment are engaged in practice at making siege materials, when the weather will admit of their being out. The steamer *Oregon* touched at the town and left late files of newspapers. There seems to be intense feeling in the States over the Presidential question, and secession seems probably by some of the southern states, should Lincoln be inaugurated. The papers are full of the subject, and to us who are so ill informed, are immensely interesting. We shall most likely be called home early in the spring, but the most of us would prefer remaining and being discharged here, now that we have spent so much of our term of service here and so well accustomed to the country. The advantages are chiefly from the profit in traveling expenses. Uncle Mark was sentenced today to 20 days in the guard house and 10 dollars fine.

Fort Steilacoom, January 30th.

The event of the season has transpired. In our rooms in he barracks this evening, a dance and oyster supper was engaged in, the oysters being the most attractive part of the entertainment, were brought from Baltimore, Maryland in hermetically sealed cans, and although not near so good as when fresh from the water, are yet quite

---

* *The American Heritage Dictionary of the English Language*: "Showing or characterized by exuberance or mirthful excitement; bright or lively." —bw

good. Our friend, Ned Cummings of Company "F" 9th Infantry, is in quarters tonight joining in the festivities and adding much to the eclat of the occasion by his drolleries.

February, 1861

Ft. Steilacoom, February 3rd.

This is Sunday, and after inspection the usual routine of lying around quarters, indulging in prognostications of the weather, politics and religion. Uncle Peter Smith had attended service and has been full of his hopes and fears for the future, and gives his views of the future for the rest of us quite freely.

February 4th.

The weather is beautiful, like spring. orders inaugurating a course of target practice and bayonet drill was read tonight. Bayonet drill three times and target practice per week in connection with our practical engineering [and] siege materials will keep us well employed. These exercises are partly intended as in the usual course of garrison duty, but Lieutenant Casey is looking to a time in the near future when they will be brought into requisition in the field.

Fort Steilacoom, February 7th.

Rain has fallen all day. The detachment doing nothing. Two of the sons of the Indian who murdered a man at Snohomish some time since, came to Colonel Casey and surrendered themselves today. They say that they had nothing to do with the murder, But they will be held for trial. It is generally believed that the father being dead, the sons are trying to put the guilt on his shoulders and get out of the scrape in that manner.

February 8th.

The steamer *Panama* came last night and brought dispatches from the States to effect that the steamer *Star of the West* had been fired upon by the people of South Carolina while entering the harbor of Charleston for the purpose of landing supplies for the garrison at Fort Sumpter. The information we have of the actual state of affairs is so meager that there is a constant state of excitement of the prospect of the country being plunged into war. The men generally believe that war will be the end of it, and it is with feelings of deep concern that they contemplate being called upon to cut the throats of brothers or our own countrymen, much as they would like a tilt with foreigners. This is a different affair.

The garrison at Fort Vancouver are reported to have revolted in consequence of not getting their pay. How far they have gone in their insubordination is not known, but rumor says the revolt is quite general.

Fort Steilacoom, February 12th.

Private Maher was remarried by a Catholic priest this evening, and it seems this [is] the real wedding, finally. And entertainment of which rum is the principal refreshment is in progress, and one or more disturbances have occurred.

February 15th.

The weather is much like April at home the last two days. The detachment were engaged packing the engineer property in cases, and making everything snug in order to be in readiness to move at any moment. This is our first step in war, if there be a war. At all events, Lieutenant Casey apprehends trouble, and thinks we will be ordered home soon.

February 19th.

The detachment commenced drilling at flying sap this forenoon. Lieutenant Casey was so kind as to pronounce my section the best executed portion of the work. We were out at bayonet drill under Lieutenant Alexander in the afternoon.

February 28th.

The last day of the month has been extremely fine. Another steamer came up from San Francisco last night, but we got no news from the States of a definite nature. Senator Seward had made a great speech on the condition of the country, but it does not seem to conciliate the southerner members. Secretary [of War] Floyd is reported a defaulter to the government to the amount of $1,000,000, and it is reported that the South is making every preparation for war. The Lieutenant is continually looking for orders for our return to the States.

March, 1861

Fort Steilacoom, March 1st.

This has been one of the pleasanter of spring days. the detachment have been engaged at sap drill in the forenoon. We commenced our first zig zag from the first parallel and find that, conducted under the directions of Casey, this is the most arduous duty we ever performed as a matter of instruction. it would seem that we were preparing for war, indeed. In the afternoon, we are out for bayonet drill under Lieutenant Alexander, and this, with the sap drill of the forenoon, develops one's muscles to the full extent.

March 9th.

We have had some blustering weather during the past week, but generally it has been fine. In changing the directions of the sap this forenoon, Sergeant Smith got the sap rooter in the sap and made a sad job of getting it righted, as he does of almost everything he undertakes. Some of the men laughed a little at his expense, and consequently he is quite hostile and disposed to attack everybody in our room.

March 10th.

The hostility of the Sergeant continues. He assumes the aggressive by moving into our room and occupying my bed, sending me to a distant part of the room. I incurred his displeasure quite innocently, but as his wrath is somewhat amusing, it is regarded as an entertainment by all of the men. Lieutenant Casey ordered him back into his own room at inspection and me to my old place in the room, therefore. Thus far, the advantage seems to be on the side of the men. The Sergeant is wrong, and will so find it.

Fort Steilacoom, March 11th.

Weather conglomerate. Men at the usual routine of duty. A rumor came to the post that southern men residing in California had seized the U.S. Mint at San Francisco in the interest of the Southern Confederacy. The rumor is not generally credited here.

March 15th.

Our duties are not changed, drill and garrison duty consume our time. The row between our room and Sergeant Smith continues, and causes considerable ill feeling. This, with the war news from the States, keeps up a continual round of talk and excitement among the men.

March 19th.

The affairs of this military community have continued about in the same old way. Sergeant McKanlus of the 9th Infantry has been tried in the Superior Court at Olympia for shooting his wife and sentenced to four years and two days at hard labor in the Territorial Prison, and the general feeling in the garrison is that he deserves all he got.

March 28th.

The weather during the past few days has been the worst of the season. Snow and rain have been frequent. It is reported that General Twiggs, commanding the Department of Texas, has surrendered all of the troops and government property in his hands to the secessionists, the troops being released on parole to not serve against the Southern Confederacy during the war. Mr. Hecter, who is clerk for his brother-in-law, Major Pagan, Paymaster, and who has been ailing some days, went entirely crazy today. Imagines himself President of the U.S., demanded the hauling down of the garrison flag, and was so insane as to require attendants.

Fort Steilacoom, March 31st.

The month ends as it has been for the last portion of it (i.e) very stormy and disagreeable. There is continuous excitement in the garrison concerning the condition of the country and now that all expect a civil war, and as a consequence, to be participants in it. The greatest excitement prevails, as all live in constant expectation of being ordered home, and that in itself is enough to create a general commotion. The prospect of seeing our friends so soon again is so gratifying that it outweighs every other consideration.

April, 1861

Fort Steilacoom, April 2nd.

Artificer Gilbert is discharged today by reason of expiration of his term of enlistment and goes home to New York. Major Pagan, who either has or will resign his position in the Army, is going home with Mr. Hector, and as Mr. Hector continues insane, the Major has engaged Gilbert to assist in taking charge of him to New York. It is quite fortunate for Gilbert, as he gets his passage money free for his services, I understand.

April 5th.

The weather continues abominable. It is about the worst of the entire season. President Lincoln's inaugural address has come today. It is called pacific in its tone, but it is believed the President will remain firm, and that he opposes secession. And with this belief, a hope arises that the South will not try to effect a separation of the States by force of arms. This is the hope of the North. Those best acquainted with the South think nothing will cause there to change their determination to go out, and fight they will.

Fort Steilacoom, April 8th.

After a long and intense excitement, which has prevailed during the whole time since news of the trouble growing out of the election of Mr. Lincoln, came a little puff of war [that] has reached us. The order so long talked of has come at last, and we are homeward bound. The order came about noon today, and everything is in readiness to go aboard the *Massachusetts* when she arrives. We go by her to Port Townsend, where the mail steamer for San Francisco calls for us. This is an interesting event for us, and the move on itself is a grateful end to most of us, for it takes us once more among friends and kindred, which we have so longed to see once more.

But it is in some respects distasteful to some, from the fact that their term of enlistment is expiring, and to get one's discharge here is quite a pecuniary benefit. Then others dislike going directly in front of the enemy, soldiers though they are. Corporal Demorest, more particulary than any other, desires to remain here and commence life anew as a citizen after his discharge. For my own particular preferences, I can hardly speak. I have long thought that if I should be discharged in this country, I would try to do something as a citizen, but if it is so that a great war is to be waged, the entire country will be required to assist in its prosecution, and one is most likely to be engaged finally, and ours is the most likely corps in the whole army to be active. At all events, we are off, and home is our destination. And let what come may, we will see our friends once more. whiskey is active.

On board Sloop of War *Massachusetts*, April 10th.

Weather beautiful. The detachment were quite busy in getting our camp and garrison equipage down to the wharf during the morning and getting it aboard of ship afternoon. We finally went aboard at 3 o'clock P.M. Nearly all of the people of Steilacoom, along with the entire garrison, were at the wharf to give us adieus. We left amid cheers and good wishes of the people, and are now steaming down among the islands and past meadowlands of one of the most beautiful sheets of water in existence.

Our campaigning in the mountains are at an end for the present. It is two years and six months since we left New York, and during that time we have been through much that has been unpleasant. Yet I do not regret it, for I have seen much that is interesting and some that is instructive, have seen enough of Oregon and Washington Territories to have a good idea of them, and shall have little desire to emigrate there after once getting home.

Major Pagan and family, including his brother Hector, are our companions de voyage. Many of the citizens at Steilacoom wished they belonged to us, in order to go to the States, for poor fellows will most likely die of drinking poor whiskey without ever seeing their friends again.

Onboard *Massachusetts,* April 11th.

We are lying in the harbor of Port Townsend waiting for the mail steamer. We arrived at 2 o'clock this A.M., [passed] the *Elija Anderson.* As we came in here, an express boat has gone up the sound to get any mail there may be aboard for us. Many of our men are ashore on pass today, and a great deal of excitement exists.

On board *Massachusetts*, April 12th.

We are still lying in Port Townsend Harbor, and the most sad event of our campaign has transpired. Corporal Demorest came aboard after being on pass in the town last evening and fell from the forecastle to the gun deck and fractured his skull. He was found lying on deck by some of the men about ten o'clock last evening, and it being thought that he was drunk, he was brought down below and left lying on the main deck, where he died at about 5:30 o'clock this A.M. He was buried at the garrison burying ground this afternoon with the usual military honors. I was in the firing party.

Poor fellow. His only fault was rum. A finer feeling man I never met, a perfect gentleman under all circumstances, with a high sense of honor. He wronged no man, and only for his one fault, I cannot conceive a better companion. After his interment, a subscription was made by the members of the detachment for the purpose of providing a stone to be erected in his memory. he stone will be purchased in San Francisco, and the officers of Company "D" 4th Infantry in garrison here promise to see it erected upon its arrival. Lieutenant Chace, in commenting upon the death of the Corporal, was quite severe, and in the opinion of some of the men, done him an injustice, inasmuch as the Corporal only injured himself by his intemperance, never interfering with others nor disturbing anyone when under the influence of liquor. Poor fellow.

It seems sad that the first death in the party should occur when homeward bound. And he seemed to have a premonition of disaster in his conversation with me on the day that the order for our return to the States. He said he had begun to hope he should be discharged in the department and commence a new life removed from his old associations. He thought maybe he could so live as to be of some use to himself and mankind again. Peace to his ashes.

On Board *Massachusetts*, April 13th.

We are still lying in the Harbor of Port Townsend waiting for the mail steamer. The weather shows signs of clearing up. Some of the men are gone to the garrison to a dance. The remainder are on pass, and most of us have been ashore in the town. I can see little to attract one here. It is a small town of two or three hundred inhabitants, lumbermen and beachcombers mostly. The town is situated on a bluff looking out on a pretty bay, which is a safe and commodious harbor for vessels, and being directly at the entrance of Puget Sound, will probably be a port of some importance in the future.

196

On Board Steamer *Cortez*, April 14th.

Weather fine. The forenoon was spent lying around ship until about 3:30 P.M., when this ship was seen rounding the promontory and entering the harbor, when all was excitement preparing for a transfer when the *Cortez* came alongside. The property and baggage was quickly put aboard of her, and we were soon steaming for Victoria, Columbia River and San Francisco. We are now, 6 P.M., bowling across the straits of Juan De Fuca in fine style. San Juan Island, the scene of last years operations, on our right is in plain view. Mount Baker, on the left, and Rainier on the right, raise their snow-capped heads like grim sentinels watching over their weaker and less magnificent neighbors, make a view that is grand and sublime. Mount Baker is one of the finest sights on the coast, and is thought to be a finer and more entertaining view than Mt. Hood.

On Board Steamer *Cortez*, April 15th, 6 P.M.

Weather very fine, wind southeast. We are about 20 miles off Cape Flattery. We ran to Esquimalt about 9 o'clock P.M. yesterday eve and remained until 9 o'clock this A.M. Esquimalt is 3 miles from Victoria and as that place has no good harbor, is in fact the port of that place. It is a small but perfectly landlocked harbor, with water good enough for the largest ships. Four British men of war were lying in the harbor when we came out. We were ashore last night and fell in with the men of wars, men, who could beat us to death with yarns, and our only satisfaction lay in having enough money to astonish them. We came out of the harbor and steamed down the Straits of Fuca and into the Pacific in fine style.

On Board Steamer *Cortez* April 16th.

We are lying at wharf at Portland, Oregon, having crossed the bar at the Columbia River at 5 o'clock A.M. and arrived here at about 4:30 o'clock P.M. The entire party are ashore most of the time, getting acquainted fast. Portland, next to San Francisco, is the largest American town on the coast. It has about 6,000 inhabitants, has fine and well-stocked stores, and two first class hotels, the Metroplous and Pioneer. The Nez Perce gold mines are the excitement now, good specimens are shown, and the usual rush is expected this season.

On Board Steamer *Cortez*, April 18th.

Weather fine, with a fair wind and smooth sea. We crossed the bar at 5 o'clock A.M., this makes five times I have crossed that bar, and are now, 6 P.M., off Umpqua River, a run of 150 miles in eleven hours, which is an excellent run, and it will take us to San Francisco, if continued, on Saturday.

On Board *Cortez*, April 19th.

Wind. Hauled dead ahead at 11 P.M. yesterday. We passed Cape Mendocino at 1 o'clock this P.M. and now, 6 P.M., are running over a sea as smooth as a mill pond, with a hope of making Frisco in the morning.

At Presidio Barracks, April 20th.

We came in at the Golden Gate at about 9 A.M., and at the dock at about 10 A.M., making a very short passage. We met the steamer *Golden Age* shortly after she left her wharf for Panama, so that we must wait over ten days for passage, and came here to remain until the sailing of the next steamer. We are badly off for room, with no table-ware, and decidedly uncomfortable.

Presidio Barracks, April 21st.

Weather beautiful in the morning, but the trade wind began to blow about 1/2 after ten. The winds blow so as to make it extremely unpleasant to be out of doors. Ones eyes, ears and nose gets filled, and for clothes, cleanliness is out of the question. The detachment were on pass. I visited fort at Fort Point. It is a brick work mounting about 50 guns and garrisoned by "A" and "B" Companies of the 3rd Artillery.

Presidio Barracks, April 23rd.

The detachment have been on pass. Richard Pryor died in hospital today. He has been on sick report for a long time and it was believed he had consumption of the lungs. Some thought that he would not live to get home. It will be a sad blow for his poor wife, and being on the trip home will make it seem doubly hard to bear.

Presidio Barracks, April 24th.

Pryor was buried at 12 M. today. I was one of the firing party. The fund subscribed for a stone for Demorest was found sufficient for two plain ones, and one has been engaged for both of our comrades and will be erected. It is a sad duty to perform, but Pryor had been in hospital so much, and we had seen so little of him during the last year and one-half that he will not be missed as much as Demorest.

We received pay to March 1st this afternoon, and tomorrow will be a general hegira to the city, and if some slight dissipation isn't indulged it will seem strange, for San Francisco offers many inducements for spending money.

Presidio Barracks, April 25th.

There was a fine shower last night, and the weather is delightful this morning. All of the men are on pass. The mail steamer arrived from Panama today and brought Brigadier General E. V. Sumner, a recently appointed General, to relieve General Albert Sidney Johnson of the command of this department. Rumors are in circulation that Fort Sumpter in Charleston Harbor has been captured by a Southern Army commanded by one Beauregard.

Alcatraz Island, April 26th.

By a general order issued at department headquarters, the order for our return to West Point is countermanded, and we are assigned to duty at this post. Lieutenant Casey came out to the Presidio at about 4 o'clock and brought the order and directed that we be at Meigs Wharf at 6 o'clock. There were only three men and myself at the quarters, and we packed up the property of the men and went to the wharf and were finally brought here. We are piled into a room and are uncomfortable. Most of the men are on pass. My pass expired tonight and I had returned for another and was trapped.

Alcatraz Island, April 27th.

This is a strong place. It mounts about 125 guns, mostly mounted on barbette in works cut in the rock which forms the island. Sergeant Wheeler [and] Corporals Walsh and Hackett have been in the town looking for the men who are on pass. Four only have come, and they say the others have left town and will not be seen until their passes expire. Lieutenant Casey has leave of absence and goes to Washington, probably will not return.

Alcatraz Island, April 28th.

The weather is fine in the morning, but a strong trade wind commences at about 10 o'clock A.M and continues until evening, which is extremely unpleasant. Company "H" of the 3rd Artillery is stationed at this post, and a detachment of Dragoon recruits intended for the 1st Dragoons duty in Washington Territory. This place is under the command of Captain Stuart of "H" Company, who is a Southern man. A sentinel is posted on the roof of the building used as barracks whose duty is to report all vessels entering or leaving the harbor. Another sentinel at the wharf allows no boat to land, and the men are all assigned positions at the different batteries in case of an attack on the island so that if, it is said, that the southern people in the city contemplate an attack and capture of the place, they will not find us wholly unprepared for them. (39)

Alcatraz Island, April 29th.

Weather continues pleasant in the mornings, but the wind is extremely disagreeable during the remainder of the day, after 10 o'clock. Lieutenant Casey visited the island today for the last time before going to the States. His adieus were limited to two or three, and a general growl went up in consequence thereof. Those [who have been] on pass are almost all reported for duty. Uncle Mark Supplee is absent and probably drunk. There is a rumor that Lieutenant McPherson of the Engineer Corps, who is on duty in the harbor, is assigned to duty as commanding officer of the detachment. It is hoped so.

May, 1861

Alcatraz Island, May 1st.

I am going on duty as a sentinel on post in a regular garrison. Very exciting news is received from the States, that in pursuance of a determination to concentrate troops at Washington, a Massachusetts regiment enroute for that place was attacked in the streets of Baltimore, Maryland, and that Lieutenant Jonas of the U.S. Army had burned the building and evacuated Harpers Ferry, and that a general engagement may take place at any time. This causes an immense amount of excitement among the men.

Alcatraz Island, May 2nd.

Today has been more than usually blustering, if it be possible. The garrison and its defenses were closely inspected today by the Commanding General, E. V. Sumner. Rumor sends reinforcements here, and it is confidently expected by some that the place will be attacked soon.

Alcatraz Island, May 7th.

The routine of duty has been much the same, being confined mostly to garrison duty. The news per Pony Express is exciting, and calculated to cause grave apprehension of the capture of the City of Washington itself. It is reported that an attack is meditated by the insurgents, and if so, the greatest fears are entertained for its safety. Baltimore is said to be controlled by the mob, and general disorder to prevail.

Alcatraz Island, San Francisco Harbor, May 10th.

The weather continues much the same. The wind is so blustering that it becomes quite disagreeable most every day. Highly sensational rumors concerning the state of affairs in the East are continually circulating and keep the men in a continuous state of excitement. The entire detachment are on extra duty enlarging the barracks accommodations for the use of reinforcements, and unless the place is soon captured, there will be some little difficulty in performing the operation.

May 11th.

There is a grand Union Mass Meeting held in the city today. The entire city is alive with the populace. Flags are flying from every building of any pretense, and it is said no such turn out by the people was ever seen. Addresses were made by General Shields and others. General Sumner and Staff were in the procession, and it was a grand demonstration for the cause of the Union. One is at a loss to know where the secession element is that will undertake the capture of this and the other works in the harbor. Captain Stewart compelled Uncle Mark Supplee to throw a citizen found in one of the works over the parapet today. It is not know what he was there for, but it would make little difference with Captain. I desired much to be on pass today to witness the demonstration in the city, but could not.

Alcatraz Island, May 12th.

The great parade of yesterday is the general theme today. It is claimed enough flags were flying to canopy the entire city, and I don't know how many thousand people were in the streets. We wonder where is the enemy that is to gobble us up, and if General Sumner has not put his foot in it just a trifle in countermanding General Scott's order.

Alcatraz Island, May 13th.

The weather continues the same. The wind, which is of the character of the trade winds, is extremely disagreeable. The garrison is reinforced by two companies of the 3rd Artillery, so that the probabilities of an attack on us by secessionists are becoming less and small, indeed. Intelligence from West Point informs of the promotion of a number of our men in the company, but as usual the detachment is ignored. This is a piece of injustice to this portion of the company who have been in the field so long to have younger members who have seen little or no active field duty promoted, and us left out in the cold, causes great discontent, and should a small portion of the maledictions found out on Sergeant Gerber be experienced, his would be an unenviable experience.

Alcatraz Island, May 14th.

The wind blows harder today than at any time before. The command of the island is held by Company "A" of the 3rd by virtue of his rank, much to the gratification of all, as Captain Stewart is such a tyrant. None love or even respect him.

Alcatraz Island, May 16th.

There is little or no change in the weather. The detachment are on extra duty excavating for quarters to be built for the accommodation of the troops lately arrived. There is barracks for one company, then some temporary buildings belonging to the Engineer Department, one of which Lieutenant McPherson, the Engineer officer in charge of the construction of the works, kindly gave for our accommodation. The men of the companies lately come are huddled together, and hence the necessity of the work.

Alcatraz Island, May 19th.

Today is Sunday, and clouds but less wind. The detachment were inspected by Lieutenant Robinson of "H" Company of 3rd Artillery, after which we were around quarters the entire day. There has been much absurd talk occasioned by a story to the effect that the commander of the war steamer *Wyoming*, Captain Mitchell, now in port, was going to run to Panama and turn the steamer over to the rebels, and that the forts were to fire on her if she attempted to go out.

An officer came from the sloop of war, *St. Mary*, landed and delivered a message to Captain Burton about 3 o'clock this P.M., and at about 5 o'clock the *Wyoming* steamed out by the forts, dipped her colors in salutation as she passed, and all of the excitement on that subject ended suddenly. The fact that Captain Mitchell is a Southern man is probably all the foundation there is for the story, but the state of mind that men are now in makes any story probable.

Alcatraz Island, May 26th.

The weather during the week has been much more pleasant than since we came here. The detachment on extra duty mostly. Wright and myself went to the city on pass last night and returned tonight. While at the What Cheer House last night, I met Fred Tyrroll, an old school mate and neighbor in Waterbury, and one who worked for my father the first summer that we lived in Fair Haven. Knowing him to be in these parts, the surprise to me was not great but with him the case was different. He did not know me at first, and the surprise was so great he could not control himself enough to speak for some time, and then could not understand me being in uniform.

We sat up most of the night and went to the mission Delores today. There is much to interest one there. The old adobe mission buildings, with their vesper bells hanging, the burying ground with the old head stones with Spanish and Latin inscriptions, appear and remind one of a past age and foreign country. The Willows are grounds laid out as a pleasure resort and shaded with willow trees. They are provided with swings, bowling alleys, etc., as well as refreshment tables and bars in convenient places about the grove. We enjoyed the ride in cars drawn by steam (I believe the only ones on the coast) much, and in fact this has been a day of events and interest to me.

Fred is expecting to return from Sacramento, where he goes tomorrow, and work on a church as a carpenter at 4 dollars per day, and I shall probably see him often. One must be from home, and friends as we have been, to understand and appreciate one's feelings in this meeting, and one who was so brought up and lived with one. I returned to the fort at 6 o'clock P.M. (40)

Alcatraz Island, May 31st.

We were mustered today by Captain Burton, and a more blustering day I have never stood on parade. We could with difficulty hear the words of command, such a hurricane prevailed. The detachment have been employed in erecting buildings for quarters for the Artillery companies arriving here. There are four companies here now besides the detachment of dragoon recruits and ourselves. Sensational rumors are continually afloat. one day we go with a command overland, and the next some other absurd rumor prevails. Meantime news from the states is all warlike.

June, 1861

Alcatraz Island, June 3rd.

Wind continues. The Pony Express brings a report from Missouri that General Harney has made a treaty with the state authorities which is extremely distasteful; first, as a General commanding the department he had no powers to treat with the state, and the terms agreed to are so unsatisfactory, amounting practically to "if you won't hurt me, I will let you alone."

Alcatraz Island, June 6th.

Weather continues bad. Detachment relieved from extra duty and on garrison duty again. One would believe there was really some danger of an attack from the stringency of orders on guard. The Pony Express brings intelligence of the shooting of Colonel Ellsworth of the New York Zouves at the Hotel at Alexandria, Virginia, when pulling down a confederate flag.

Alcatraz Island, June 11th.

Weather has been somewhat fine today. The party that left for Monterey are returned, and a General Order read at parade this morning directing that the detachment of Engineers detained in California when enroute proceed at once to West Point, New York, in charge of Sergeant Wheeler, and an order from General Sumner directs that we leave by the *Senora* on her return trip. She sails on the 21st. General Sumner gets a rap on the knuckles for detaining us. Everyone is elated at going home. The men are full of excitement and talk loudly enough.

Alcatraz Island, June 19th.

Our party have done no duty [for the last 8 days] since the order for our move was published. Today everything that can be is packed, and the men have done their washing and been provided with 40 rounds of ammunition in anticipation of meeting any of the Confederate cruisers, a number of which are afloat in the Atlantic, and rumor says one is on this coast for the express purpose of capturing ships of this line. Day after tomorrow will see us off for good from this coast. The last two months have been as disagreeable as any since we came.

On Board Steamer *Senora*, June 21st.

We left the Island at 6:30 o'clock this A.M. and embarked at about 7:30. Our stay at Alcatraz has been extremely unpleasant, and the most disagreeable part of our campaign on this coast. Our last day was about the worst, and the detachment left without a regret. We left the wharf at about 10:30 and are running down the coast with a fair wind and smooth sea. The ship seems like an old comrade to us, although she has undergone some alterations and repairs since we came up from Panama in her. She has her old Captain Baly. Also the First Officer, Mr. Mewen, is yet in her. Instead of the fifteen hundred passengers who came up in her with us, she has only about one hundred and fifty, among whom is the notorious and wealthy Sam Brennan [*sic*],* who once was an Elder in the Mormon Church, and since then been considered the most wealthy man in San Francisco.

We are now homeward bound, and if the elements are propitious, will be in New York by the middle of next month, and everybody is in good humor over the prospect of so soon meeting friends, and at no time since leaving home has so much real good feeling prevailed. It is a singular coincidence that there are two of our passengers who were fellow passengers out with us, and now returning. There is an unusually large shipment of gold by the steamer by reason of the protection we are supposed to afford against capture by rebel cruisers. (41)

On Board *Senora*, June 22nd.

At 2 o'clock P.M. we were in Latt. 33° 35' N, Long. 115° 00'W., distance run 240 miles. A good run and fine prospects of crossing the gulf [of California]. A disgraceful row took place between Lieutenant Lease and one of the crew tonight. Thurn was caught too near some of the ship's stores.

---

*This would be Samuel Brannan (1819-1889) a pioneer who adopted Mormanism in 1842 then led a colony of Mormons to San Francisco in 1846. He published the *California Star* in 1847, the first newspaper in San Francisco. Brannan Street is named for him. —bw

On Board Steamer *Senora*, June 24th.

Today's reckoning shows us in 27° 34' N., 11° 10' West, distance 240 miles. Nothing new transpired, except that a guard is detailed in consequence of the affair of Lease and the ship. He is full of bluster over it, but like all of his splurges, will end in gas. General and Ex-Governor Isaac. I. Stevens is aboard, going to Washington to tender his services to government. It is said he is the most thoroughly shaken from the effects of rum drinking of any person I ever met, rarely being seen out of his stateroom, only when going to the bar for his drinks, and then seems to almost totter on his legs, he trembles so. (42)

On Board Steamer *Senora*, June 25th.

Observation 24° 35' N., 112° 15' West, distance 239 miles. Sighted a steamship at 11 o'clock this A.M. A fog hung over us during the night and a portion of the forenoon, but have a smooth sea and seems making a uniform rate of speed.

On Board Steamer, June 26th.

Observation 21° 56' N. , 108° 59' West, distance run 240 miles. Sea smooth and weather quite warm. Am confined between decks most of the day by reason of being on guard. Nothing unusual occurred.

On Board Steamer *Senora*, June 27th.

Observation 19° 28' North, 105° 22' West, distance run 245 miles. The sea has been as smooth as a mill pond and we have [not] made more than our usual ten miles per hour, as we have made a stop at Manzanilla Harbor, discharged freight and took aboard quite a quantity of silver. The city of Manzanilla is inland some distance, and quite important for the mining interests in the vicinity. The harbor is the principal point from which supplies are received and silver shipped, but seems of little importance in itself. There are a few small huts on the shore, but the ground rises abruptly from the shore into quite steep and formidable hills. One can see little from the ship decks of the general features of the country, only as sailing down the coast running in full view of it, as we have done during today. One gets an idea that it is barren and sterile, seeming overgrown with chaparral and of no use unless for its mineral resources, whatever they may be.

On Board Steamer *Senora*, June 28th.

Observation 17, 102° W., distance run 223 miles. We are running along with a smooth sea and in full view of [land]. The weather is quite warm, but clouds obscure the sun most of the time, so we have not to endure the scorching sun's rays, and the decks of the ship are more endurable from being less heated.

On Board Steamer *Senora*, June 29th.

Observation 16° 36' North, 99° 36' West, distance run 165 miles. We run into the harbor of Acapulco, Mexico at 6:30 o'clock this A.M. and, moored alongside an old hull, took in coal and water. It is an amusing spectacle to witness the coaling going on with all of the traffic around the ship. The natives carry the coal aboard in sacks from the lighter, and the native bingos are lying alongside with fruit and pastry for sale, but there is less interest felt by the scene by the passengers, most of them having witnessed the thing in their outward bound trip.

The U.S. War Steamers *Sian* and *Naragansett* are lying here to protect American, and particularly [those carrying] U.S. [troops], vessels. We remained in port until 10 o'clock and sailed, giving the war vessels a salute. They returned the compliment with cheers from the crews, who manned their yards and gave us three times three in answer to our guns and cheers.

On Board *Senora*, June 30th.

Reckoning 14° North, 90° 34' West, distance run 200 miles. A severe storm broke during the last part of the night and raged a portion of the forenoon, causing heavy seas and rough times. Sea sickness showed itself quite plentifully.

July, 1861

On Board Steamer *Senora,* July 1st.

Reckoning 13° 51' North, 92° 58' West, distance run 240 miles with head wind and some rain.

On Board Steamer *Senora,* July 2nd.

Reckoning 11° 27' North, 90° 33' West, distance run 223 miles. Sea somewhat rough with occasional rains. The atmosphere is cool and pleasant. We had quite a gale during the night. A sail in sight caused some excitement, as there is a bright lookout for Jeff Davis privateers are reported cruising for craft of this line, the object being the specie aboard.

On Board Steamship *Senora,* July 3rd.

Reckoning 9° 45' North, 85° 57' West, distance run 240 miles. Cloudy weather, but sea more smooth than for the last two days. Passed the steamer *Golden Age* in her upward trip.

On Board Steamship *Senora,* July 4th.

Reckoning 7° 25' North, 82° 47' West, distance run 260 miles. It is only 240 miles to Panama. The day has been celebrated on board with enthusiasm. A platform was erected on the after part of the upper deck and addresses delivered by Ex-Governor Isaac I. Stevens [and] Samuel Bernnan who was also President [...]. We were favored with songs and speech, and resolutions of patriotism were offered. The detachment had reserved seats and flattering allusions [were] made to our future. Brennan had large quantities of brandy-punch made for us, enough to make us drunk for a month, had we drank it, and on the ship the day has been spent much as it usually is on shore. Certainly sentiments of patriotism prevailed, and the authors of the present war denounced heartily.

On Board Steamship *North Star*, July 5th.

We arrived in Panama Bay at 10 o'clock A.M. and were transferred to a lighter at once, and came ashore and went at once aboard the train for Aspinwall and [then we] left Panama almost immediately. The sights and scenery along the line of the railroad was much the same as on the outward bound trip. Upon arriving at Aspinwall, we were allowed to go aboard and deposit our accouterments and pass on and off at will, so that the 4 hours of stay here has been pleasantly passed by us, and at 6 o'clock a signal gun announced the sailing of the ship.

The Brigadier of War *Bainbridge* is lying here and manned the yards and gave us three times three hearty cheers as we run by her in leaving. The night is dark, and we are running without lights, a not very safe operation, but deemed judicious by our captain, in view of the rebel craft supposed to be in these waters. We are at last headed towards home, and [in] a few short days will see New York and home, we hope, if this confounded war does not deprive us of a furlow. There is less enthusiasm among the men on the approach of home than would be expected.

On Board Steamship *North Star,* July 6th.

No bulletin of today's observations was published today. There are Southern resigned naval officers aboard, and it is said Capt. Jones of this steamer is in great fear of our being captured by privateers. We were near running down a vessel during the night, and [this] created considerable excitement among the passengers, who felt sure we had encountered a privateer ship. We were inspected this morning, the first since [leaving] Alcatraz Island. It is ascertained that we made 204 miles in the 18 hours.

On Board Steamship *North Star*, July 7th.

We are running up against a strong head wind with a rough sea, and it is said we made 225 miles, but nothing definite is known.

On Board *North Star,* July 8th.

Weather is warm and sea smooth, 220 miles for the 24 hours, and it is said we will be up with and pass the island of Cuba tonight on the north side. Some excitement was created among the passengers today by sighting two vessels. The ship is running along the island's shore entire[ly] out of the track usually followed by steamers of this line. This for fear of the *Jeff Davis* or some other privateer cruising for booty. This is the steamer built by Commodore Vanderbilt and used as a private yacht on an European trip with himself and family. She is staunch and trim and considered a first class sea boat.

On Board Steamship *North Star*, July 9th.

We have run 206 miles. The weather is very warm, and there seems little life on the ship. A complete lassitude seems to pervade everyone, and the greater quiet prevails.

On Board *North Star*, July 10th.

Made 231 miles. Encountered quite a gale about 12 M. today, took water over the weather bow, split a top sail and created some little excitement, and under the influence of cooling atmosphere, the passengers seemed to be inspired with more life. We must be nearing Hattaras, and once by that point, the run to New York will be short. There is less talk among the men of home and anticipated pleasures than was expected. Each one seems inclined to indulge in his own anticipation without communicating his feelings to others.

On Board *North Star*, July 11th.

Made 240 miles, been raining, and sea considerably rough. Met a fore and aft schooner. Expect to be in New York on the day after tomorrow.

On Board *North Star*, July 12th.

Run 275 miles. Continues to rain. Encountered quite a storm at midnight last night. Everyone is on deck and the passengers and crew are growing more animated as we near home. Tomorrow we shall be in port and undoubted [shall] go at once to West Point, and then such as can will get furloughs. I shall try hard for one.

On Board Steamship *North Star*, July 13th.

We arrived in port and alongside the wharf at 3 o'clock this P.M., distance 320 miles. The sailing up the narrows and bay was a delightful one, notwithstanding a falling rain. I am on guard, and by reason of the Quarter Master's Office being closed [it was Saturday], the Sergeant is unable to provide quarters for us, and we are to remain aboard until tomorrow or Monday. I am on guard, therefore compelled to remain on the ship. But everyone but us three are away up town; for us it is extremely dismal.

On Board Steamship *North Star*, July 14th.

We have been decidedly uncomfortable. Sergeant Wheeler left the ship this morning. The men remained aboard all of the forenoon, not knowing what disposition would be made of us. Finally, during the afternoon, the men began to straggle off. Myself, Schlagg and Wright went up town and spent the afternoon and evening. New York appears more strange to me than ever it did before. Distances seem much less some way. Not having any acquaintances in the city and it being Sunday and raining, there has been little to interest me. Had I known we were to remain aboard, I should have gone to Jamaica and spent the day with brother George. The strangest thing of all is to see the men so seemingly indifferent about seeing their relatives after being so anxious to get home. Those having families seem in no haste to meet them. But we go to the Point tomorrow morning.

West Point, N.Y., July 15th.

And here we are at the home of the Corps [of Engineers] and the Army once more, after an absence of 2 years, 9 months and 10 days. We arrived here at 10:30 A.M., left N.Y. at 6:30 by the steamer *Armenia*. The trip [up] the river was a delightful one. The boat had a goodly number of passengers. The weather fine, and the men in the best of spirits. There are two Italian children aboard pursuing the calling of strolling musicians. The often heard of song, "Dixie Land," was listened to for the first time by the members of our party, much to their delight and [the] profit of the musicians.

As we neared the Point, all were on the lookout for familiar scenes, and on coming up to Bennie Maven's* place, the Captain was induced to run his boat out of the usual course and in towards Bennies Wharf.

The calliope with which the boat is provided played "Home Again." Uncle Bennie came down on his wharf and handsomely responded to the cheers of the detachment. It was a sight worth seeing, as the old gentleman stood on the wharf, hat in hand, his long white hair blowing in the wind, and him greeting us with hearty cheers.

After arriving at quarters and getting our baggage properly stored, all hands started for Buttermilk Falls to see friends and relative. Us who have no intimate friends or relatives soon found ourselves at

---

* It is unclear if this is "Maven" or "Haven" as appears a few lines farther in the diary. –bw

Uncle Bennie Haven's hospitable board, and with his good cheer, passed an enjoyable evening and afternoon. I have applied for a pass for the purpose of visiting my friends in Connecticut, but the detachment, having been granted four days leave of absence, reporting each morning at eight o'clock, the application will not be considered until the end of that time. Lieutenant Cymer is detailed in charge of the detachment. The men spend their entire time among their relatives and friends.

West Point, New York, July [...] 1861.

And now ends the campaign on which we started nearly three years ago. We have traversed over a great amount of the great northwestern territories, and seen and learned much that ought to be useful to us in after life. For myself, I shall never regret having joined the Corps, feeling that my experiences in this campaign will repay me for the many inconveniences I have suffered. The erroneous opinions and fancies I had of that mysterious and enchanted great North Western portion of our continent is dispelled. The gilding is all off, and I know the facts as they really exist. While there is much to commend the country to the emigrant, there [are] many trials and hardships to be undergone in establishing a home in that far away country.

To recapitulate, we traveled from West Point to New York, thence to San Francisco, thence to Fort Vancouver, W. T., thence to Fort Dalles, Oregon, thence in a south easterly direction by the Blue Mountains, returning to the Dalles and Fort Cascades, thence to San Juan Island, thence to Fort Cascades, thence to Fort Steilacoom near the head of Puget Sound, thence to San Francisco and West Point.

After the expiration of the four days leave of absence granted the detachment by the Commander of the Post, I obtained an eight days furlough and visited Connecticut. [On] returning found the detachment gone to Washington. I was ordered to proceed to join them at once, but in consideration of O'Donoghue being absent and his leave to expire two days later, I was allowed to remain and go in company with him. We arrived and found the detachment.

The following day after our arrival, we commenced on works for the defense of the Capitol and were engaged on eighteen of the forts, Pennsylvania at Ternby Town being the largest, twelve of the eighteen being on the Virginia side of the Potomac, several at Uptons and Mason's Mills.

In November we returned for winter quarters, the Corps having been augmented by an act of Congress, allowing four companies of

212

one hundred and fifty men each, instead of one company of one hundred men. Recruiting parties had been sent, and before January, the old Company "A" joined us and Companies "B" and "C" came, making quite a battalion.

Epilogue

On the nineteenth day of February, 1862, I was discharged from the Corps by reason of disability occasioned by the hurt received while at Steilacoom [from the mule]. The Corps of Engineers performed important and honorable duties during the war of the Southern rebellion.

On the 15th of April, 1863, I reported to Captain Thomas Lincoln Casey, in charge of sea board works for the defense of the coast of Maine. I was assigned to duty on Fort Scanimell in Portland Harbor, and appointed Receiver of Materials for that work. My duties were to receive, have charge of, and issue all materials and property at the work.

In 1866 I was placed temporarily in charge of the work, and in 1867 was made overseer, or Superintendent. I remained at Portland until November, 1868 at which time appropriations failed, the funds were exhausted, and I left. (43)

In August, 1878, I took charge of dredging the channel in New Haven Harbor as Inspector, and continued on the work until completed, appropriation $25,000. I was in charge of improving Bridgeport harbor, Connecticut, in the fall of 1879, appropriation $10,000, and in charge of dredging in New Haven, Connecticut during the whole of the season of 1880, appropriation $30,000.

(1881). I commenced duty in charge of the improvements in Milford Harbor on the 21st day of March, and finished on the 15th or June, same year, $2,000. Reported for duty to relieve I. J. MacKinly in charge of improvements in Bridgeport on the 25th of June, 1881. Finished the work on the first day of July, 1881, appropriation $10,000.

Commenced work on channel in New Haven Harbor July 27th, finished Oct. 20, 1881, appropriation $5,000.

Commenced dredging at Bridgeport, Nov. 9th, 1881, finished Dec. 30th, 1881, appropriation $10,000.

On the first day of September, 1882, I reported for duty in charge of removal of wrecks obstructing navigation in the harbors of Bridgeport and New Haven, and completed the same Nov. 15th of the same year.

May 1st, 1883, I reported for duty with H. B. Gorham on the construction of the dike at Sandy Point, and breakwater from lighthouse to Quixies Ledge, both at New Haven. I continued on this until the 1st of Sept., when I was sent to Clinton, Connecticut, in charge of the construction of a dike in that harbor. On the 25th of May, Colonel Barlow was relieved of duty in this district by Major Brot, Colonel Walter McFarland, Engineer Corps. The work at Clinton was finished Dec. 5th, 1574 tons of rip rap granite being put in place at $1.41 per gross ton. $2,219.34.

September 15th, 1884.

Commenced work on New Haven breakwaters and continued until Oct. 1st, when Mr. Gorham arrived from Omaha and assumed charge. I reported for duty on the breakwater at Greenport, [Long Island], New York on the 31st of Oct., 1884, and continued on that work until the contract was finished, on the 10th day of February, 1885, putting 1,387 tons of stone in the breakwater. Price $1.38.

Long Island, New York.

I went to Flushing Bay on the 12th of April, 1885. Was in charge [of] removing 44,633 cubic yards of mud from the channel, price 17 and 8/10th cts per yard. Finished on the 8th of June.

Went to Engineer Office at New Haven, Connecticut on the 22nd of June. Went to South Norwalk and took charge of dredging 34,824 cubic yards of mud, finished July 14th.

I was employed in the New Haven office again until the 28th day of July, when I took charge of removing 4,000 yards of material from the bar at the mouth of the Housatonic River, Connecticut, finishing Sept. 9th, 1885. Commenced charge of dredging channel in New Haven harbor on the 10th. Removed 44,192 yards, finished on the 8th of October, 1885, at 8 1/2cts, and reported for duty on Rolling Hills dike on the 12th inst. and finished that work on the 24th of October, 1885. Remained in the office until November 1st, and that finished the season.

I commenced working as copying clerk in the New Haven office. On the 1st of February, 1886, Colonel D. C. Houston, the officer in charge of our detachment going to and in Oregon, relieved Colonel McFarland of the works on Long Island Sound in February, and the office was transferred to the Army Building Corps on Houston and Green street, New York City, early in March. I remained in the office until April 30th, when I went to Hartford, Connecticut, and took charge of dredging on the bars below Hartford, and finished that work on the 5th of July, 1886. I took charge of the dredging at the mouth of the Housatonic River, Connecticut the following day, the 6th of July, 1886. Finished at Housatonic River August 20. Commenced dredging on the Connecticut River below Hartford Sept. 2nd, and finished October 10th, 1886.

Detailed in charge of dredging in Bridgeport Harbor Oct. 20th and commenced work Nov. 2nd, 1886. Finished May 16th, 1887.

Commenced dredging at Norwalk River, Connecticut, May 30. Finished June 24th, 1887.

Commenced at Flushing, New York, May 28th, left on leave of absence July 14th, ended Aug. 15th. Reported again Oct. 28th, suspended work again Dec. 19th.

Reported for duty at Montville January 7th, 1889. This work was located on the Thames River 6 miles above New London, Connecticut. I left here March 8th. Reported to East Chester, New York, March 11th. Finished the contract, 11,207 yds., April 25th.

Reported for duty at South Norwalk, April 26th, finished May 6th. Reported for duty at Bridgeport May 7th, finished there July 16th. Assisted in gauging vessels for New Haven breakwater and dike until August 1st, when I went on Housatonic River, dredged the several bars between Milford Beach and Derby, finished Nov. 10th. Went on New Haven Harbor Nov. 29th, finished Dec 21st, dredging, 1889.

Commenced dredging at Black Rock, Connecticut, June 9th. Finished June 23rd, 1890.

Commenced putting stone in Flushing dike August 15th. Finished August 25, 1890.

Commenced enlarging Greenport breakwater March 1st, 1891. Finished Aug. 26th. Commenced dredging Greenport Harbor, Sept. 3rd, finished Oct. 31st, 1891.

Commenced dredging Mystic River, Connecticut, Oct. 8th, 1892. Work suspended Dec. 31st on account of ice.

Commenced dredging in Clinton Harbor, March 24th, 1892. Finished May 10th, 1893.

Commenced dredging at Cos Cob, Connecticut, May 16th. Finished August 8th, 1893.

Commenced dredging at Five Mile River, Sept. 16th. Finished for good, Oct. 20th-

Commenced dredging at Black Rock harbor, Connecticut, Nov. 16th. Finished January 8th, 1894.

Commenced at Milford, June 14th. Finished August 2nd, 1894.

Commenced dredging Connecticut River between South Glastonbury & Rocky Hill, August 30th. Finished September 17th, 1894.

Commenced dredging in Bridgeport, Nov. 6th. Finished Dec. 9th, 1894.

May 9, 1895, commenced dredging Connecticut River. Left June 8th to take charge of dredging at Milford. Commenced June 10th. Finished July 24th.

Nov. 5, 1895, commenced at Five Mile River. Finished Dec. 30th, 1895. Jan 9th, 1896. Commenced gauging barges. Baugs Bros., Hughes, for New Haven breakwater. Finished 15th January, 1896. June 25th, 1896. Commenced dredging in Milford. Finished July 31st, 1896.

Oct. 8th, 1896. Commenced dredging at Port Chester, New York. Finished December 4th, 1896.

THE END

Notes

❖ To help readers locate original text while referring to the Notes, the page number where the note occurs in the text is shown as parenthetical after the Note number.

1. (p.15) William A. Peck, Jr. was born in September 1834, in Waterbury, Connecticut. His occupation was a burnisher. He enlisted in the U.S. Army on August 21, 1858 for a term of five years. He had gray eyes, brown hair, light complexion, was 5 feet 10½ inches tall. His enlistment form was signed by Henry M. Robert, Brig. 2nd, U. S. Engineers. (Peck, Wm. A.: *U. S. Army Register of Enlistment's*, Year 1858, vol. 53, page 193.)

Goetzmann pp.13, 20-21, points out that the Military Academy at West Point had been under the direction of the Engineer Corps and was oriented toward the education of engineer-soldiers and the Corps had a great interest in exploring the West.

2. (p.19) There is a difference between written English and spoken English – a difference between the spelling of a word and the pronunciation. Peck recorded the events of the day in spoken English. There are other words that are just different. Some of these are in the *Dictionary of Slang and Unconventional English*, so I have left them as they are. It seems likely that some of the differences in spelling are due to Peck not having a dictionary. The likelihood of a "mud-soldier" in the field in this period of history having a dictionary seems remote. There are words which are either spelled incorrectly, or are hard to decipher in the hand-written work. Many of these occur where Peck made the entries for several days on a single page, and especially at the bottom of the page where he was trying to squeeze in an entry. The hard to decipher entries I have typed using the dictionary spelling. Where Peck used a whole page to record the events of a day there are few mistakes. Basically, Peck's handwriting is very good.

To facilitate reading, all of Peck's abbreviations are spelled out as Lieut. becomes Lieutenant. He also spells Lieutenant Robert's name as Roberts, which was the way he pronounced it. He spells the Deschutes River as Des Chutes, which Captain Wallen did in his report. I have changed Roberts to Robert but DesChutes, where it appears that way, is retained.

3. (p.35) An excellent but brief account of Colonel Steptoe and Col. George Wright and the Indian wars is in Relander pp. 96-98: Another source is Manring. In summary, the Indians defeated Colonel Steptoe therefore Colonel Wright mounted a punitive expedition and by all means at his disposal won the war. It has been said that the death of Wright on July 30, 1865, when he drowned during the foundering of the steamer *Brother Jonathan* off Crescent City was "divine retribution" for his treatment of the Indians. The quotation is on p.45 in Webber, *Battery Point Light*.

4. (p.38) Fort at Upper Cascades. Sign on Highway 830, above the Upper Cascades:

> Fort Rains. A blockhouse was built on the point just east of here by H. D. Wallen, Lt. H. D. Hodges and soldiers of the U.S. Army in November, 1855. It was named for Maj. Gabriel Rains and overlooked the racing water of the Cascade Rapids.

Overhanging second story wall pierced with gun holes and a mounted howitzer provided protection for the transfer of military supplies and pioneer cargo over the portage road from the upper landing to the river boat landing three miles below the Fort. Indians in this area were friendly, but on the morning of March 26, 1856 hostile Indians attacked the Cascades to protest against the increasing encroachment of white settlers on their traditional territories. Sgt. Matthew Kelly and eight soldiers of Co. H, 4th U.S. Infantry successfully defended the Fort for three days. Two soldiers and several settlers were killed. The siege was lifted by the arrival of Col. E. J. Steptoe with a detachment of regulars from the Dalles, and Lt. Phil Sheridan with his dragoons from Fort Vancouver. Later this site was referred to as Sheridan's Point.

—Skamania County Historical Society

5. (p.39) Below Celilo Falls the Columbia River narrowed to where it was only two hundred feet wide – "an agitated gut," wrote explorer William Clark in 1805, "swelling, boiling and whorling in every direction." Lavender pp. 343-345. The rapids were five or six miles long.

6. (p.39) George Horatio Derby was a Lieutenant in the U. S. Army Corps of Topographical Engineers which had been established in 1838. This Corps was composed entirely of commissioned officers, who made the reconnaissances and surveyed the routes for all of the military roads in the West. The term "military road" has been used to classify them because they were paid for by the U. S. Army, but the Army Engineers recognized that the primary importance of these routes was to emigrant and pioneer settlers. In 1853, the Corps was authorized to construct a military road from Walla Walla to Fort Steilacoom. The route for this was found to be too difficult, and in 1855 Lieutenant Derby was authorized to use his own judgment in deciding whether he should build this road or one from Fort Vancouver to The Dalles. Derby decided to build the one from Fort Vancouver. Lieutenant Derby was also a humorist of the first water who wrote many sketches which were published in magazines and for which he probably was paid. He used pseudonyms of "Phoenix," "Squibob," "Butterfield," and others. In so doing, he was probably eliminating any conflict in interests as Army officers were supposed to be 100 percent Army business. It seems obvious that he signed his latest article as "Doesticks." See: Carey: p 483; Randall V. Mills: "Frontier Humor In Oregon And Its Characteristics," in *Oregon Historical Quarterly,* Vol. XLIII December, 1942, pp. 350-352; W. Turpentine Jackson: "Federal Road Building Grants for Early Oregon," in, *Oregon Historical Quarterly,* Vol L March, 1949 pp.3-29.

7. (p.40) Wet weather is common in western Washington and Oregon in winter. Why this occurs is in Renner. (See bibliography)

8. (p.61) General Harney wrote Colonel S. Cooper, Adjutant General of the U. S. Army, Headquarters, Department of Oregon, Fort Vancouver, W.T., January 17, 1860:

I have the honor to inclose the … reports of the expedition made from this command the past summer, to open a wagon road to the Salt Lake from the Dalles of the Columbia River; and also to protect the emigration from the Western States to Oregon and Washington Territory. —36th Congress, 1st Session, Senate, Ex. Doc. No. 34: Report of Back, p. 1.

The Secretary of War, communicating, in Compliance with a resolution of the Senate, the *Report* of Captain H. D. Wallen of his expedition, in 1859, from Dalles City to Great Salt Lake, and Henry Davies Wallen (– -1886 was born in Georgia and appointed to West Point from Florida Sept. 1, 1836. He was appointed 2nd Lieutenant, 4th Infantry, Oct. 4, 1840.) See: Bischoff, p. 173. Wallen was promoted to Captain. In 1860 he was stationed at Fort Cascades, W. T. in Command of Company H, 4th Infantry. He was transferred to San Francisco in June 1861, was promoted to Major of the 7th Infantry on Nov. 25, 1861 with which he went in the 7th to New Mexico, where he served as acting Inspector General during the rest of the Civil War. See: *War of the Rebellion,* Series L, Vol. L, Part I – Reports, Correspondence 1897, pp. 116, 512, 517, 620.

9. (p.66) Wallen's *Report*, p. 7, states that his total strength consisted of nine officers and 184 enlisted men.

10. (p.77) Wallen's *Report,* p. 7:

From our inexperience in the use of pontoons, and the difficulty in crossing the animals, four days were consumed in making the necessary preparations, and in crossing the river. The error that we first committed was in attempting to cross a loaded wagon on the pontoon flat, without putting a sufficient amount of freight as ballast, before rolling on the wagon. The flat being extremely light, and, in consequence, taking such a slight hold of the water, just as it reached the point where the current was deflected from the opposite bank with great violence, it was whipped over in an instant, and the contents of the wagon lost.

11. (p.78) Wallen's *Report*, p. 8 declares they camped on Trout Creek on the night of June 17th and that

The delay in reaching this camp was caused by the difficulty in getting up the hill on the east bank of the Des Chutes. The wagons had to be unloaded and the contents packed up the hill by the mule trains.

12. (p.79) The emigrant train that came down the Crooked River and went through the ordeals that Peck mentions crossed the continent in 1845. Clark and Tiller describe the circumstances of the wagon train: Stephen H. L. Meek, said he could guide the emigrants on a route that was better and shorter than the Oregon Trail, thereby escaping the ordeal of crossing the Blue Mountains. Some 300 emigrants, with wagons, cattle put their trust in Meek to guide them. They moved along until they got to about Harney Lake where, out of water and food, many perished.

Hoffman wrote that during this so-called "Meek Cutoff" gold was discovered. But as this was 3 years before the great discovery at Sutter's Mill in California, these pioneers did not know for certain what it was. Believing the metal was nothing out of the ordinary, the discoverers dumped it in a bucket that had been painted blue and failed to document where the gold had been found. It was not until the early 1970's that a scientific expedition was successful in retracing the steps of this 1845 route. See Hoffman's *Search For Oregon's Lost Blue Bucket Mine.*

13. (p.79) Knuth, Priscilla, Ed.: "Cavalry in the Indian Country 1864," in *Oregon Historical Quarterly,* March 1964, p. 27. This is the *Journal* of the Drake expedition in 1864. Drake stated that the "Crooked River is small, with water a little brackish, hills on each side high, with here and there precipitous cliffs."

14. (p.80) Clark and Tiller: p. 78

15. (p.81) Wallen's *Report*, p. 9:

On the 16th we left our camp on the branch of Crooked River.... The road had to-day been good; indeed, the entire distance from Trout Creek to our present camp is over the best natural road I have ever seen.

16. (p.82) Wallen's *Report,.* p. 9:

Having left Fort Dalles on the 4th of June, and not arriving at my present camp until the 27th, I deemed it a proper point to disencumber myself from the ox-train and divide my command. Lieutenant John C. Bonnycastle, 4th Infantry, was left in command of the depot and party, to explore the route and work on the road back to the Columbia river.

Wallen's *Report,* pages 18-19: on June 29, 1859, Wallen instructed Bonnycastle:

That portion of the command returning to the Columbia river will be under your orders, and after making the preliminary surveys over the several Indian trails leading across the spur of the Blue mountains, in the direction of Scholl's Butte you will select the shortest and best for the wagon road to Fort Dalles. ... Your success will enable me to explore the country east of the Blue mountains and return to the Columbia river by a different route than the one already passed over.

17. (p.84) Wallen stated page 20:

Lieutenant Johnson reported that: 'The impassable hills on the John Day's river are here connected with the spur of the Blue mountains by a chain of volcanic hills, over which it is impossible to take wagons and which cannot be turned in any direction.'

(See also:) Wallen's *Report*, page 21:

Bonnycastle returned over the same road over which the command of Captain Wallen had passed in going out, hoping, from explorations to the north of the road, to find some practicable route over the spur of the Blue mountains, which, enabling me to pass to the westward of the volcanic hills referred to by Lieutenant Johnson as barring further progress down the John Day's ... should enable me to strike the John Day's further down, and thus cut off more distance. In this, however, I was disappointed...

220

18. (p.86) *The War Of The Rebellion: A Compilation of the Official Records of the Union and Confederate Armies.* Series I – Volume L – In Two Parts, Part I "Reports, Correspondence, Etc.": Chapter LXII. "Operations On The Pacific Coast. January 1, 1861 – June 30, 1865": Part I. "Summary Of The Principal Events." p. 336. "Expeditions To Southeastern Oregon."

Two persons were found (Mr. Louis Scholl and Mr. George Rundell) who had been employed as guides with similar expeditions into that country in the years of 1859 and 1860. From them I learned that the natural route of travel into the Harney Lake country in fact, into any part of the country lying south of the Blue Mountains – was by the road traveled by Captain Wallen in 1859 by the valley of the Crooked River.

19. (p.90) Wallen's goal was finding and making a good wagon road from Fort Dalles to Great Salt Lake. When he reached the south fork of the Crooked River he decided to leave the wagons and go on an exploring trip to Great Salt Lake which was an abandonment of the original objective. Wallen went on to find a good road, except for a couple of places which wagons could not cross. A branch of his force went northward to find a good road, and did, except for a couple of places. These roadblocks made the route impassable. Then, on the way back to Fort Dalles, Bonneycastle and Johnson hoped to find a traversable roadway over the Blue Mountains to the John Day River, and thus find a shorter route. Again, they failed. On the other hand, back on November 25, 1858, Peck recorded in his *Journal*: "I wish to penetrate far into the interior." The Wallen expedition did that.

Priscilla Knuth, editor for "Cavalry in the Indian Country, 1864," in *Oregon Historical Quarterly,* March, 1964, fn pp. 5-6, cites the Wallen expedition in 1859, then the Steen and Smith expedition in 1860, the expedi-tion of John M. Drake in 1864. After this there were numerous expeditions to locate routes for a railroads as well as wagon roads.

20. (p.93) In 1818 the boundary line between the United States and Canada was extended along the 49" parallel to the Pacific Ocean. The British wanted the line to follow the flow of the Columbia River to the ocean. In 1846, the U.S. and Great Britain made an agreement to extend the line west to salt water on the 49°. This put all of the western half of present Washington State in U. S. territory but left all of Vancouver Island, the most desirable part of it, below the 49th degree as part of Canada.

Gibson argues that this agreement was the crucial part of the boundary settlement for by it Great Britain gave up not only the lower part of the Columbia River, but also the harbors of Puget Sound. Gibson feels that Canadians should not forget that they were dispossessed of part of their rightful Columbia heritage, a heritage whose economic potential in general, and agricultural possibilities in particular, were initially and successfully demonstrated by the Hudson's Bay Company, as Great Britain was left with the poorer northern part of the Oregon country which was primarily a fur trade area and that Canada badly needs the more productive area it gave up for its economic welfare.

Bancroft, in his work on British Columbia p. 605: points out:

...the 1846 treaty specified that the boundary line would run down the <u>middle</u> of the channel which separated the continent from Vancouver's Island, thence through Fuca Straits, to the Pacific Ocean, providing navigation of said channel and straits remain free and open to both parties. But there were two channels, the Strait de Haro and the Strait of Rosarios. Between them were the group of islands forming the Archipelago de Haro. In 1790 the Spanish explorer de Haro made a voyage to the area and his map showed only one route, which lay directly east of Vancouver Island.

In 1792 Captain Vancouver explored the region and decided that the Strait of Rosario was the major waterway. In 1841 Lieutenant Charles Wilkes made an exploring trip and decided that the Channel de Haro was the major waterway. This was seven miles in width, while Rosario Strait was less than half of that. Louis McLane, who was the U.S. Minister to Great Britain, asked for the channel 'de Arro' but he accepted the indefinite terms of the proposed agreement, which was essentially the British proposal. He wanted to dissipate British hostility to Americans, because the Mexican War had just started. Both sides regarded the Archipelago de Haro, which was the San Juan Islands, as belonging to them.

Following this agreement, the Hudson's Bay Company moved its headquarters from Fort Vancouver on the Columbia River, which was now in the United States, to Victoria on Vancouver Island. Then The Grand Company started to graze sheep on San Juan Island. The operation was put in charge of Charles John Griffin, who added cattle and pigs to his sheep herds. He did not fence in the animals because he considered that the whole island was his territory. This led to a growing interest in the islands. In 1854 the U.S. Collector of Customs for Puget Sound went there and asked Griffin to pay customs duties. The collection was not enforced until 1855, when the sheriff of Whatcom County seized some thirty or more of the sheep. Then came the Fraser River gold rush. Thousands of Americans participated in it. Most did not find much gold and they faced the hostility of the local government – British – so most of them left. At this time, the U.S. government sent a surveying party to San Juan Island and said that the land could be preempted.

In 1859, some 16 Americans settled on the island. The one who lived closest to Griffin's ranch was a man named Cutlar, so the official report states. He developed about two-thirds of an acre into a garden where he grew potatoes. A British pig got in, so he built a fence around the garden. Then a predatory hog broke through the fence and ravaged the potatoes. Cutlar saw this, grabbed his gun, and shot the black boar. As it turned out, this was the only casualty of the Pig War. Cutlar went to Griffin to complain about the damage and offered to pay $10.00 for the animal provided that Griffin would fence them. Griffin refused, and went to the British authorities, who accused Cutlar of trespassing on British land and fined him $100.00. Cutlar wouldn't pay. This episode led to what has been called "The Pig War."

General William S. Harney, the commandant of the American troops in the Department of Oregon, was making a routine inspection of all the American forces under his authority. In the process, he visited Fort Bellingham, which had been established to protect the settlers from marauding Indians, who came down from the north in their canoes to raid the local Indians and the white settlers. It was here that Harney heard about the death of the trespassing pig, and how the British had reacted to the incident.

Haller, p. 7, tells how Harney made a courtesy call on Governor Douglas at Victoria and then sailed to San Juan Island to personally investigate the issue. He went to the farm and talked with Cutlar who told him how the British had threatened to arrest him and take him to Victoria for trial.

Murray, p. 35:

The General made a snap decision to occupy the island with American troops but he needed some kind of justification before he took such a rash action.

He called a meeting with the settlers, where he told them that they should draft a petition expressing their fear of Indian raids and their need for protection of their rights as settlers from the British authorities. This was to be signed by every settler on the island. Murray states that this decision to occupy the island without any authorization from the U.S. government was the same kind of action he had attempted in Texas and Mexico in 1846, therefore his action was not out of character. A few days, later General Harney wrote General Winfield Scott that San Juan should be taken because

...at the southeastern extremity [of the island] one of the finest harbors on this coast is to be found, completely sheltered, offering the best location for a naval station on the Pacific Coast.

This was Griffin Bay. Next, Harney went to Fort Vancouver, where he had a conference with Isaac Ingalls Stevens, who was the Governor of Washington Territory. They must have felt that if they sat down gracefully, waiting for an amicable agreement on the boundary line to be worked out, they would see American rights to the islands vanish thus they needed to take vigorous action and quickly to assert the interests of the United States there.

Stevens, Vol. II, p. 288:

Undoubtedly the governor, in his earnest and convincing manner, fully imbued the general with his views of the American rights, and the duty of the authorities to defend it.

General Harney ordered the commandant of Fort Bellingham to move his troops to the island. In July 1859, Captain George E. Pickett Company D, 9th Infantry, landed on the island with all 68 of his men. It could also be noted that wherever Isaac I. Stevens was, there was always a certain amount of hysteria.

Snowden, Vol. IV, p. 52: Pickett was instructed "to protect the inhabitants of the island from the incursions of the northern Indians." But he was also to have a "more serious and important duty" and that was:

to afford adequate protection to the American citizens in their rights as such, and to resist all attempts at interference by the British authorities residing on Vancouver Island, by intimidation or force,

in the controversies arising out of the conflict of the settler's interests with those of the Hudson's Bay Company. In case a second threat was made to seize an American citizen and carry him to Victoria for trial, on any pretense, he was "to meet with the authorities from Victoria at once and inform them that they cannot be permitted to interfere with our citizens in any way."

21. (p.96) With reference to "mad as our own Harney," there was a widespread feeling that General Harney would go off on all sorts of activities. Concerning General Harney, The *Dictionary of American Biography*, vol VIII, p. 280, lists:

Harney, William Selby (Aug 22, 1800 – May 9, 1889), born in Tennessee. On Feb. 13, 1818 he entered the army as Second Lieutenant of the 1st Infantry. He quickly showed his fitness as a soldier in the numerous expeditions into Florida against the Indians and rose rapidly in rank until on Aug. 15, 1836 he was made Lieutenant Colonel of the 2nd Dragoons. On June 30, 1846 he was promoted Colonel of the 2nd Dragoons. This promotion, which came about the time of the Mexican War, made Harney the ranking cavalry officer under General [Winfield] Scott. Harney and Scott were not on good terms, and Scott, who had never been able to manage Harney, and who thoroughly distrusted his judgment and impetuosity, attempted to detach Harney from his command. Harney appealed to his superiors in Washington with the result that Secretary of War Mercy, with President Polk's approval, upheld Harney's position against Scott. Harney was rewarded with the command of the Department of Oregon and the rank of Brigadier (1858). But his anti-British and expansionist proclivities, especially his seizure of the Island of San Juan, claimed by the British, soon caused his recall.

Meany. p.244:

General W. S. Harney was visiting Puget Sound at that time, and seeing the flag on land he knew was in dispute, landed to investigate. Here was an excuse for action.

General George B. McClellan is the authority for the statement that the saving of San Juan Island was not the only motive of General Harney at that time. McClellan wrote:

It is a fact not generally know, that the movements which are referred to here in the occupation of San Juan had their origin in a patriotic attempt on the part of General Harney, governor Stevens, of Washington Territory, and other Democratic Federal officers on that coast, with the knowledge and zealous concurrence of Captain Pickett, to force a war with Great Britain in the hope that by this means the then jarring sections of our country would unite in a foreign war, and so avert the civil strife which they feared they saw approaching.

Haller: p. 4

Now the South, with Texas, was about ready to fight the North, if not allowed to secede, and a war with England, then, would, without doubt, have greatly helped to secure their independence. General Harney's conduct is inexplicable, unless it was a design and object with it, the Southern secession from the beginning.

The editor notes that Haller's account appears to make more sense than Meany's.

22. (p.98) Thompson p. 55: On August 23rd Captain Haller and his Company

224

I, 4th Infantry, came ashore from the *Massachusetts* and 2nd Lieutenant Henry M. Robert, with a detachment of engineers, arrived to begin work on a redoubt for the placing of the eight 32-pounders that had been removed from the *Massachusetts*. On p. 131, Thompson states that the troops and civilian laborers manhandled the 32 pounders to the top of the ridge and that by the end of the month, Colonel Silas Casey had 15 officers and 424 enlisted men under his command.

Haller p. 12, shows that in August, General Harney reported to General Scott on the number of troops on the island:

Companies A and C, Fourth Infantry, and H, Ninth Infantry (from Steilacoom) 139

Companies A, B, D and M, of the 3rd Artillery 181

Company I, 4th Infantry 44

Detachment of Company A, Engineers 11

Total troops: 461

Miller p.90 says the British were aware of these arrivals. Captain Hornby reported to Admiral Baynes:

> I think it is requisite to draw your attention to the position that the United States Authorities are now taking up as it differs so materially from their original one. At first they landed 50 men and professed their object was to protect their citizens, especially from the Indians. Now they have 400 soldiers on shore with six (6) Field-pieces, eight 32pdr. mounted, and, it is said, six more iron guns under cover in their camp. Six of their heavy guns are placed on the ridge of the hill overlooking the harbor; and by throwing up a parapet they could command the harbor; even in their present position they would be difficult to silence. The other two heavy guns and field pieces are placed to defend their camp. They seem to me therefore, not only to be prepared to defend themselves but to threaten us.

23. (p.100) The official name of the settler was Lyman A. Cutlar, but the people who live on the San Juan Islands today say his name was Sawyer. (Statement by Gary Grendahl, who had many contacts with San Juan Island and now lives on Lopez Island, 1986).

The petition that General Harney wanted was to be drafted by the American settlers on the island and signed by every one of them. Cutlar (Sawyer) disappeared just before this was done. Harney's instructions to Pickett cite a "second threat." It could well be that Sawyer felt that this could come at any moment and that his only hope of getting out of sight was by leaving the island.

Murray p. 35, says the petition was drafted on July 11th, two days after Harney's visit. It enumerates several murders alleged to have been committed by bands of marauding Indians.

Haller p. 8, states there was not a word in it praying for protection against "the outrages perpetrated upon them by the British authorities" and the Hudson's Bay Company.

The pig episode was the spark that ignited the confrontation. General Harney could not justify military intervention without being able to cite it as a cause for action so it was sent back to the settlers. He directed them to amend the petition to include protection against British authorities. It was at this point that Lyman A. Cutlar took over the role of Sawyer and drafted an account of the pig episode, which had taken place on June 15th, and included all of his grievances against the Hudson's Bay Company.

Thompson pp. 15, 16, 18, 19, 20 records that Cutlar wrote his account at the urgent of Paul K. Hubbs, the U.S. Inspector of Customs on the island. It could be that Hubbs, who probably had the best knowledge of the situation on the island by reason of his office, provided a lot of the information.

24. (p.101) Governor Stevens' Inspectors, who lived on the island, claimed there were 4,500 sheep. See: Murray p. 29.

25. (p.102) Bio-sketchs of Pickett appears in *The Dictionary of American Biography,* and in *Webster's Biographical Dictionary* and in other sources.

Pickett, George W. Edward (Jan. 25, 1825 – July 30, 1875) was an American Army officer who had been appointed in 1842 to the United States Military Academy and graduated in 1846 but did not have an outstanding record at the Point finishing last of his class of 59. He went directly into the Mexican War and was commissioned 2nd Lieutenant, in the 2nd Infantry on Mar. 3, 1847. For gallantry at Contreras and Churubusco he was brevetted 1st Lieutenant, Aug. 20, 1847. From 1849 to 1856 he was a garrison officer in Texas and was promoted to Captain on Mar. 3, 1855. In 1859 Pickett was ordered to take possession of San Juan Island, W. T. which he did with 60 soldiers. Three British warships anchored broadside to his camp and ordered him off the island. A British Magistrate aboard the flagship summoned him for trial, but Pickett politely thumbed his nose at both demands. (Similarly, in World War II, Colonel Anthony C. McAulliffe, surrounded by Germans in the Battle of the Ardennes, when ordered to surrender, replied, "Nuts!" –McCombs, Don and Fred L. North *World War II Super Facts.* Warner. 1983.)

The British threatened a landing for joint military occupation but Pickett answered this time proclaiming "I am here by virtue of an order from my government, and shall remain till recalled by the same authority." He admonished the magistrate that he would fire upon any landing force. However, joint occupation by British and American forces became the solution reached and Pickett remained in command of the American forces there almost continuously until 1861 when he resigned from the Army to accept a commission in the Confederate Army. He served with distinction for the South but lost two major battles one of which was at Gettysburg on July 3, 1863.

26. (p.102) Thompson, p. 133 states that the Fort, or redoubt, was constructed on the summit of the hill lying south of the first American camp.

Bancroft, *British Columbia,* in a long footnote on pages 624-625, described the fort:

The earthworks extended on the west waterfront 350 feet, on the southeast 100, on the east 100, and on the northeast 150 feet, on the north side being left open, with the garrison ground in its rear. The embankment had a base of twenty-five feet, and a width at top of eight feet. Inside of the redoubt were five gun-platforms of earth, reaching to within two feet of the level of the parapet, each twelve by eighteen feet, two of them being at corners of the redoubt. The parapet was seven feet above the interior, and the slope of the interior twelve to fifteen feet, the exterior slope being twenty-five to forty feet, with a ditch at the bottom from three to five feet deep.

27. (p.102) The soldiers had been sent to San Juan Island to protect the American settlers, so a visit to them could be a reasonable activity. Five days later, on October 2nd, he made a second trip to visit other settlers. Very little is known about these people. Thompson, p. 182, found that about 25 American settlers had arrived on the island before Pickett and his soldiers landed. Thompson provided this roster (p. 191-192) of 22 settlers who signed the petition on July 11, 1859:

J. M. Haggard	Samuel MacCauley	J. E. Higgins
Charles H. Hubbs	Lyman A. Cutlar	William Butler
J. D. Warren	Alex McDonald	H. Warton, Jr.
Peter Johnson	John Witty	Angus McDonald
B.S Andrews	William Smith	John H. McKay
Charles McCoy	Noil Ent	D. W. Oakes
Michael Farris	K. Hubbs, Jr.	George Perkins
Paul K. Hubbs		

Three settlers had left the island before the signing. One of them was Sawyer, the person who shot the pig. About sixteen of these had taken up preemption claims. As to where these claims were located. Thompson p. 118, quotes a letter from W.F. Tolmie, the Chief Factor of the Hudson's Bay Company, stating that the Americans had "squatted" on all the best parts of the Sheep Stations of the Bellevue Farm. Peck's going ashore "about 12 miles from camp" suggests that the ranches were stretched for miles along the shore of the island. Thompson p.18. also quotes Charles J. Griffin, who managed the Bellevue Farm, as stating that one of the settlers had landed 20 head of cattle and a mare therefore they were trying to raise livestock. Haller, p. 8, asserts as for housing, Dallas, the governmental official from Victoria, who visited to the settler who shot the pig, and who was accused of threatening to arrest him and take him to Victoria for trial, stated that the squatter lived in a hut or tent.

28. (p.105) Thompson, pp. 62, 70 182: When Pickett landed, in addition to his soldiers, he brought some 50 civilian workers. Immediately, people settled in what was to become San Juan village to supply food and other goods to these workmen. Businessmen, knowing that soldiers consume a lot of whiskey, included this staple with their goods. After the American reinforcements arrived, this made almost 500 troops on the island. In the next few weeks more people located in the village which now sprouted about 20 tents. All this became a grave concern to the British. With all these people, hundreds of northern Indian women landed to work as prostitutes.

An historic signpost:

Old San Juan Village Whiskey drinking seems to be the principal occupation.

29. (p.107) Signpost in the San Juan Islands National Historic Park:

Lt. H. M. Robert
Lt. Henry Martyn Robert supervised construction of the redoubt. This was the first major assignment for the 23-year-old engineer just out of West Point. Robert served with the Union Army during the Civil War. He remained in uniform and retired as Chief of the Engineers in 1891.He is best known, however, for his work in a more peaceful capacity. The field of parliamentary procedures fascinated him and led him to write the final work on the subject: Robert's Rules of Order.

Henry M. Robert was an excellent student at the Military Academy graduating 4th in his glass. Bio-sketches of Robert appear in various sources one of which is Thompson p. 57:

> Henry Martyn Robert, a native of South Carolina, graduated from West Point in 1857, fourth in his class. He spent his entire career in the Corps of Engineers, remaining with the North during the Civil War. In 1901 he became Chief of Engineers with the rank of Brigadier General. He retired a month later. His task on San Juan was erecting the redoubt for the 32-pounders.

30. (p.108) Thompson: pp. 37, 40, 47, 51-52, 60, 128-130; Bancroft: p.619; Haller is a reprinted from the *Tacoma Sunday Ledger* January 19, 1896, p.12.

Captain Pickett and company D, 9th Infantry, a total of 68 men, landed on San Juan Island on July 27th. He first camped near the shore of San Juan Harbor, about 200 yards inland and a little to the west of the Hudson's Bay Company wharf. The next day the British warship *Tribune* arrived, anchored, and watched the Americans.

Pickett did not feel comfortable under the guns of the *Tribune,* which was a thirty-gun frigate, and there was no drinking water where Pickett encamped. Pickett decided to move his camp for two reasons: 1) He needed water so within a week, he moved his camp to the opposite side of the island, near a spring that Griffin had been using for his sheep. 2) The move put him out of sight of the *Tribune's* lookouts. Captain Prevest, of the British navy, whose ship, the *Satellite,* had replaced the *Tribune,* wrote that the second camp was very strongly located on the most commanding position on the southeast end of the island and was well sheltered by a commanding eminence. For the first time the Americans now held a position that offered defensive values. The British responded by immediately anchoring four war-ships here. At 7:00 A.M. on August 10th, Colonel Casey and three companies of infantry and the 3rd Artillery, about 139 men from Fort Steilacoom, arrived at the south side of the island, near the new American camp. Casey landed his troops and eight howitzers there, rather than at the wharf on the north side of the island. His stated reason was be claimed a dense fog re-duced visibility to about 50 yards and, being at low tide, the water off San Juan Village was not very deep. Casey also noted that there was a smooth place on the land with the crest so depressed as to make the ascent from the shore to the top of the ridge easy. Thompson felt that the real reason for the decision was the presence of the

H.M.S. *Tribune* in San Juan Harbor. Colonel Casey, the ranking officer now on the island, immediately assumed command from Pickett, but named the site Camp Pickett. Shortly, more American troops arrived to make a total of 461 soldiers.

The British military situation on the island was the opposite of that of the Americans. They had only 125 men but with the arrival of the naval force with 5 warships, the British power totaled 167 guns and 2,140 men. The British decided not to land the naval troops on the island.

31. (p.109) The *Satelite* was stationed in San Juan Harbor to spy on American activities. Thompson, p. 63, tells that the officers on the island exchanged social calls with the British. He cites Colonel Casey and his staff attending a dinner party on board the ship. Peck's *Journal* establishes that this hospitality extended to the common soldiers. Sarah Emma Peck in "Reminiscences of Sara Emma Peck to Robert Sepetowski," January 1, 1974 recalled that her father said he had dinner on board a British warship, just a small party of Americans, say three officers and three enlisted men. They ate in the same room, the officers seated with the British commander and the enlisted men, including Peck, at the lower end of the table, Peck making the point they had real silverware.

32. (p.132) Thompson p. 137: Lieutenant Henry M. Robert, the engineer who had constructed the redoubt, surveyed and staked off the boundaries of a military reservation. This was to become an issue on the island because, somehow, his map was lost.

33. (p.132) On Oct. 22nd, Peck noted in his *Journal* that he had been on the road from camp to a spring with a party of men repairing it.

Thompson p. 128, states that Pickett began moving his tents to a spring on the south side of the peninsula, near the shore, as early as July 30. The *Colonist* reporter on that date described the scene:

The whole of this side is prairie, extending to the end of the island. In the middle of it, near the springs, were three tents, erected by Captain Pickett's company, to which teams were hauling army stores.

34. (p.136) Murray pp.57-58; Miller: p.115; Thompson: pp. 64-65. At this point the Federal Government entered the picture. On September 19th, General Winfield Scott left New York for the North West Frontier where he would take command over General Harney. On September 22, 1859, President Buchanan's administration told the British diplomats in Washington, D.C., that it would reduce the American command on San Juan Island to one company but no final decision could be made until General Scott, Commander in Chief of the U.S. Army, could make his personal investigation.

General Scott arrived at Portland and on October 21st discussed the issue with General Harney. Murray p.58, states:

This was the only time the two men met face to face during Scott's entire visit.

Obviously, both found the other's company distasteful.

The next day Pickett went to Portland and reported to General Scott that everything was quiet on the island. On October 25th, General Scott, the "Great Pacificator," who later stated that he "found both Brigadier Harney and Captain Pickett proud of the *conquest* of the island,, arrived at Port Townsend where he wrote to Governor Douglas at Victoria, proposing joint military occupation of the island with each nation furnishing not over one hundred men toward the total force to protect the nationals of both Britain and the United States "in their persons and property, and to repel any descent on the part of hostile Indians."

Douglas made a counter-proposal that American troops be withdrawn from San Juan entirely. If, however, in Scott's opinion, this was impossible, he would agree to a military occupation. If the Americans removed "the large military force with its eight heavy guns and numerous field pieces," the British would remove the *Satellite* from San Juan Harbor and not occupy the island. General Scott agreed, and on November 5th he announced the reduction of American troops on San Juan to one company and stated that work on the redoubt had been stopped.

35. (p.141) Captain Hunt was the commanding officer at Camp Pickett for about six months after Colonel Casey and most of the soldiers left. Thompson p. 138, states that just before he left San Juan, Captain Hunt gave a brief description of his quarters:

My men are all comfortably housed and I am established in as neat and snug a cottage as you could wish to see. It is built of hewn logs, closely fitting and lined within, a piazza in front, the columns of which are decidedly rustic being cut from the forest, peeled and the knobs left some inches long.

A visitor to Camp Pickett, the Boundary Commission's William Warren, made observations about the post.

Camp Pickett is in a very unfinished state. The men were at work cutting down the large trees in the vicinity of the Camp and finished the erection of log houses for quarters.

Thompson cites as the source Lucille McDonald's article on San Juan, in *Seattle Times*, Nov. 16, 1955.

36. (p.145) Bancroft, *Oregon*, Vol. II, p. 69, fn 5:

The transport *Massachusetts* entered the Columbia May 7th, 1849, by the sailing directions of Captain Gelston, without difficulty.

The *Honolulu Friend*, quoted by Bancroft, reported on Nov. 1, 1849 that the *Massachusetts* "...was the first government vessel to get safely into the [Columbia] river." How could this be accurate when there are various sources on Oregon history that note that approximately three years earlier, the U. S. Navy sloop *Shark* had been there in 1846 and was wrecked on trying to pass outbound over the bar on September 10. In Webber, *Beachcombing* –1978, is found that the City of Cannon Beach gets its name from the fact that:

...a few weeks later a portion of the ship's [*Shark's*] deck, to which was attached a cannon and capstan, washed ashore.

Oregon Historical Quarterly, June 1936, fn 35, states that the steamer *Multnomah*, in the fall of 1852, was put on the Portland and Cascade route under the command of Captain Fauntleroy.

This footnote suggest that Captain Fauntleroy and the *Massachusetts* was involved in developing navigation on the Columbia River. For detailed history of navigation on the Columbia, see Mills.

37. (p.163) Bancroft, *History of Wash., Ida. and Mont* pp.88-89, mentions that appropriations were obtained for Washington from the federal government:

An appropriation of $25,000 was made for the construction of a military road from Fort Dalles to Fort Vancouver, and of $30,000 for a road from Vancouver to Fort Steilacoom.

This was the start of building what was to become Highway 99, and ultimately Interstate 5.

38. (p.184) While Peck mentions the injury to his leg, he was simultaneously seriously injured in the abdomen suffering a hernia. As a result, he did no general duty afterwards. As we have seen, shortly after the accident, the Engineer Detachment was transferred to Washington, D.C. to build defenses. At the start of this duty, it was apparent that Peck was incapable of doing any hard labor. On February 19, 1862 he was given an honorable discharge from the Corps of Engineers where he ranked as Artificer, because he had an "inguinal hernia." On the same day he was granted a pension of $4.00 per month.

There is an obvious connection between the discharge and the pension. One can also reason that this was a partial disability pension which was increased to $8.00 on April 3, 1884. Two years later, Peck applied for an increase in his pension to $12.00 per month because by that time he suffered from a double inguinal hernia. At that time, certifying to an adjudication board and presenting a sworn statement on August 23, 1886 (U.S. Government Records of Veterans Administration: Pension Application File No. WC 457-911, pertaining to William A. Peck.), Ralph Wright, New Haven, Connecticut, testified that Peck

...was driving a six Mule Team ... and was thrown form the Saddle Mule by reason of the animal falling, and was caught with his left leg under the mule and dragged in this position a considerable distance, receiving injuries that caused him to be under the Surgeon's care for some time, and subsequently he was discharged from the Company for disability to perform the duties devolving upon members of the Corps. The disability was caused by abdominal trouble commonly known as ruptures. I was witness to the accident and know personally of him being under Surgeon's care.

39. (p.200) Wayne Holm, a National Park Ranger on Alcatraz Island, stated in 1989 that the island was once a barren, rocky outcrop in San Francisco Bay.

The United States acquired the island in 1848 and during the 1850's built fortifications on it. In the 1860's Alcatraz was an impressive fortress. Along with Fort Point, on the San Francisco side of the Golden Gate, the guns on the island guarded the entrance to San Francisco Bay. There were 84 large cannon with 15 inch bore on the island each weighing 45,000 pounds

Holm also said that during the Civil War there were many Southern sympathizers in San Francisco. The National Park Service *Alcatraz Island, Self-Guide Trail,* states that the island became a Military Prison in 1907 and soldiers jailed there for hard labor chipped rock, built roadways and buildings. They moived soil from neighboring Angel Island which was used for foundations, landscaping and in the process, all of the gun emplacements Peck helped build were covered.

40. (p.203) Peck's visit as a tourist to Mission Delores is notable as most off-duty soldiers did not spend their time in such pursuits. Peck was not a run-of-the-mill soldier in his free time since a very large proportion of the Army's officers and men were regular drinkers. It is obvious although Peck took a few drinks, drinking was not his usual way of life. Although one unpublished account suggests that Peck, in not going to taverns as soldiers did, was a "Sunday School teacher," this is an unsubstantiated judgment. Some soldiers, Peck included, had other interests and did not spend their time in taverns. Data in the Veterans Administration shows reference to Peck being a member of the Episcopal Church in Connecticut.

41. (p.205) With reference to the stay at Alcatraz being unpleasant, Peck had noted on May 10th that the detachment was enlarging the barracks to house more soldiers. This suggests that the reinforcements had arrived before there were any accommodations for them – not unusual. As a result, the men were all packed together in inadequate housing.

42. (p.206) Stevens, in his biography of his father: Vol. II, p. 299, writes in contradiction of the charge of Stevens being a drunkard:

Governor Stevens rapidly overcame – lived down – the prejudice excited by the charges and reports against him and won the respect of his fellow members. Several of them expressed to him their surprise at finding him so different a man from what they had been led to believe. Said one gentleman, 'I expected to find a loud-voiced, tobacco-chew-ing, drinking, swearing, violent man and instead I find a gentlemen of quiet manners, education, ability and high aims and ideals.'

43. (p.213) Peck was no longer a member of the U. S. Army Corps of Engineers but he continued to work as a civilian doing officer work – not manual labor – and as a supervisor, under Captain Thomas Lincoln Casey, who had been in charge of the road building survey from Fort Vancouver to Fort Sterilacoom.

Appendix

Books at the Friday Harbor Library
About the Pig War

It is often that visitors have extra time when in the San Juan Islands especially while waiting for ferry boats. The San Juan Island Library District offers these items about the Pig War for use in the Library.

Bailey-Cummings, Jo. *San Juan: the Powder-Keg Island; the Settlers' Own Stories.* NW Sec. 979.7/BAILEY

Baker, Betty. *The Pig War.* [EASY BOOKS CHILDREN'S ROOM]

Bave, Emelia L. *San Juan Saga: A Unique History of the San Juan Islands and the Pig War Told in Words and Pictures From the Long-Running Historical Pageant.* NW Sec. 979.7/BAVE

Coulter, C. Brewster. *The Pig War and Other Experiences of William Peck – Soldier 1858-1862 - U.S. Army Corps of Engineers - The Journal of William A. Peck, Jr.* NW Sec. 979.7/COULTER

Dawson, Will. 1909- *The War That was Never Fought.* NW Sec. 973.6/DAWSON

Ferguson, Linda L. *Miscellaneous San Juan Islands Reports 1912-1926,* [Excavations - archaeology] 1975. DOCUMENTS SEC. SJ25

Johnson, C. [Cindy]. *Miscellaneous San Juan Islands Reports 1976-1977.* [Excavations - archaeology] DOCUMENTS SEC. SJ26

McCabe, James O. *The San Juan Water Boundary Question.* [REF] 979.7/McCABE

Merk, Frederick. *The Oregon Question, Essays in Anglo-American Diplomacy and Politics.* NW Sec. 327.73/MERK

Murray, Keith A. *The Pig War.* NW Sec 979.9/MURRAY

Richardson, David Blair, 1926- *Magic Islands, A Treasure-Trove of San Juan Islands Lore.* NW Sec. 979.73/RICHAR

_____. *Pig War Islands.* NW Sec. 979.7/RICHAR

Schmoe, Floyd Wilfred, 1895- *For Love of Some Islands; Memoirs of Some Years Spent in the San Juan Islands of Puget Sound.* NW Sec. 917.97/SCHMOE

Pig War National Historical Park, Hearing, 89th Cong. 1st Sess on S-489, Apr. 17, 1965 [REF] 973/PIGWA

San Juan Island National Historical Park. (Pig War National Monument) San Juan Island, Washington. DOCUMENTS SEC WA 1

—This list was supplied by The San Juan Island Library District—

Bibliography

Bancroft, Hubert Howe. *History of British Columbia.* History Co., 1887.

_____. *History of Oregon.* History Co. 1888.

_____. *History of Washington, Idaho and Montana.* History Co. 1880.

Bischoff, William N. S.J. Ed. *We Were Not Summer Soldiers: The Indian War Diary of Plympton J. Kelly, 1855-1856.* Wash. State Hist. Society. 1976.

Carey, Charles H. *General History of Oregon.* Binford and Mort. 1971.

Clark, Keith and Lowell Tiller. *Terrible Trail: the Meek Cut-Off, 1845.* Caxton. 1966.

Goetzmann, William H. *Army Exploration in the American West, 1803-1863.* University of Nebraska Press. 1979.

Gibbs, James A. *Oregon's Seacoast Lighthouses.* Webb Research Group. 1992.

Gibson, James R. *Farming the Frontier: The Agricultural Opening of the Oregon Country, 1786-1846.* Univ. of Washimhton Press. 985

Haller, Granville O. "San Juan and Secession" in *Tacoma Ledger* Jan. 19, 1896.

Hart, Herbert M. *Pioneer Forts of the West.* Superior. 1967.

_____.*Tour Guide to Old Western Forts.* Pruett. 1980.

Hansen, Harry (Ed.) *California; A Guide to the Golden State.* [Federal Writers' Project – American Guiide Series] Rev. Ed. Hastings. 1967.

Hitchman, Robert. *Place Names of Washington.* Wash. State Hist. Society. 1985.

Hoffman, Charles S. *The Search For Oregon's Lost Blue Bucket Mine; The Stephen Meek Wagon Train of 1845 – An Oregon Documentary.* Webb Research Group. 1992.

Johansen, Dorothy and Charles M. Gates. *Empire of the Columbia.* Harper & Row. 1957.

Lavender, David S. *Land of Giants, The Drive For the Pacific Northwest 1750-1950.* Doubleday. 1958.

Manring, Benjamin Franklin. *The Conquest of the Coeur d'Alenes, Spokanes and Palouses; the Expeditions of Colonels E. J. Steptoe and George Wright in 1858.* YeGalleon. 1975.

Meany, Edmond A. *History of the State of Washington.* Macmillan. 1909.

Miller, (David) Hunter. *San Juan Archipelago: Study of the Joint Occupation of San Juan Island.* Windham Press. 1943.

Mills, Randall V. *Stern-Wheelers Up Columbia.* Pacific. 1947.

Murray, Keith. *The Pig War.* Wash. State Hist. Society. 1968.

Relander, Click. *Drummers and Dreamers.* Caxton. 1956.

Renner, Jeff. *Northwest Mountain Weather.* Mountaineers. 1992.

Snowden, Clinton A. *History of Washington.* Century History Co. 1909.

Stevens, Hazard. *The Life of Isaac Ingalls Stevens.* Houghton Mifflin. 1900.

Thompson, Edwin. *Historic Resource Study, San Juan Island National Historical Park, Washington.* Dept of the Interior. 1972.

Wallen, H. D. (Capt. U.S.A.) *The Report of Captain H. D. Wallen of his Expedition, in 1859, from Dalles City to Great Salt Lake, and Back.* Senate Doc. Wash. D.C. 1860.

Webber, Bert and Margie Webber. *Battery Point Light & the Tidal Wave of 1964.* Webb Research Goup. 1991.

_____. *Beachcombing and Camping Along the Northwest Coast.* YeGalleon. 1978.

Index

Principal persons, ships and places continually mentioned are not Indexed.

Page numbers in *bold italic* are illustrations

It is acknowledged that many first names missing as these do not appear in the *Journal*

Colophon

The work on the Peck Journal *went through the hands of many technicians and workshops situated in Oregon's peaceful Rogue River Valley, noted for its pear orchards, being 30 miles from the California line and 90 miles from the Pacific Ocean.*

Typesetting of the text was from prepared double-spaced typed manuscript sheets into a 14-inch PENTAX IQ flatbed scanner operated by R. Marshall Webber. The scanner automatically fed into a Diamond Flower IBM-compatible 486-SX25 computer in a system custom-designed by Matthew Hill then installed by Richard Webber. The first sheets were printed on a Panasonic KPX1123 24-pin printer. Following initial proofing by Margie Webber, for corrections and augmentations, the camera-ready sheets were printed on a Hewlett-Packard LaserJet IIIp printer. The text is on 24-pica lines in 10 point English Times Roman with some English Times Boldface and ship's names in English Times Italic. The on-page footnotes are English Times Roman in 8 point but the NOTES section is in 9 point. Chapter headings are 13 point bold face Thomas Paine as is the first letter in each chapter. The legends and special boxed features are in computer-Arial (Helvitica) in 9 point but some, for better fit, are in 8.5 point. Bert Webber did page makeup on a custom-made fluorescent light table (built by Dale Webber) with accommodation for the Lectro-Stik waxer.

For the pictures, the photo laboratory technicians were Joseph Frodsham (lead); Jack Fowler, custom darkroom and Noritsu Systems quality control; Kathy Fowler laboratory work-flow coordinator. Senior photo-lab technicians were Laurie Horton, Marne Hale, Dulcie McDowell, Cari Hutson, Diana Hall, Angela McGowan.

Thomas Chadwell, graphic artist, did the 100-line screening for the photographs on a Model 2750 Kenro camera.

At the printing works, Peter Dale was general coordinator. Brad Barton and Stanley Pothoven handled pre-press stripping, plating on a 30 x 40-inch NuArc light table as well as did the camera work; Al Bower and Kevin Tobin, pressmen, operated the 36-inch single color Miehle and 28-inch 4-color Akiyama presses. The pages are 60-pound Husky book stock, a Weyerhaeuser sheet with the cover on 10-point CIS, a Federal sheet. The Herzog & Heymann folding equipment was operated by Glenn Johansen, Gail Stading and Loria Charlton who also did the adhesive binding on a Mueller-Martini 7-pocket perfect binder. Andrew Hinds made the final trim on a 45-inch FC Itoh cutter then he and Chino Pumpelly boxed the product and delivered it

All of the work went smoothly.